GW00372705

Leek Trade Bills
c.1830-1930

*A source book of trade and business in Leek
and surrounding areas c.1830-1930,
using letterheads, adverts and directories*

Vol. II I-P

From the collection of the late
Stuart Hobson

with notes by
Ray Poole

CHURNET VALLEY BOOKS
1 King Street, Leek, Staffordshire, ST13 5NW 01538 399033
www.leekbooks.co.uk
© Churnet Valley Books 2005
ISBN 1 897949 34 X

Part of an aerial view of Leek in 1956, which changed little between the turn of the century and the 1960s.
Clockwise from the top left is seen the old factory in Bath Street, the little shops at the top of Ball Haye Street, Regent Street School and Bethesda Methodist Chapel. On the right is part of the huge Brough, Nicholson & Hall factory site, and the row of shops on Ashbourne Road, above the Talbot. Completing the circle are the Smithfield Cottage and Coffee Tavern.

INTRODUCTION

This second selection of billheads and ephemera covers I to P. It therefore includes a number of non-trade organisations and enterprises whose titles start with 'Leek'. Here will be found reminders of the former local authority, Leek Urban District Council forerunner of the present Staffordshire Moorlands District Council. These were the days when the local authority was responsible for its own public services, so they include gas, water and electricity. Likewise there are a number of local building society and newspaper letterheads.

A hallmark of these Victorian and Edwardian letterheads and billheads is the high quality of the printing and engraving of the designs. It happens that a number of prominent local printers fall into this volume, and the headings of Thomas Mark, M.H. Miller, David Morris and George Nall are fine examples of the art and craft of the printer.

In printers' parlance a billhead is usually deemed to be used for sending out invoices or statements. A letterhead is for correspondence and an elaborate engraved design would create a good impression and raise the prestige of the sender. Today such business stationery is usually computer generated and lacks the imagination and flair of its forebears. The art of the compositor and engraver has been superceded.

Most of the letters and bills were of course hand-written, and a good copperplate handwriting was a great asset to a clerk seeking employment. The offices of larger companies were very labour intensive with armies of clerks bent diligently over their work. By the late Victorian era the fountain pen was the symbol of their trade, ideally with a 14ct gold nib, and names like 'Onoto', 'de la Rue', 'Parker', 'Swan' and 'Waterman' were household names, and Stephen's Ink was used by the gallon.

THE DIRECTORIES

The directories used in this volume are a considerable advance on their predecessors. William White followed his ground-breaking Directory of 1834 (included in Vol I) with a considerably expanded update in 1851. By this time the railway had arrived on the scene, many municipal developments had taken place and trade and industry had expanded. These were the high Victorian years and industrial growth was the hallmark of the age. In his preface, William White (a Sheffield man) states that he and his team of assistants had worked for 18 months to revise the Directory, with the support of more than 3500 subscribers and also "a large number of literary and official gentlemen."

Slater's Directory of 1862 lacks the long historical preambles of White but it is well-organised and very comprehensive with details of public services, local government officers and churches listed. Some of the spellings sccm odd but they are reproduced here as they appear in the original.

CHARLES SLAGG'S MAP OF 1862

Charles Slagg was appointed Town Surveyor to the Leek Improvement Commissioners on 17th November 1857. He served for about five years and towards the end of his period in office he produced his Plan of the Town and Environs of Leek, which reflects the growth of the town at that time. He was able to show the railway and a number of new streets mainly on the fringe of the old town, but the basic street pattern of the earlier map can still be seen.

Slagg's map shows a large area of open land lying between London Street and the present Ashbourne Road, where an extensive scheme of infill housing would see the construction of Southbank Street, Fynney Street, Shoobridge Street, Leonard Street, Cromwell Terrace, Livingstone Street, Talbot Street, Moorhouse Street, Wood Street and Grosvenor Street - terraced houses of style and quality for all classes of the growing population. This area of land was owned mainly by Mrs Shoobridge and Mr James Nixon.

To the north of Derby Street, the Ford Street and Bath Street area was awaiting development when Slagg drew up his map. On the western side of the town, land off Canal Street, owned by Hugh Sleigh, was designated for Hartington Street, Hugo Street and Dampier Street. Off Britannia Street, Chorley Street and Gladstone Street would be constructed on the late T. Atkinson's land, and further west, Grove Street and Westwood Grove would stretch out over open land owned by the Earl of Macclesfield. Slagg was also able to include the railway, the gas works and the cattle market at the junction of Ashbourne Road with Derby Street.

The map showed the town as being enclosed within a perfect circle. This was because, under the terms of the Leek Improvement Act of 1855, the area of the town was defined by a circle of a radius of 1500 yards centred on the lamp in the middle of the Market Place. All the land within that circle was the responsibility of the Leek Improvement Commissioners - the local government of the day.

As in the first volume, the material in this second volume is from the collection of the late Stuart Hobson and we are grateful again to his widow, Barbara Hobson, for permission to use this material and preserve it for a wider public. We are also grateful to Mrs Christine Chester and Mr Robert Cartwright for the use of a few items and to Mr John White for Slagg's 1862 map.

Ray Poole, Leek

This work will be produced in three volumes, approximately covering 1830-1930:

Volume I - Names A-H, the 1838 map of Leek, and two directory sections for Leek, from Parson and Bradshaw's, 1818, and White's Directory, 1834.

Volume II - Names I-P, Slagg's 1862 map of Leek, the Leek section of White's 1851 Staffordshire Directory, and Slater's 1862 Leek Directory.

Volume III - Names Q-Z, Stephens & Mackintosh 1908 Town Map of Leek, and several Leek Town Directories, including 1876, 1898, 1916 and 1934.

Volume II

Names I - P
Slagg's 1862 map of Leek,
Leek section of White's 1851 Staffordshire Directory,
and Slater's 1862 Leek Directory

St Luke's Church

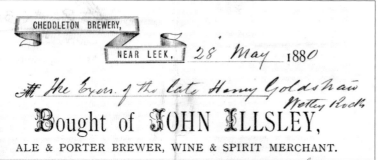

CHEDDLETON BREWERY,

NEAR LEEK, 28 May 1880

At the Exors. of the late Henry Goldshaw
Wetley Rocks

Bought of JOHN ILLSLEY,

ALE & PORTER BREWER, WINE & SPIRIT MERCHANT.

CHEDDLETON BREWERY, 6 Aug 188 5

Mr T. Russell Esq

Bought of JOHN ILLSLEY & Co.

ALE AND PORTER BREWERS,

Wine and Spirit Merchants.

Casks not returned within a reasonable period, in good condition, will be charged for

	Quality.	Per. Brl.	£	s.	d.
2397					
1 Fir Bitter	BB	54	-	13	6
Settled with thanks	Ale 2				6

QUEEN'S HEAD INN YARD,

Leek, _____ 186

Adams Alsop Esq.

To W. JACKSON & W. BOOTH,

PLUMBERS, GLAZIERS, GAS FITTERS, PAPER HANGERS, PAINTERS, &c.

1864		£	s.	d.
Mar 11	To 1 Cup joint in pipe	-	-	4
"	" Solder washer for Tap	-	-	5
	Mans time	-	1	3
	£	-	2	-

Settled 12th March

William Cardens

Ilsley's brewery was located at Cheddleton near the Flint Mill and the Canal

Jackson and Booth had their workshop in the yard of the Queen's Head Inn in Stanley Street.

Johnson brothers were an old-established (1817) firm of dry cleaners and dyers. Their Leek branch shop was in Gaunt Buildings in Derby Street, and the main heading here would also be used by their many other branches throughout the Country.

This appears to be a bill made up of very small items covering a full year. Such extended credit, by agreement, no doubt would make for cordial business relationships.

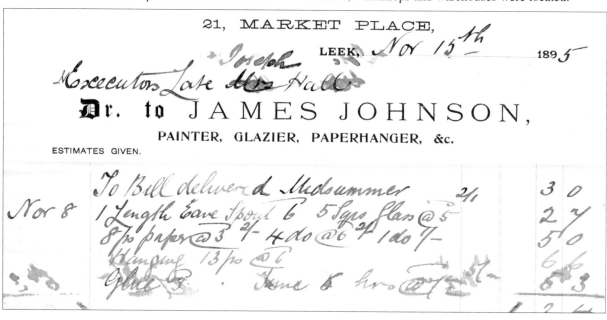

Golden Lion Yard, Leek,　*Oct 2nd* 188 4

Mrs Bradshaw,

To JAMES JOHNSON,

Painter, Grainer, Paper-hanger & House Decorator.

			£	s	d
To Painting & Papering House in Compton Terrace as per agreement			5	1	0
To Extras 6 ps paper @ 8				4	
To Hanging ditto				3	
Flour 4					4
			5	8	4

Johnson's main shop would be entered from the Market place (No 21). His working address was given as Golden Lion Yard, at the rear. The Golden Lion public house (a former coaching inn) stood near the top of Church Street, just around the corner from the top of the Market Place. There was a complex of yards and alleyways at the rear of Market Place shops where a number of small businesses, workshops and warehouses were located.

21, MARKET PLACE,

LEEK, *Nov 15th* 189 5

Executors Late Mrs Hall — *Joseph*

Dr. to JAMES JOHNSON,

PAINTER, GLAZIER, PAPERHANGER, &c.

ESTIMATES GIVEN.

				£	s	d
	To Bill delivered Midsummer	2/1			3	0
Nov 8	1 Length Eave Spout 6　5 Sqrs Glass @ 5				2	7
	8 po paper @ 3　4 - 4 do @ 6　1 do 7-				5	0
	Hanging 13 po @ 6				6	6
	Glue 3　Time 8 hrs @ 7½-				6	3

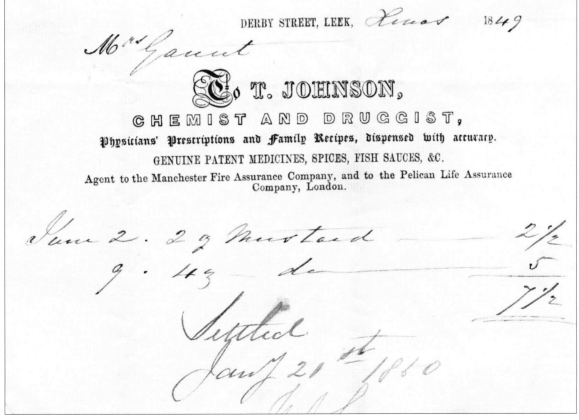

T. Johnson was an old established and highly respected chemist and druggist. Like many Victorian traders, in addition to his main line of business, he served as agent for two insurance companies.

99.

DERBY STREET **Leek** Xmas 1867.

Sam Clowes Esq

Bought of Johnson & Sons,

Family and Dispensing Chemists.

July	18	1½ doz	Lemonade		6 –
Aug	15	2 doz	do	✓	8 –
Oct	3	½ doz	do		2 –
					– 16 –

Received
with thanks
Dec 2/68
Wm Johnson

CORNWELL'S EUCALYPTUS FOOT POWDER

For the PREVENTION and CURE of OVER-HEATED and TENDER FEET, without injury to health.

4½d. per Canister. **4½d. per Canister**

Sole Agent for Leek and District:

MESSRS. JOHNSON & SON,

CHEMISTS,

STANLEY STREET, LEEK.

Many local chemists were appointed agents for patent, branded medicinal products. These would be featured in their stationery and advertising - particularly if they were the sole agent. Johnsons have moved by this time from their old premises in Derby Street to Stanley Street.

Derby Street **LEEK.** 1st May 1854

Mr. Bradshaw.

Bot. of T. Johnson.

Chemist & Druggist.

Genuine Patent Medicines

HORSE & CATTLE MEDICINES

Soda & Seidlitz Powders

PERFUMERY, &c

Physicians Prescriptions accurately dispensed.

HAVANNAH CIGARS & FANCY SNUFFS.

Agent to the Manchester Fire Assurance Company
and the Pelican Life Assurance Company, London.

June 26	1/2 pt. Vinegar Best			2½
28	Tooth Brush			4
July 4	Tooth Powder 10 ¼ lb Mustard 5		1	3
	1 oz Nutmegs 8 Matches 1			9
5	Refilly Smell g Bottle			2
8	Calomel Pills & Blk Draught			10
10	Tincture & Mixture		1	4
	¼ lb Mustard			5
14	Seidlitz Powder			2
15	2 do do			4
Aug 14	Pot. Polish g Paste 2 g Matches 4			7
Sep 4	Olive Oil 4 13 d 1 oz Nutmegs 8		1	
13	Liquid for Mark g Ink			3
30	Seidlitz Powder			2
Oct 2	¼ lb Mustard 5 Flour Brimstone			4
	Pot. Polish g Paste 9 Pill & Draught 10		1	4
	Carried Over		9	9½

This interesting bill lists a wide range of family medicinal requirements purchased over a
period of 5 months - the total being less than ten shillings.

9, Stanley Street, Leek, *Nov 1st* ____ 189 3

M The Exors of the late Mrs Prince

Bought of L. & G. JOHNSON,

LADIES' & BABY LINEN WAREHOUSE,

BERLIN & FANCY REPOSITORY.

Agents for G. Wright & Sons, Dyers & Cleaners to the Queen.

Dr. Jaeger's Sanitary Woollen Clothing.

DEPOT OF THE BRITISH & FOREIGN BIBLE SOCIETY.

1893			
July 10	Darning Cotton ³ Ditto Wool ³		6
"	Hair Pins ² Dress Preservers 6'		8
24	Night Dress	3	10
26	Night Dress 1 Comb Bag	3	4
	Silks & Cottons		6
Aug 6	Darning Wool ⁴ Cotton ²'		8
10	1 Pair Canvas Slippers	2	10
"	Silks 6' Transfer paper ⁴		10
Sep. 4	2 Pair Dress Preservers 6'	1	0
" 10	2 Ditto 1/-	2	6
12	Darning Wool		2
		16	4

Received with thanks
L. Johnson
Dec 18/93

The proprietors of this small business were Misses Lydia and Gertrude Johnson. This type of shop flourished in the Victorian era when the personal services of the proprietors (usually ladies) were greatly valued by local mothers.

1876

Contrasting forms of transport are seen in this early 20th century view of Derby Street.

SAMUEL F. JOHNSON,

GENERAL BUTCHER,

DERBY STREET, LEEK,

Tenders his best thanks to the Public for the patronage he has received since he commenced business in Leek, and begs to say that he will always endeavour to deserve the confidence hitherto placed in him.

HOME-CURED HAMS & BACON

And PICKLED TONGUES always in Stock.

FRESH SAUSAGES DAILY.

Leek was a town of small family butchers - 17 were listed in the 1862 directory and 23 in 1898, where old established names such as Bayley, Burnett, Godwin, Knowles and Meakin appear. Most butchers displayed their meats in the open air, with poultry game and joints hanging outside the shop. This 'natural refrigeration' would have worked well enough in winter but the summer months must have presented a problem. Ice was delivered regularly by the railway.

Minton, - - Wedgwood or Wilton Ware. -

Nothing could be more charming or give more pleasure.

....

Obtainable from

Mrs. JOHNSON, The CHINA DEPOT, St. Edward St., Leek.

8, Sheep Market, Leek, *6 Nov* 1867

Mess. *Challinor*

DR. TO C. R. JONES,

(LATE HILLIARD)

BOOKSELLER, STATIONER, BOOKBINDER AND PRINTER,

LONDON AND COUNTRY NEWSPAPERS SUPPLIED.

Agent for the Union Insurance & Whittington Assurance Companies.

July 15	100	Forms 4to Summons		4 6
	100	„ Drunkenness „ backed		5 6
	100	Poor rate appeals		3 6
29	100	„ Town Summons		5 6
	100	„ Leet Town Act backed		6 6
Aug 5	100	„ 4to Overseers Jury Lists		4 6
10		Inkstand		1 6
14	100	Forms fo. Summons		5 6
	100	Dᵒ Bastardy backed		6 6
Sep 13	200	„ 4to Witness Sum.		6 6
	100	„ backed		5 6
Augᵗ		Binding Master & Servant Act	£	2 15 6
				2 6
			£	2 18 -

C.R.Jones took over the old established printing business of W.M. Hilliard in the 1860s.

8, Sheep Market, Leek, *Midsummer* 1871

Mr. Challinor & Co. (*Justices Clerks &c.*)

DR. TO C. R. JONES,

ACCOUNT BOOK MANUFACTURER,

BOOKSELLER, STATIONER, BOOKBINDER AND PRINTER.

DEALER IN PAPER HANGINGS.

4

Date	Qty	Description		£ s	d
Jan 7	100 forms	Notice of Appeal	✓	3	6
Feb 13	150 Do	List of Constables	✓	7	6
	250 Official envelopes- directed	(oversewn)	✓	7	6
18	100 forms	"Common" Summonses	✓	5	6
	100 Do	Do backed	✓	6	6
	25 Do	Do in blank	✓	3	
	25 Do	Do Do	✓	3	6
April 1	100 Official envelopes	Surveyors	✓	3	6
	100 forms	Summons to Constables to take oath of office		4	6
3	100 "	(money paid) Bastard	✓	5	6
	100 "	" backed	✓	6	6
5	100 "	Appeals against rates	✓	3	6
	100 "	Constables appointments		4	6
15	100 "	Summons Assault	✓	4	6
	100 "	" backed	✓	5	6
26	50 "	" in blank	✓	3	
	50 "	" in blank backed	✓	4	
May 3	75 "	Appts of Sp Sessions for Highways	✓	3	6
19	100 "	Commitments "Penalty & Costs"		5	6
			£4	11	0

The great proliferation of printed legal notices, posters and other material required by the Victorian legal profession is illustrated in this invoice. C.R.Jones also produced account books to customers' requirements.

All KODAK Supplies.   **Films developed & printed in a few hours.**

All Surgical Appliances	**EDWARD JONES, M.P.S.**
Health Insurance Dispensing	CHEMIST & DRUGGIST.
Patent Medicines	**13, DERBY ST., LEEK.** PHONE 329
Toilet Luxuries	

April 10th 1934.

Messrs J Breasley & Sons.

Dear Sirs,
Enclosed please
find cheque in payment
of I quarters rent.

Yours faithfully

E Jones

Edward Jones was a popular local chemist who was still trading in the 1950s - and eventually taken over by Boots Chemists. Local people often referred to him affectionately as "Dr Jones", and his 'free' advice was greatly valued.

This heading of J.L.Jones illustrates one of those old trades and specialist skills that were very much in evidence in Victorian times. Here, a one-man business, probably operating from home, offers as well as his main business, a service to homes and businesses for the supply and maintenance of bells.

4,   DEANSGATE,

LEEK, *June 6* 1891

Mr Russal

DR. TO J. L. JONES,

GUN   AND   TRUSS   MAKER,

BELL-HANGER, &c.

Houses, Hotels, &c., fitted with Electric and other Bells.

Repairing Bells   £ s d
                        5

John Jones
Settled

Another part of an aerial view of Leek, showing Leek livestock market in Heywood Street. It was moved to its present position in Barnfields in the 1960s and the Smithfield retail centre and Bus Station was built in its place.
The Leek Baths in Derby Street, the Leek Town Hall in Market Street, and the Brunswick Methodist Church
are other buildings seen here in 1956 which are now gone.

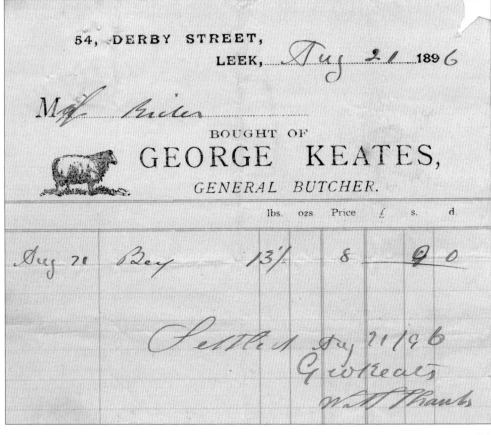

6, MARKET STREET,

LEEK, *Mar 17ᵗʰ 1900*

Mʳ Woolly

Bought of E. KEATES,

CONFECTIONER, ETC.,

MANUFACTURER OF SAUSAGES AND PORK PIES

1909		£	s	d
Sep 3ʳᵈ	2/- *Pork pie*		2	0

54, DERBY STREET,

LEEK, *Aug 21 1896*

Mr Miller

BOUGHT OF

GEORGE KEATES,

GENERAL BUTCHER.

	lbs.	ozs	Price	£	s.	d
Aug 21 *Beef*	13/				8	0	0

Settled Aug 21/96
G W Keates
With Thanks

Butchers were very numerous in the Victorian years, most of them in small shops. Many did
their own slaughtering, often on the premises.
Provision and corn merchants also often sold butchery products.

✤ KEATS ✤ BROTHERS, ✤

Houghwood Quarries, nr. Bagnall, Stoke-on-Trent, *20 april* 18*88*

To Messrs Challinor & Co Leek

We have your letter of 24th but our Mr C Keats is ill at home and so we cannot reply for a few days. You shall hear from us as soon as he is well enough to return to business which we hope will be in a few days more.

In the great building boom of the mid and late Victorian years, when Leek was enjoying economic growth and stability, the demand for bricks and stone was high. Much of these were sourced locally, and brickyards and quarries flourished.

rec'd 18 May 1888.

ᛟ MEMORANDUM. ᛟ

188

From

HENRY KEATES,

✤Wholesale and ✤Retail ✤Boot and ✤Shoe
✤Manufacturer,

8, Sheep Market, LEEK, Staffs.

To *Mr Howard*

....

....

Sir

I will Pay Challinor & Co a/c next week certain

Your a/c

H Keates

504

8, Sheep Market, Leek,   May 9 190 1

Mr Newall for Mrs Smith

Bought of Henry Keates,

BOOT MAKER.

Shooting, Fishing. Walking, Hunting & Coachmen's Top Boots made on the Premises.

A staff of the most skilful workmen in the district to do repairs, and nothing but the best material used.

Travelling Trunks, Railway Portmanteaux, Travelling Bags, Ladies' Fancy Satchels, Rug Straps, Hat Cases, Purses, Cloth, Canvass and Leather Gaiters, Farmers' Strong Leggings, Fancy Leggings in great variety.

1901

Feb. 16	Youths Boots	10	6
„ 27	Dau. Shoes	6	2
„	Allens Slippers	2	11
March 9	Canvas Shoes	3	2
„ „	Button Shoes	10	9
„ „	Jessies Boots	9	6
„ „	Willies Boots	11	6
„ 23	Jessies Boots	7	4
April 20	„ Canvas Shoes	3	2
		£ 3 5	0

Recd May 18/1901

H Keates

T. Smith

This detailed heading indicates a wide range of footwear, plus a variety of other leather goods, often made to order. Henry Keates was in business as a bootmaker in 1888. In the 1860s a William Keates was also a bootmaker in Russell Street.

Boot and shoe makers, dealers and repairers were prolific in these years - the Directory of 1916 lists no less than 43, an indication that people did much more walking in those days.

The Executors of the Late Mr Broadington

LEEK WHARF,   1841

Bought of W. KEATES,
MALTSTER,
DEALER IN HOPS, CORN, &c.

				£.	s.	d.
Ap 22	45	lb Cow Grass	10½	1	19	4½
	15	" Trefoil	6½		8	1½
Middleton	15	W. Clover	9½		11	10½
Grange	15	Oat Grass	9		11	3
		Vetches 1 Bushel		3	10	7½
					12	0
	Barley 10 Bags at 7.2 per Bag					0
Nov 26 Cut.				4	14	7½

Leek, Midst. 1877.

The Repr. of Mrs Heath Bradnop.

To J. Kenny, Surgeon, &c., Dr.

To Professional Attendance and ~~Medicine for the~~ in June /77.

£2 7 6

Oct 12th/77.   Recd J. Kenny

Dr Kenny's address was Clerk Bank. In the 20th century there was a Dr Depree, and then a Dr Fry, on Clerk Bank. It was not usually necessary for professional persons to show their full address.

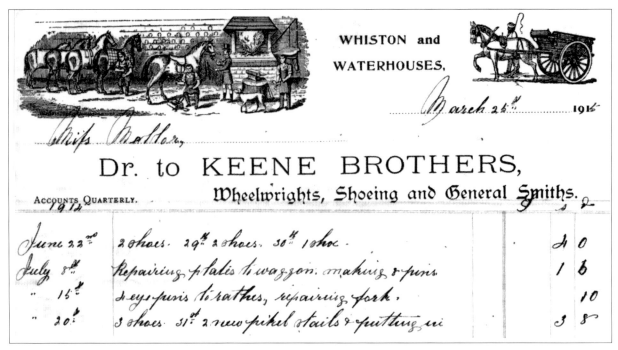

An example of the diversity of many Victorian businesses. As well as his coal merchant business, Mr Kent made bricks, pipes and pots and supplied horticultural items. Alfred Key, opposite, was a similarly diverse Endon business.

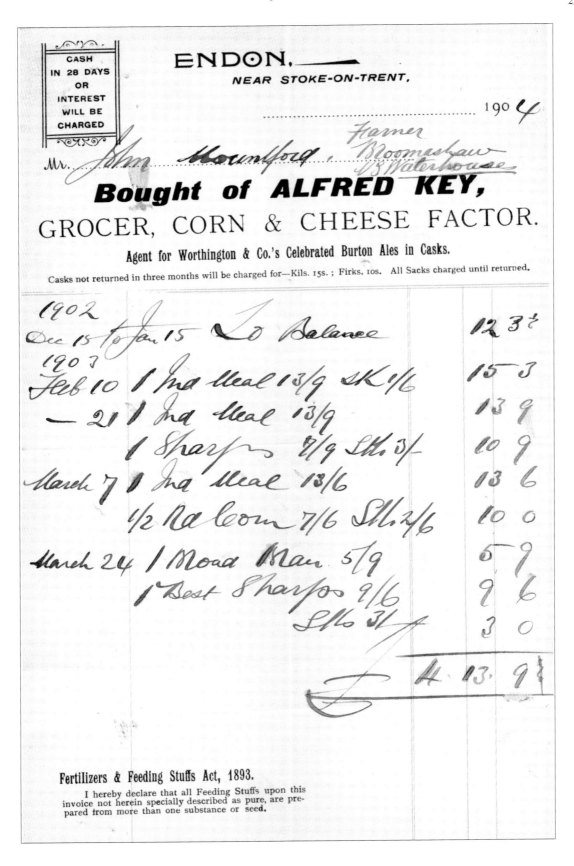

CASH IN 28 DAYS OR INTEREST WILL BE CHARGED

ENDON,

NEAR STOKE-ON-TRENT,

190 4

Mr. *John Mountford* , *Farmer Bloomshaw V3 Waterhouse*

Bought of ALFRED KEY,

GROCER, CORN & CHEESE FACTOR.

Agent for Worthington & Co.'s Celebrated Burton Ales in Casks.

Casks not returned in three months will be charged for—Kils. 15s. ; Firks. 10s. All Sacks charged until returned.

1902
Dec 15 to Jan 15   To Balance   12   3¾
1903
Feb 10 1 Ind Meal 13/9 Sk 1/6   15   3
— 21   1 Ind Meal 13/9   13   9
        1 Sharps   7/9 Sk 3/   10   9
March 7 1 Ind Meal 13/6   13   6
        ½ Na Corn 7/6 Sk 2/6   10   0
March 24 1 Mond Meal 5/9   5   9
        1 Best Sharps 9/6   9   6
        Sk 3/   3   0
                                     £4 13 9¾

Fertilizers & Feeding Stuffs Act, 1893.

I hereby declare that all Feeding Stuffs upon this invoice not herein specially described as pure, are prepared from more than one substance or seed.

LITTLE BIRCHALL FARM,
LEEK, *July 21* 189 4

Mr J G Smith

DR. TO **ARTHUR KIRKHAM,**

COAL MERCHANT,

General Carter, and Furniture Remover.

July 17.19 two Boat Loads Stone 46 tons cut yes £2 6 0
Carted to Albion St & Ulsop St

Paid
July 24 94
Arthur Kirkham

TELEGRAMS:—"KIRKHAM, LEEK."

MEMORANDUM

Leek, *May 14 1888*

From

CHAS. KIRKHAM,

Letterpress and Lithographic Printer,

WHOLESALE & RETAIL STATIONER.

STEAM WORKS:—DERBY STREET.

To *Messrs Challinor & Co.,*
Solicitors
Leek.

Dear Sirs
I shall be greatly obliged by a settlement of the printing & advertising account rendered Mch 31 last, (amount £13-10-) at your earliest convenience, & shall be pleased, also, to receive your further orders, which shall have my best attention
I remain
Dear Sirs
obediently yours
Charles Kirkham

These polite but firm chasers were typical of the Victorian way of business.

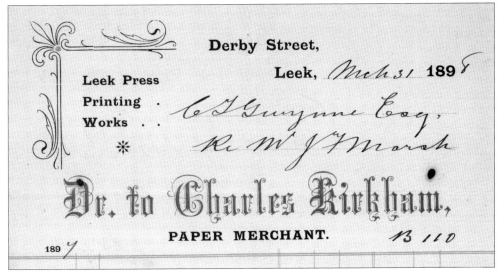

27 & 29, DERBY STREET,
LEEK, *June 30 1890*

Mr W Howard   Leek
for Executors of late Miss Ellen Walker

Dr. to CHARLES KIRKHAM,

Printer, Stationer, Bookbinder, and Newspaper Agent.

PATTERN CARD MAKING IN ALL ITS BRANCHES.

Funeral Cards and Invitations Printed at an Hour's Notice.

1890					
Feby 10	100	Cards in Memory of Ellen Walker Ptd to Copy with Black border		8	
	100	Envelopes Printed with Black border		2	6
				10	6

Rec'd July 17th 1890
pro Charles Kirkham

Derby Street,
Leek, *Mch 31 1895*

C S Gwynne Esq,
Re Mr J F Marsh

Dr. to Charles Kirkham,

PAPER MERCHANT.

£3 11 0

189

The business of Charles Kirkham was established about 1850 and besides offering a full range of printing services, he was a stationer, bookseller and newsagent. A comprehensive range of books was stocked, on all sorts of subjects, and the shop was the local depot for the Oxford University Press. Magazines and periodicals were also stocked. As with all local printers at the time, funeral work was given great priority - compositors standing by to deliver, even to "an hour's notice".

This 1956 aerial view shows the centre section of Derby Street, with the spire of the Congregational Church dominating the scene. On the right is Market Street where the prominent buildings are the Town Hall and Brunswick Methodist Church.

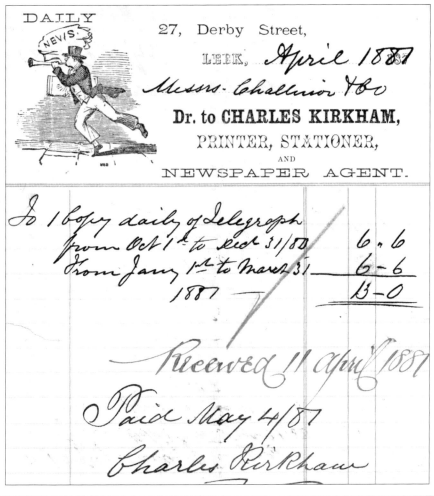

DAILY NEWS

27, Derby Street,

LEEK, *April 1887*

Messrs. Challinor & Co

Dr. to CHARLES KIRKHAM,

PRINTER, STATIONER,

AND

NEWSPAPER AGENT.

To 1 copy daily of Telegraph
from Oct 1st to Dec 31/86 — 6 " 6
from Jany 1st to March 31 — 6 - 6
1887 — 13 - 0

Received 11 April 1887

Paid May 4/87

Charles Kirkham

Telegrams "KIRKHAM, LEEK." **29, DERBY STREET, Leek,** *March 10th* 190 0

To Executors of the late William Reade

In account with *Charles Kirkham.*

Steam Printer,

Manufacturing Stationer & Paper Merchant.

To printing 48 Memorial Cards for the
late William Reade & Envelopes — 7 0
1 doz Invitation — 8
7 8

Paid with thanks

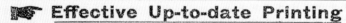

☞ Effective Up-to-date Printing

AT A MODERATE COST, GO OR WRITE TO

GEORGE KIRKHAM'S

Stationery Warehouse,

SHIRLEY BUILDINGS, LEEK,

Where you will find a charming stock of Wedding Cards, Invitations, Bride Cake Boxes.

PLAIN & FANCY STATIONERY IN BOXES FROM 3D. TO 1/- IN GREAT VARIETY.

OUR 6½d. BOX OF VELLUM STATIONERY IS WONDERFUL VALUE.

Party Tickets, Handbills, Circulars, Posters, Programmes, Catalogues, &c., &c.

COMMERCIAL, SCHOLASTIC & LEGAL STATIONERY a Speciality.

MOURNING ORDERS

Have prompt attention.

A choice selection of FUNERAL CARDS, MOURNING STATIONERY & INVITATIONS always in stock.

Mr. Charles Kirkham,
Bookseller, Stationer, Letterpress and Lithographic Printer, 27 and 29, Derby St.

The above mentioned firm control one of the oldest bookselling, stationery, and steam printing establishments of Leek and its vicinity. During the forty years of its existence the house has had a career of substantial prosperity, and of late years especially its operations appear to have increased in a most gratifying manner. Much of the firm's success is doubtless due to the fact that the present principal is a thoroughly practical man in the art of printing, and gives his personal attention to every order, thus ensuring not only the excellence of workmanship, but promptitude. The front premises are situate in Derby Street, the shop being spacious and attractive. The windows contain suitable items for display purposes, the interior of the establishment is fully stocked with all the usual lines pertaining to the business in which Mr. Charles Kirkham is engaged. The selection of literature is very exhaustive, and embraces the standard works in science, art, biography, theology and fiction. There is also a large assortment of religious and liturgical literature, this being the local depot of the Oxford University Press. In magazines, periodicals, and newspapers the business done by the firm attains considerable proportions, and in the general and fancy stationery department will be found all the leading lines and the fashionable novelties. At the rear are the printing and lithographic departments, these being equipped with machinery and appliances affording every facility for high class printing. Here are turned out billheads, circulars, price lists, business cards, visiting cards—in short, every class of printing from the ball-room programme to the three sheet double royal poster. By giving close personal attention to the work, Mr. Kirkham, the present head of the concern, is able to effect substantial economies, of which customers reap the benefit in the exceptionally low quotations he is able to make. The firm publish the *Leek Congregational Magazine*, a monthly record of church work.

SHIRLEY BUILDINGS, Leek, _____ Aug 12 _____ 190 8

Messrs Challinors & Shaw

BOUGHT OF GEORGE KIRKHAM,
PRINTER, STATIONER, PAPER AND GENERAL SMALLWARE MERCHANT.

1	Ebony Ruler 9/1 in		9
1	" " 12/1½	1	1½
1	Wests Patent Ink Stand	1	
		2	10½

Settled by credit in contra
August 12 1905

Messrs Challinors
& Shaw
Leek

Dr. to GEORGE KIRKHAM,
Manufacturing Stationer, Printer, Publisher, etc.,
HIGH STREET, LEEK.

April 17 190

All Newspapers sent by post must be Prepaid, otherwise the usual Credit Rate will be charged.
Any irregularities in Town or Country deliveries should be reported in writing direct to us without delay.

5 Reams Commercial Note Original Government Vellum	3/6	17 6

Messrs Challinors & Shaw
Solicitors
Leek

Aug 20 1912

BOUGHT OF
GEORGE KIRKHAM & Co.,
Manufacturing Stationers, Printers, Publishers and
GENERAL MERCHANTS.
21, QUEEN STREET, LEEK.

TELEGRAMS:
"George Kirkham. Leek."

ORDER No.

1000	Superfine Bankers' Manilla Envelopes Large Pass Book size Pocket Shape Extra Strong	13	6
	Cash Dis 5%		8
		12	10

Mill Street, Leek, _____ *Xmas* _____ 189*1*

Miss Mellor

Dr. to THOS. KNIGHT,

DEALER IN MUSICAL INSTRUMENTS

PIANOS, HARMONIUMS, VIOLINS, FLUTES, CONCERTINAS, STRINGS, FITTINGS, &c.

Lessons given.   Pianos Tuned and Repaired.   String Band for Balls, Parties, &c.

Miss Forrester		
Instruction on Violin	11	-
E. String		4
"Faust" 2 Violins & Piano 2/	1	8
	13	.

Paid May 6 - 9 2

Thos Knight

PHONE : 273

T. KNIGHT & SONS

PIANOFORTES FOR HIRE.

AGENTS FOR THE NEW 'HIS MASTER'S VOICE' AND COLUMBIA GRAMOPHONES AND RECORDS.

PIANO and ORGAN DEALERS
EXPERT TUNERS and REPAIRERS
30, BUXTON ROAD, LEEK
STAFFS.

AGENTS FOR ROGERS, CREMONA, BROADWOOD, CHAPPELL, CHALLEN WITTON WITTON ALLISON, ETC. PIANOS & PLAYER PIANOS

Mrs Dakeyne Stockwell S _____ *Sept* 193*1*

To one year's tuning	15	0

Knight's old established music business later moved to Derby Street. It was a comprehensive business, not only selling musical instruments but offering tuition and tuning - and it was an early supplier of gramophone records.

T. KNIGHT & SONS

For PIANOS and

Agents for
Rogers,
Broadwood,
Moore & Moore,
Cremona,
Witton,
Monington & Weston
etc., etc.

Agents for
Columbia Grafonolas,
and New Process Records.
Also
"Regal" Gr
and R
"Decca"
etc.,

GRAMOPHONES

30, BUXTON ROAD, LE

"The House for Value"

'PHONE 273.

T. Knight & Sons formerly traded in Mill Street and later had a shop at 30 Buxton Road. This is a sleeve from an old 10" 78 rpm record sold under their name. Knights finally moved to a shop in Derby Street, near to the old public baths, now demolished.

Have you tried our Accumulator Charging Service?

Leave YOUR Accumulator at one of our collecting depots.

KNIGHT'S
The MUSICAL People
for PIANOS of QUALITY.

You also get the best in

Gramophones

Records

and

Radio

FROM

Phone 273 **KNIGHT'S** Buxton Road.

The MUSICAL People.

KNOWLES & SON,

Pork & General Butchers,

Derby St., Leek.

1900-30

This is Our
30th Christmas
in business and we are
as determined as ever to
provide

XMAS FARE that is

SECOND to NONE.

The name of Knowles was prominent amongst Leek's butchers for many years. George Knowles is listed in Derby street in the 1860 directory. Thomas Knowles appears in Kiln Lane and Overton Bank in 1888, moving to North Street by 1896 and later trading as Harriet Knowles. Messena Knowles was at 54 Derby Street in 1904, where Knowles & Son later came under the ownership of Charles Sherratt, and is now Boulds. Another Knowles - Matthew (known as "Matty") - traded at 13 West Street and 6 St Edward Street. There were Knowles butcher's shops in West Street and on Compton until the late 1980s.

18, North Street & 1, Overton Bank,

LEEK, ...1

Mr Isaac Heath

Bought of M. KNOWLES,
Harriet

FAMILY BUTCHER.

Home-cured Hams and Bacon a speciality.
Pickled Tongues, Home rendered Lard,
Pork. Sausages, Dripping, Brawn.

			£	s	d
1902					
March 1	To Dishonoured Cheque & Expenses		25	2	8
	Court fees on same		3	8	=
June 2	To Cheque not Due		25	=	=
		£	53	10	8

2, CHURCH LANE,

Leek, *July 13* _____ 187*1*

M~ *The Trustees of the Late Chas Flint Esq~*

Dr. to WILLIAM KNOWLES,

BUILDER, &c.

Feb 23	To Repairing Roof in Stackwell St	£	s	d
	Bricklayer ½ day		4	10
	Labourer 1 day		3	
	2 Pecks of Cement		1	8
	40 Roof tiles		1	9

LEEK, *2 Oct 27* _____ 187*6*

M~ *W. B. Badnall Esqre*

Dr. To WILLIAM KNOWLES,

BUILDER &C.

Oct 7	To repairing reading Schools Miss Mellow	£	s	d
	To 2 men 7 days each at 4/	2	16	
	To 3 Bags of portland cement & carting at 14/	1	17	6
	3 Barrows of hair mortar		4	
	80 Bricks 2/6 · 40 roof tiles 2/3 · & carting 1/3		6	
	3 Buckets of lime putty flag 2 feet 6 by 2 foot		3	6
	10 Slates Laths & nails		4	11
	Carting dirt away 3 loads		4	6
	Self ½ day		2	11
	£	5	19	4

William Knowles' address was 46 Derby Street, an address later occupied (1887)
by J.R. Morton, jeweller and silversmith

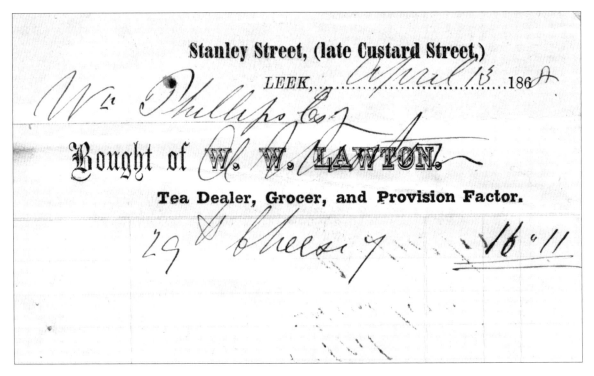

Stanley Street, (late Custard Street,)

LEEK, *April 13* 186*8*

Wm Phillips Es^q

Bought of W. W. LAWTON.

Tea Dealer, Grocer, and Provision Factor.

This billhead shows the earlier name of Stanley Street, Custard Street. The most likely explanation of the origin lies in the proximity of the street to the Market Place, in and around which the stalls of the costermongers would be found.

TELEPHONE No. **66.**

TELEGRAMS: "LEEK, ENGINEERS, LEEK."

Invoice from

CHARLES LEEK & SONS,

BRITANNIA ENGINEERING WORKS,

LEEK, ... 19 ....

STAFFS.

Machinists to Silk, Smallware, and Allied Trades.

WINDING FRAMES FOR COTTON, SILK AND ARTIFICIAL SILK.   SPINNING AND THROWING MILLS.
SMALLWARE LOOMS.   TAKING-UP MOTIONS FOR LOOMS.   SHUTTLES AND PLATE SPRINGS.
ALL CLASSES OF SILK MACHINERY.

To ....

TELEPHONE No. **66.**

TELEGRAMS: "LEEK, ENGINEERS, LEEK."

Memo.
from

Charles Leek & Sons,

(H. B. LEEK.   HARVEY LEEK.)

BRITANNIA ENGINEERING WORKS,

LEEK, Staffs. .... 191 ....

To ....

The growth of the silk industry in Leek created work for millwrights, foundries and light engineering works. The complex nature of most silk machines, like spinning machines and looms, meant that inevitably they would break down, and many tools and spare parts often had to be made to order. The ingenuity and skill of these respected craftsmen enabled them to solve almost any such problem and the necessary parts were usually "fettled" to order. Charles Leek's heading lists their various speciality services to the silk industry. Leek's are still in the town today at the corner of Ashbourne Road and Springfield Road.

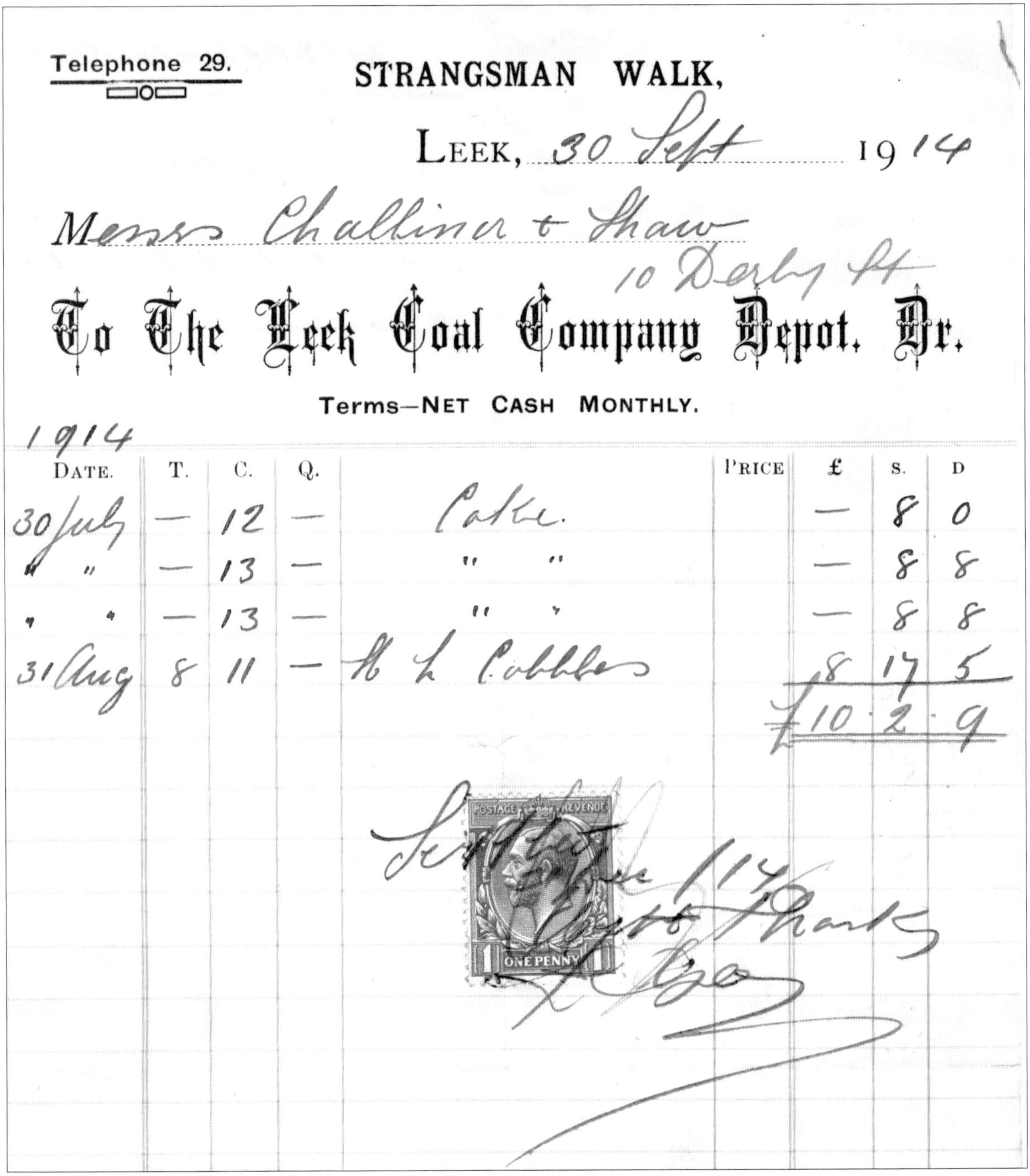

Telephone 29.

STRANGSMAN WALK,

LEEK, *30 Sept* 19*14*

Messrs Challiner & Shaw

10 Derby St

To The Leek Coal Company Depot, Dr.

Terms—NET CASH MONTHLY.

1914

DATE.	T.	C.	Q.		PRICE	£	S.	D
30 July	—	12	—	Cake.		—	8	0
" "	—	13	—	" "		—	8	8
" "	—	13	—	" "		—	8	8
31 Aug	8	11	—	H L Cobbles		8	17	5
						£10	2	9

Presumably Strangsman Walk is a mis-spelling. Strangman's Walks formerly led off St Edward Street, following the present Strangman Street and continued down to the canal terminus and railway station at the bottom of Broad Street (in the area of the present day Morrisons and Focus).

Telephone 29.

STRANGSMAN WALK.
LEEK,

10 Jan 19*12*

Messrs Challinor & Shaw 10 Derby St

To THE LEEK COAL COMPANY DEPOT. *Dr.*

Terms—NET CASH MONTHLY.

DATE.	COAL.		COBBLES.		SLACK.				Price	£	s.	d.
	T.	C.	T.	C.	T.	C.	T	C.				
5 July 11			1	0¾	& Carriage				18/6	0	18	11

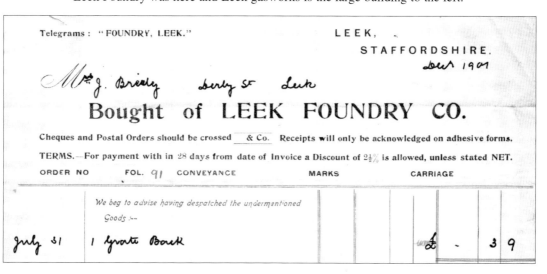

Leek Canal Basin in the 1950s, the area where many local coal merchants had their depots.
Leek Foundry was here and Leek gasworks is the large building to the left.

Telegrams : "FOUNDRY, LEEK."

LEEK,
STAFFORDSHIRE.
Dec 1901

Mr J. Brealy Derby St Leek

Bought of LEEK FOUNDRY CO.

Cheques and Postal Orders should be crossed ___ & Co. Receipts will only be acknowledged on adhesive forms.

TERMS.—For payment with in 28 days from date of Invoice a Discount of 2½% is allowed, unless stated NET.

ORDER NO	FOL. 91	CONVEYANCE	MARKS	CARRIAGE		
		We beg to advise having despatched the undermentioned Goods :—				
July 31	1 Grate Back			£	3	9

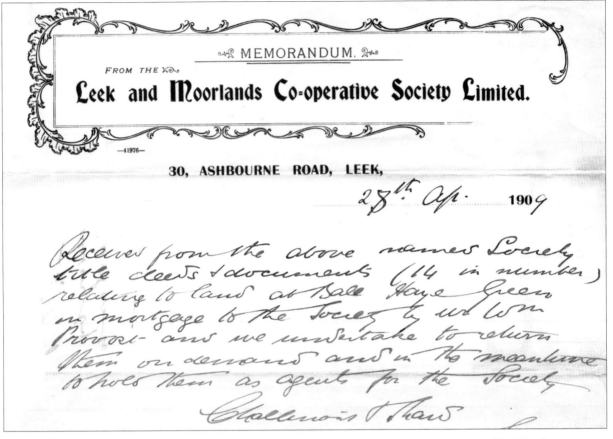

The Co-operative movement was established in Leek in 1859, firstly in a small cottage on Clerk Bank, soon to move to a shop on the opposite Overton Bank. Business expanded rapidly, and other branch shops were opened in different parts of the town - Ball Haye Green (1882), Picton Street (1895), Buxton Road (1904), Mill Street (1907) and Compton. This heading shows the address of the Central Premises on Ashbourne Road, designed by Larner Sugden, built by Thomas Grace and opened in 1899. The premises comprised offices and boardroom, grocery, provisions and bakery, and a large hall upstairs used for meetings and functions.

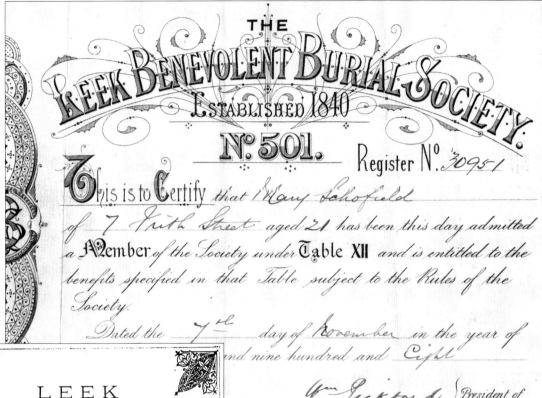

LEEK
BENEVOLENT BURIAL
SOCIETY

REGISTERED No. 501.

FIFTY-THIRD
ANNUAL REPORT
AND
ADVERTISER,

For the Year ending 31st December, 1893.

REGISTERED OFFICE:
RUSSELL STREET, LEEK.

HOURS OF ATTENDANCE,

6-30 to 7 every Evening (Saturday excepted.)

WILLIAM BOTT,
Secretary.

JOHN. C. FOGG, PRINTER, LEEK.

The Leek Benevolent Burial Society was established on December 13th 1840. In its first year it had 1155 subscribing members and paid out £93 for 26 funerals. It was run by a committee of local business men and was probably motivated by the problem for the poor in burying their children. At the time nearly 1 in 5 of all babies born in Leek would have died by the end of a year! Conversely throughout the 1890s the Annual Report of the Leek Medical Officer of Health (MOH) was repeatedly railing against the organisation, implying that the insurance system increased the death rate of small babies because of the financial gain, and frustrated his efforts to reduce the Infant Mortality Rate.

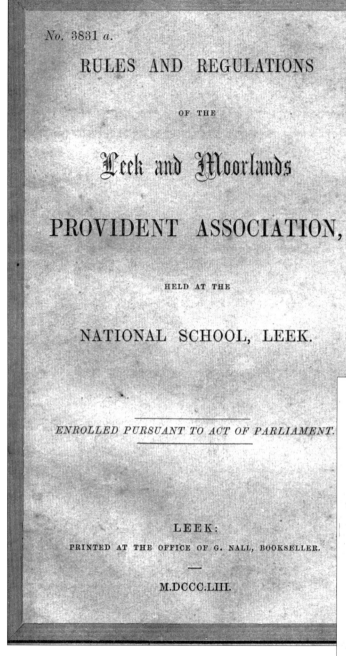

No. 3831 a.

RULES AND REGULATIONS

OF THE

Leek and Moorlands

PROVIDENT ASSOCIATION,

HELD AT THE

NATIONAL SCHOOL, LEEK.

ENROLLED PURSUANT TO ACT OF PARLIAMENT.

LEEK;

PRINTED AT THE OFFICE OF G. NALL, BOOKSELLER.

—

M.DCCC.LIII.

The Leek & Moorlands Provident Association was one of many friendly societies, either local or more national, that provided insurance against illness and injury. Many had ancient connections, with names like Ancient Order of Foresters, or Buffalos, and the Masonic movement gave similar cover. Waterhouses had the Waterfall Friendly Society.

With Lloyd George's 1912 National Insurance Act all working men were covered by the Government scheme (the 'Dole'), but the women and children were not and the societies mainly picked up this cover. The societies were still active until the late 20th century but have rapidly declined since with the improvement in government benefits and the growth of private health insurers.

The Friendly Societies Act of 1793 laid down the foundations for these mutual benefit associations, where members made regular contributions which enabled a pay-out in times of ill-health or a death in the family. It was from such 'self help' organisations that the building society movement later evolved.

Leek and Moorlands
BUILDING SOCIETY.

Established 1856.   Incorporated 1879.   Protected by Act of Parliament.

Trustees.

JOSHUA BROUGH, Esq., J.P.   ARTHUR NICHOLSON, Esq., J.P.
JOHN WARD, Esq.

Bankers.

MANCHESTER & LIVERPOOL DISTRICT BANKING Co. (Ltd.) Leek

Solicitors.

Messrs. CHALLINOR & Co., Leek.

Secretary.

Mr. THOMAS BREALEY.

Surveyors.

Messrs. THOMAS BREALEY & SON.   Mr. EDWIN HEATON.

Annual Income £50,000.
The Society has advanced upwards of £475,000.
The Reserve Fund exceeds £9,000.
Bonuses have been allotted to the extent of £21,600.

ADVANTAGES:

1.—The Society is Incorporated under the Building Societies' Act, 1874, whereby the liability of Members is limited.

2.—Persons in all ranks of life, including females and children, may become Investing Members at any time.

3.—Money promptly advanced to Borrowers at moderate rates, and without the necessity for previous membership.

4.—No Entrance Fees. No deductions from loans, nor addition to mortgages, for premium or commission.

5.—No publicity. Fixed Law Charges for Mortgages.

6.—Investors may withdraw Shares, and Borrowers redeem mortgages on giving notice.

7.—Profits periodically divided equally between Investing and Borrowing Members entitled to participate.

8.—Bonuses paid in full without forfeiture or loss on withdrawal or redemption at any time.

9.—A large reserve Fund, and ample security.

10.—Management expenses economical, and all payments by calendar month, being 12 only in the year. It appears from the Building Societies' Directory, that (with the exception of the small Societies) this is the most economically conducted Society in the Kingdom.

Office:—1, Stockwell Street, Leek.

INVESTORS.

The Shares are divided into Subcription Shares and Preference Shares.

CLASS 1.—SUBSCRIPTION SHARES OF £25 EACH, realizable by calendar monthly payments of **2s. 6d.** in 12 years and 9 months, **with profits.** Any number of Shares may be taken at any time. **Compound Interest at £4 10s. 0d. per cent. per annum is allowed in addition to Bonuses.** The following Example illustrates the system—

The Leek and Moorlands Building Society was first established on a permanent basis in 1856, largely due to the efforts of William and James Challinor, with Thomas Shaw, who became the first Secretary of the Society.

The original 1856 offices of the Leek & Moorlands Building Society in Stockwell Street, now the Leek Town Council offices. The society grew inexorably from its formation in 1856, through amalgamation to form the Leek & Westbourne in 1966, then the Leek and Eastern Counties in the 1980s and finally by the end of that decade emerging as the Britannia - now one of the largest societies in England.

Leek features greatly in the building society movement. Not only does it have the Britannia, but also the Leek United which although it has remained local is still an important employer. One of its chairmen, Enoch Hill went on to the Halifax and was at the helm as chairman throughout the 1920s and 1930s when the society grew into the most successful society in the Country.

1925

1876

STILL THE SAFEST INVESTMENT OF THE DAY,

and the safest investment of **any** day, yesterday, today o
to-morrow. The investment that **never** depreciates. Th
investment that **always** maintains its full capital value an
invariably pays the highest rates of interest, free of Tax

THE
LEEK UNITED
AND MIDLANDS
BUILDING SOCIETY

AS IMPREGNABLE AS THE PYRAMIDS.
INTEREST FROM 3½ to 5 per cent. FREE OF TAX.

Investments of any amount may be made at any time.

The offices of the Leek United and Midlands Building Society seen in 1937 celebrating the coronation of George VI.

The offices were originally the site of Hacker & Allen, solicitors, and the society is still there today, although it has expanded considerably along Strangman Street and into the old corn mill of Whittles.

HEAD OFFICE: 50 ST EDWARD STREET, LEEK.

LEEK

Floral and Horticultural Society.

ANNUAL STATEMENT OF ACCOUNTS, &C.,

FOR THE YEAR 1861.

President :

JOHN CRUSO, ESQ.

Committee :

Mr. JOHN BREARLEY.	Mr. T. MYATT.
,, J. CRITCHLOW.	,, JAMES RIDER.
,, W. GALLIMORE.	,, W. H. SQUIRE.
,, J. M. HAMMERSLEY.	,, W. H. WOOLEY.
,, T. MASKERY.	,, R. WOOLLISCROFT.

Treasurer and Secretary :

Mr. W. S. BROUGH.

REPORT.

THE Committee of this Society have again the pleasure of tendering to their Friends and Subscribers their ANNUAL STATEMENT OF ACCOUNTS.

The Exhibitions of past years have generally been successful, and have given the public great satisfaction. They have caused a generous competition to arise amongst the growers, and have promoted the extension of a very delightful and healthy occupation amongst Cottagers and others.

It will be the aim of the Committee to make the coming Show as attractive as that of any former one, and they trust such friends as possess choice or rare plants will kindly lend them for the decoration of the room. Care will be taken of them and they will be returned in safety.

An appeal will again be made to the Friends of the Society for funds to defray the expenses of the present Autumnal Show, which is intended to be held at the usual place, on TUESDAY, the 16th SEPTEMBER, 1862.

LEEK, August, 1862.

LEEK

Floral and Horticultural Society.

••

THE

ANNUAL EXHIBITION

WILL BE HELD ON

THURSDAY & FRIDAY, AUGUST 28 & 29, 1884,

IN A FIELD IN WEST STREET.

Occupied by Mr. Goodfellow.

Patrons :

THE EARL OF MACCLESFIELD.

ARGLES F. A. ESQ.
BROUGH JOSHUA ESQ., J.P.
CRUSO MRS.
CHALLINOR W. ESQ.
CHALLINOR J. ESQ.
CRAIG W. Y. ESQ., M.P.

DAVENPORT H. T. ESQ., M.P.
DEACON REV. G. E.
GLOVER E. C. ESQ.
MILNER R. S. ESQ.
ROBINSON JOHN ESQ., J.P.

SMITH MISS
SLEIGH H. ESQ., J.P.
SNEYD D. H. ESQ., J.P.
WORTHINGTON ERNEST A. ESQ., J.P.
WARDLE T. ESQ.

President :

H. L. JOHNSON ESQ.

Treasurer :

MR. B. FLANAGAN.

Committee :

CHAIRMAN OF COMMITTEE : MR. T. H. BISHTON.   VICE-CHAIRMAN : MR. H. GIBSON.

BARNFATHER W.
BENNETT J.
CLEMESHA J. C.

GARNER W.
MATHEWS J.
MILLER M. H.

E. WALKER, Secretary.

W. CLEMESHA, STEAM PRINTER, LEEK.

LEEK SELF-SUPPORTING AND CHARITABLE

DISPENSARY.

The Objects of this Institution are,

First.—To encourage a provident and independent spirit amongst the working classes, by allowing such of them, as support themselves without parochial assistance, to become Subscribers to this Institution, under the denomination of " FREE CLASS," on paying after the rate of one penny per week for persons above fourteen years of age, and one halfpenny per week for persons under that age; thereby entitling themselves to medical and surgical aid, when required, and to certain privileges to be enjoyed exclusively by this class.

Secondly.—To provide medical and surgical assistance for such poor persons as are unable to afford the means of subscribing to the Free Class, and who shall receive Tickets of recommendation from Honorary Subscribers.

Thirdly.—To provide surgical assistance for poor married women, during their confinement.

Fourthly.—To enable Overseers of the Poor to contract with the Committee, and the Surgeons of this Institution, for the purpose of providing Medical and Surgical Assistance for the Paupers belonging to their respective Townships or Parishes.

Lastly.—To consult the feelings, and to promote the comforts of the poor, by allowing, to all classes, the choice of being attended by any of the Surgeons of this Institution which may be most agreeable to them; and by providing them with medical attendance at their own dwellings, when severe illness renders them unable to attend at the residence of the respective Surgeons.

R U L E S

OF THE

LEEK SELF-SUPPORTING

AND CHARITABLE

DISPENSARY.

ESTABLISHED APRIL, 1832.

PRESIDENT,

THE REV. T. H. HEATHCOTE, M.A.

COMMITTEE.

MR. JOSEPH ABBOTT	MR. RICHARD GAUNT
MR. THOMAS CARR	MR. MATTHEW GAUNT
MR. TOFT CHORLEY	MR. SAMUEL PHILLIPS
MR. J. CRUSO JUN.	MR. ANTHONY WARD
MR. FRANCIS CRUSO	MR. JAMES WARDLE
MR. LILLEY ELLIS	MR. SAMUEL YOUNG

CONSULTING SURGEON, (*GRATUITOUS*)

MR. FLINT.

ACTING SURGEONS,

MR. CHADWICK.   MR. COOPER.

TREASURERS,—MESSRS. FOWLER AND GAUNTS.

SECRETARY,—MR. NALL.

G. Nall, Printer.

LEEK DISPENSARY.

ESTABLISHED APRIL, 1832.

PRESIDENT,
THE REV. G. E. DEACON, M.A.

VICE-PRESIDENTS,
Mr. ALSOP, | Mr. CRUSO.

CONSULTING SURGEON, (Gratuitous)
Mr. FLINT.

ACTING SURGEONS,

Mr. COOPER,	Mr. RITCHIE,	Mr. WALTERS.
Mr. HEATON,	Mr. TURNOCK,	

COMMITTEE,

Mr. BADNALL,	Mr. G. CRITCHLOW,	Mr. MOLLATT,
Mr. CARTWRIGHT,	Mr. J. GODDARD,	Mr. W. WOOD,
Mr. JOSEPH CHALLINOR,	Mr. J. HOWES,	Mr. WOOLLISCROFT,
Mr. CHELL,	Mr. T. JOHNSON,	Mr. E. WRIGHT,

TREASURER,
Mr. ROBERT NALL.

SECRETARY,
Mr. JOHN RUSSELL, Jun.

REPORT FOR THE YEAR ENDING MARCH, 1862.

THE Committee in issuing their Report for the year just concluded, are gratified to be able to observe that, notwithstanding the recent great depression in trade—a cause which affects, of all classes, most nearly the working population of the town, for whom alone the Dispensary was established—the number of Subscribers to its " Free Class " has been so well maintained, that their payments of a penny per week have amounted, as will be seen in the Accounts, to the sum of £372.

This fact tells more forcibly than anything the Committee can say, how well the system of the Dispensary is adapted to the circumstances and requirements of its Free Members, and how highly its advantages are appreciated by those, who by its means are rendered to a great extent independent of parochial relief or casual charity in time of sickness, and are in some degree directed into habits of providence and method, the practice of which in themselves—setting aside the advantages of their end— cannot but have a beneficial influence on the character of those who cultivate them.

But although the Dispensary has now been in existence for a many years in the town, there seems to be in the minds of some persons (of those classes from which the Dispensary asks only a friendly countenance), considerable misapprehension as regards its purposes and aim, and the Committee think the present a fitting opportunity for correcting such mistaken views as may have been formed, and for placing before the public what the real character of the Institution is, confident that when its object is clearly perceived, it will cordially commend itself to the support and approbation of all.

As Leek does not possess the advantage of a Hospital or Infirmary, like many other towns, the Dispensary was instituted to meet in some degree this necessary requirement, and at the same time to encourage a provident and independent spirit among the working classes, by making it mainly self supporting—allowing such of them as do not apply for parochial relief, to obtain medical and surgical aid from any surgeon they may choose, on payment of one penny per week. In a population like that of Leek, there will always be some who, from various circumstances, will need the assistance of their wealthier neighbours, and to meet this requirement there is, in addition to the Free Class already mentioned, a Charity Class, consisting of persons who on presenting to the Surgeon a Subscription Ticket, receive a month's attendance and medicines, which they would otherwise be unable to obtain. The Committee believe that a ticket of this kind if judiciously given, is frequently a very great boon to many poor people, particularly in the case of married women needing attendance in their confinement, and they would urge the claims of this class to more attention than they have hitherto received. The whole of the money subscribed by the Free Class, with the exception of the expenses incurred in collecting it, is divided amongst the Surgeons. A Subscriber receives four Tickets for each guinea subscribed; and to meet the general expenses of the Institution, collections have been made annually in the Churches and Chapels, the half of whatever sum is obtained being returned to the respective Minister of each place of worship in the shape of Subscriber's Tickets. Having thus briefly placed the main objects of the Institution before the public, the Committee feel sure that a careful consideration of them, and a perusal of the Rules, will show that there does not exist in the town a more useful organization, or one more worthy of the support of the charitably disposed.

Dr.   THE TREASURER OF THE LEEK DISPENSARY IN ACCOUNT.   Cr.

FREE CLASS SUBSCRIPTION ACCOUNT.

	£	s.	d.		£	s.	d.
1861—62.				1861, Sep. 25.			
Balance brought from last year.........	0	9	1½	Paid Surgeons for 1832 Tickets at 1s. 10½d.	171	15	0
Subscriptions received	372	0	11	Ditto, for 4 Midwifery Cases, under Rule 9,			
Transferred from Cash Account for 10				at 10s. 6d	2	2	0
Midwifery Cases under Rule 9, at 2s. each	1	0	0	Ditto, for 27 Ditto, under Rule 10, at 5s. 6d.	7	8	6
Ditto, for 41 Cases under Rule 10 at 1s. 6d.				1862, March 23.			
each	3	1	6	Paid Surgeons for 1930 Tickets at 1s. 8d ..	160	16	8
				Ditto, for 6 Midwifery Cases under Rule 9,			
				at 10s. 6d.	3	3	0
				Ditto, for 14 Ditto, under Rule 10, at 5s. 6d.	3	17	0
				Collecting Subscriptions one year	22	6	5
				Registering Patients one year	3	3	0
				Balance	1	19	11½
	376	11	6½		376	11	6½

HONORARY SUBSCRIPTION ACCOUNT.

	£	s.	d.		£	s.	d.
Balance brought from last year.........	14	6	9	1861, Sep. 21			
Honorary Subscriptions received, (*Tickets*				Paid Surgeons, for 92 Tickets, at 5s.	23	0	0
issued, 112)	29	8	0	1862, Mar. 23.			
Proportion of Collections made in places				Ditto, for 59 Tickets, at 5s...........	14	15	0
of worship, for which Clergy have re-				Transferred to Cash Account.........	10	0	0
ceived 39 Tickets...................	10	4	9	Balance in hand	9	4	6
Transferred from Cash Account for 12							
Cases relieved by Committee.........	3	0	0				
	56	19	6		56	19	6

CASH ACCOUNT.

	£	s.	d.		£	s.	d.
Balance in Bank last year	56	19	11	Last year's Balance transferred to Free			
One Year's Interest on Ditto...........	1	14	1	Class Account	0	9	1½
Balance in Treasurer's hands last year ..	10	17	7½	Ditto, to Honorary Subscription Account	14	6	9
Proceeds of Sermons, £21 7s. 7d., less				Allowed on 10 Midwifery Cases, under			
£10 4s. 9d. value of Tickets given to the				Rule 9, at 2s.....................	1	0	0
Clergy	11	2	10	Ditto, on 41 Cases, under Rule 10, at 1s. 6d.	3	1	6
Donations	0	13	6	Leeches	0	7	0
Messrs. Bermingham, Witness's Fee in a				Printing and Stationery	6	7	11
Prosecution	0	5	0	Transferred to Honorary Subscription Ac-			
Donation from Trade Protection Society..	2	2	0	count for 12 Cases relieved by Com-			
Rules Sold	0	1	10	mittee	3	0	0
Amount transferred from Honorary Sub-				Sundries	1	6	0
scription Account..................	10	0	0	Balance in Bank	58	14	0
Balance of Free Class Account	1	19	11½	Ditto, in Treasurer's Hands	16	8	11½
Ditto, of Honorary Subscription Account..	9	4	6				
	105	1	3		105	1	3

HONORARY SUBSCRIPTIONS.

	£	s.	d.		£	s	d.		£	s.	d.
Alsop Mr.	1	1	0	Brought forward	13	18	3	Brought forward	22	11	6
Badnall Mrs	0	10	6	Flint Mr........	1	1	0	Rowley Mr.......	0	5	3
Badnall Mr.	0	10	6	Gaunt Miss	1	1	0	Russell, Mr.	0	5	3
Bermingham Mr..	1	1	0	Grosvenor Mrs ..	1	1	0	Russell Mr. J. Jun	0	5	3
Birch Mrs......	0	10	6	Hammersley Mr.				Shaw Mr. T.	0	10	6
Bloore Mr......	0	10	6	Robert........	0	5	3	Smith Miss	0	10	6
Booth, Mr. T....	0	10	6	Hammersley Mr.				Smith Mr. G....	0	5	3
Brough, Mr. Josh.	0	10	6	W. H.	0	5	3	Tarr, Miss	0	5	3
Brough, Mr. John	0	15	9	Heath Mr. G....	0	5	3	Walmsley Mr. J..	0	10	6
Bull Mr. George..	0	5	3	Howes Mr	0	5	3	Wamsley Mrs. ..	0	10	6
Carse Mr.	0	10	6	Johnson Mr. H. L.	0	5	3	Wardle Mr.......	1	1	0
Cartwright Mr...	0	5	3	Lawrence Mrs. ..	0	5	3	Wardle Mr. T....	0	10	6
Challinor Mr. J..	0	5	3	Lawrence Miss ..	0	5	3	Winfield Mr.	0	10	6
Challinor Mrs. ..	1	1	0	Lightfoot Mr.....	0	5	3	Wright Mr. E....	0	5	3
Challinor Mr....	0	10	6	Pidcock Rev. B..	0	15	9	Worthington Mrs.	0	10	6
Cooper Mrs. G...	0	15	0	Phillips Mr......	1	1	0	Weston Mr. (the			
Cruso Mrs......	2	12	6	Phillips Mr. John	0	5	3	late)	0	5	3
Deacon Rev. G.E.	1	6	3	Pollock Rev. T. B.	0	15	9	Young Mr.	0	5	3
Dean Mr. R. R...	0	5	3	Redfern Mr.	0	10	6				
Carried forward	13	18	3	Carried forward	22	11	6		29	8	0

DONATIONS.

	£	s.	d.
Astley Mrs	0	1	0
Challinor Miss ..	0	2	6
Critchlow Miss ..	0	2	6
Clarke Mr.......	0	1	0
Eaton Mrs	0	1	0
Faville Mr.......	0	1	0
Gould Mr., Union			
Street	0	1	0
Mollatt Mr.	0	1	0
Sutton Mr.......	0	1	0
Swindells Mr. J..	0	1	0
	0	13	6

The Dispensary movement throughout the country set out to provide medical treatment for the working classes in the new industrial towns and cities. In Leek it eventually led to the building of the Leek Memorial Hospital, part of the charitable Infirmary movement providing free or affordable in patient care to working people. It was completely separate from the Workhouse movement run by 'local guardians' for the destitute

The MEMORIAL HOSPITAL, LEEK.

JUBILEE YEAR APPEAL.

The Committee of Management of the above Hospital desire to draw the attention of the inhabitants of LEEK and surrounding districts to the serious financial position with which they are faced, and to suggest that a special effort be made during this year, in which their Majesties the King and Queen celebrate their Silver Jubilee, with the object of,

1. Wiping off the present deficit on the General Account amounting to £532   12   9.

2. Providing funds for the building of a new Hospital.

The Hospital, which is supported by voluntary contributions, ministers to the needs of the inhabitants of the town of LEEK and neighbouring country districts, and the demands now made upon it have grown out of all proportion to the total amount of the annual subscriptions received with the result that the present indebtness is, as stated above, £532.

During the past year 353 patients have been admitted and cared for, 130 operations have been performed and 466 X Ray cases have been treated, at a total cost of £2294   5   7.

The Hospital is fortunate in having on its Honorary Consulting Staff, Specialists in Surgery, Medicine, Ear, Nose and Throat, Radiology, Orthopaedics and Anesthetics, whose valuable services, so freely given, the Committee very highly appreciate.

The recently appointed Matron has commenced duties, the Nursing Staff is being reorganised, and every endeavour is being made by the Committee to ensure the comfort and skilled nursing of the patients.

Notwithstanding the increasing number of patients treated in our own Hospital, we have, in the past, been largely dependent on the North Staffordshire Royal Infirmary, which Institution has rendered great service to the inhabitants of LEEK.

In order to remedy this the Committee are very desirous to commence the building of the proposed new Hospital, the site for which has been secured by the purchase of the Ball Haye Hall estate.

The cost of the erection and equiping of an up-to-date Hospital cannot at present be accurately estimated, but will be in the region of £20,000. It is hoped to include a much needed Maternity Section, thus adding materially to the services which the Hospital is able to render.

It is with very great confidence that the Management Committee appeal to the public for subscriptions and contributions for the two very worthy objects above mentioned and suggest there can be no more commendable way in which to commemorate the Silver Jubilee of their Majesties than by contributing to the funds of this worthy Institution.

Contributions may be earmarked either for reduction of debt or for the New Hospital fund, whichever is desired, and may be sent to the Hon. Secretary, Mr. JOHN WARD, LANGFIELDS, LEEK or to the DISTRICT BANK, LEEK.

"WHO GIVES QUICKLY GIVES TWICE."

1882.

Annual Report

OF THE

Leek Memorial Cottage Hospital.

NAMES OF TRUSTEES, OFFICERS, AND COMMITTEE FOR 1883.

Trustees (ex-officio Members of the Committee.)

ALSOP JOHN,	BERMINGHAM HENRY,
CHALLINOR JOSEPH,	CRUSO MRS.,
JOHNSON H. L.	NICHOLSON ARTHUR,
RITCHIE MRS. J. J.,	WARDLE THOMAS.

Medical Officers (ex-officio Members of the Committee.)

DAKEYNE T. E. GAILEY EDGAR. GAILEY J. A. KENNY JOSEPH.
RITCHIE J. J. SOMERVILLE A.

Officers and Committee elected for 1883.

President—ROBINSON JOHN, | Vice-President—BROUGH JOSHUA,
Treasurer—WHYATT A. R., | Secretary—CARR CHARLES.

CHALLINOR MRS. J.,	GIBSON MRS. S.,
SUGDEN MRS. W.,	BERMINGHAM HENRY,
BIRCH GEORGE,	CARR H. G.,
FARROW ROBERT,	MILNER ROBT. S.,
MORTON JAMES,	SMITH G. H.,
WARD JOHN,	WINFIELD J. S., JUN.

Auditors elected for 1883.

ANDREW JOSHUA, | SHAW THOMAS.

Matron.

McROBBIE MARY.

LEEK:
PRINTED AT THE OFFICE OF SAM RIDER, DERBY STREET.

The Cottage Hospital and surrounding
areas in 1879.

The Cottage Hospital, the Leek Memorial and the Alsop Memorial were all names for Leek's independent hospital. It was built in 1870 to a Sugden design in memory of James Alsop JP with an endowment from his widow. A new wing was added by public subscription in 1909. As the letter on the opposite page demonstrates, during the 1930s a project to raise money for a new hospital was enthusiastically pursued. It is said that by 1939 £80,000 had been raised. When the NHS arrived in 1948, the money was swallowed up. The hospital persisted as a general, and later general and maternity hospital, with outpatients and operating list, until the 1980s.

LEEK PUBLIC BATHS.

COMMISSIONERS.

MR. JOSHUA BROUGH, *Chairman.*
MR. THOMAS BIRCH, *Treasurer.*

MR. THOMAS CARR,	MR. JOHN RUSSELL,
MR. ROBERT HAMMERSLEY,	MR. HUGH SLEIGH,

MR. JOHN WARD.

AUDITORS. | SECRETARY.
MR. ALSOP, | MR. MILNER. | MR. CHALLINOR.

LEEK PUBLIC BATHS.

The Commissioners have the pleasure of reminding the Public that these Baths are open daily (except Sunday) from half-past Six o'clock in the Morning, until half-past Eight o'clock in the Evening, and will so continue from the 1st of April to the 1st of October. The remainder of the year they are open from Eight o'clock in the Morning to Eight o'clock in the Evening.

The Establishment has been fitted up with every necessary convenience. On the Men's side there are large First and Second Class Swimming Baths, six Private Baths, and one Shower Bath. On the Ladies' side (which is approached by a distinct entrance) there is a large Plunge Bath, three Private Baths, and a Shower Bath. Hot and Cold Water is always ready, so that Tepid or Hot Private Baths can be had at any temperature. A continual flow of fresh Water has been secured for the Swimming Baths to the extent of near 13,000 gallons a day, and they will be also emptied, cleansed, and refilled weekly.

The First Class Swimming Bath is reserved on Mondays, Weds, and Fridays, exclusively for Annual Subscribers and Strangers.

The Ladies plunge or swimming bath is reserved for 1st class bathers until 1 o'clock each day, after which it is open to 2nd class bathers.

To the GUARDIANS of the LEEK UNION and the RURAL
DISTRICT COUNCIL.

GENTLEMEN,

Referring to our letter of the 25th ult. as to the appointment
of a Clerk in succession to our late Partner, Mr. Wm. Challinor, we beg
to observe that the main consideration in desiring the appointment for
our Mr. Thomas Shaw was the continuance of the long connection of
nearly 60 years which has existed between our Office and the Guardians,
during the whole of which period we are not aware of a single instance
of unpleasantness or complaint; nor has there, we believe, been any
litigation or loss. On the other hand some legal work which could not
be undertaken by other than a Solicitor has been performed without charge.

Although the ordinary detail work may have been done by clerks in
our Office, Mr. Challinor and his predecessors, Mr. Badnall and Mr. F.
Cruso, superintended and were responsible to the Guardians for the proper
conduct of the business, and this would have been actively continued by
our Mr. Thos. Shaw, who would have had the services of our Office staff
and the use of the present offices free of expense to the ratepayers.

We intimated to Mr. Joseph Shaw our desire to continue his services
on a permanent basis and at increased remuneration; but we now under-
stand that the Guardians wish their Clerk personally to perform all the
duties, and contemplate a reduction of the salaries. If this be the case
the appointment of Mr. Thomas Shaw would result in little or no
pecuniary benefit, but would leave us with all the responsibility—our
application is therefore withdrawn.

As there may be some misunderstanding we beg to add that
Mr. Joseph Shaw has been receiving from our firm, including the sums
paid to him by the Guardians and Council since the reduction of Mr.
Challinor's salary, about £160 per annum, on an average of the last three
years, independently of liberal pecuniary provision by Mr. Challinor personally,
and that we have also paid the salary of another clerk whose time has
been chiefly occupied in assisting Mr. Joseph Shaw.

Regretting the severance of our connection with the Guardians and
Council,

We beg to remain

Your obedient servants,

CHALLINORS & SHAW.

Leek, 9th April, 1896.

No. 210

CATTLE DISEASES PREVENTION ACT, 1866.

LEEK UNION, COUNTY OF STAFFORD.
TOWNSHIP OF ENDON, LONGSDON, AND STANLEY.

RECEIVED the 26th day of *September* 1866, of
Mr. *John Read* the sum of
pounds, 17 shillings, and 8 pence, in respect of Rate
at Threepence halfpenny in the pound, made the sixteenth day of August, 1866, for the
above Township, by authority of the Cattle Diseases Prevention Act, 1866, viz :—

	£	s.	d.
Landlord's Share		8 -	10
Tenant's Share		8 -	10
TOTAL		17	8

W Hale OVERSEER.

The offices of the Leek Union were at 6 Russell Street in 1866. The Board administered the
health and medical requirements of a wide area of the moorlands, from Smallthorne to Longnor,
from Biddulph to Butterton - an area of over 75,000 acres with a population of 42,000 in 1901.
The Leek Workhouse was run by the Union and was by then in Ashbourne Road.
Below: North block (the Infirmary) at Leek Workhouse in 1896.

Workhouse Street (now Brook Street) was the site of Leek's second workhouse. The first was in Derby Street, which was later Morton's jewellers (see page 151)

The new workhouse was erected in 1838 in London Road (later became Ashbourne Road). In this section of Slagg's 1862 map the area has a number of brickyards.

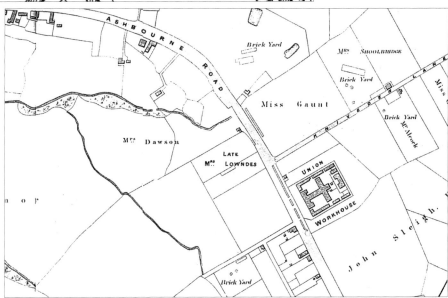

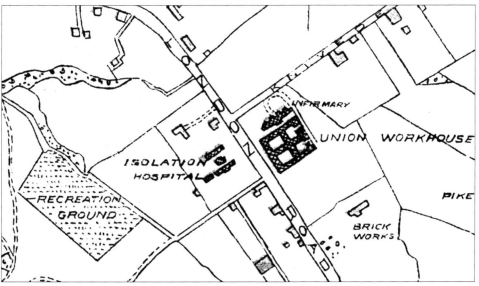

This early 20th century map shows the Isolation Hospital which was built for the Leek Commisioners in 1880.

The Recreation Ground (Pickwood Recreation Ground) was presented to the Town by William Challinor of Pickwood Hall in Queen Victoria's Golden Jubilee year, 1887.

THE
LEEK ANNUAL

BEING

AN ALMANACK, DIARY AND DIRECTORY,

for the year 1916, and including a Guide to the Public Bodies and Institutions of the Town and Neighbourhood of Leek.

FIFTY-FIRST YEAR OF ISSUE

Printed and Published by W. H. EATON,
at the Moorlands Press,
LEEK: ANNO 1915.

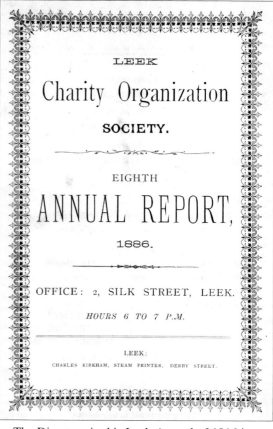

LEEK

Charity Organization

SOCIETY.

EIGHTH

ANNUAL REPORT,

1886.

OFFICE: 2, SILK STREET, LEEK.

HOURS 6 TO 7 P.M.

LEEK:
CHARLES KIRKHAM, STEAM PRINTER, DERBY STREET.

The Directory in this Leek Annual of 1916 is reproduced with others in Vol. III of Leek Trade Bills

Public services such as gas, electricity and water were originally the responsibility of the local authority - first the Leek Improvement Commissioners, then the Leek Urban District Council.

GAS WORKS, LEEK,

Mess.rs Challinor Badnall & Challinor,

To the Leek Gas Commissioners.

18 50		£	s.	d.
Nov.r 9	1 - Two-light Gas Meeter	1	15	0 -
	Nov.r 22nd Paid Geo Hall			

"LEEK IMPROVEMENT ACT, 1855."

RATES FOR 1859—60.

M _C Brassington_ _____ Street.

Premises.	Assessment		£	s.	d.
House	£4 0	General Purposes Rate...........at 6d. in the £		2	
		Paving and Sewerage Rate, at 6d. in the £		2	
Land	£	Cemetery Rate......................at 3d in the £		1	
		District Rate....................at 4d. in the £			
		£		5	

The above Rates are due, and are hereby demanded.

WILLIAM BARKER, Collector.

Under the terms of the Leek Improvement Act of 1855 the Town was defined by a perfect circle with a radius of 1500 yards taking as its centre the lamp in the middle of the Market Place, and this was the area administered by the Leek Improvement Commissioners.

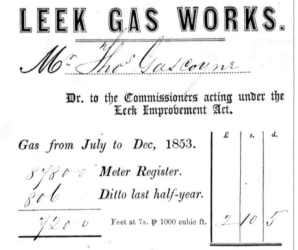

LEEK GAS WORKS.

Mr _Thos Gascoyne_

Dr. to the Commissioners acting under the Leek Improvement Act.

Gas from July to Dec, 1853.

		£	s.	d.
8780 0	Meter Register.			
80 6	Ditto last half-year.			
720 0	Feet at 7s. ℔ 1000 cubic ft.	2	10	5

N.B.—You are particularly requested to pay the above Gas Rent to R. HAMMOND, *Clerk to the Gas Commissioners*, within 14 days after the Account has been delivered, in default of which, your supply of Gas may be discontinued.

The Gas Commissioners hereby give Notice, that they will not be responsible for any loss which may be occasioned by explosion or other accidents arising from the imperfect state of the Gas Fittings in the interior of the buildings.

It is particularly requested that when there is any smell of Gas, immediate notice thereof may be given to the Manager of the Gas Works; and that in the mean time, every precaution may be taken to prevent any person approaching the place with a light, where the Gas is escaping, especially in a cellar or other confined place.

The water in the Meter is liable to be frozen, and the supply of Gas through it, to be stopped in consequence; care should therefore be taken to prevent this.

All consumers of Gas are to burn by Meter, which Meter the Commissioners will supply them with at prime cost. Meters, not exceeding three-light size, are lent to consumers, by the Commissioners, at a charge of five shillings per annum.

Access is to be given to the Meters, for the purpose of examining them, at all reasonable hours.

By Order of the Commissioners.

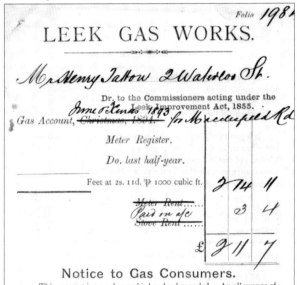

Folio **198**

LEEK GAS WORKS.

Mr _Henry Tatton 2 Waterloo St._

Dr. to the Commissioners acting under the Leek Improvement Act, 1855.

Gas Account, ~~Christmas, 1894~~ _Some or Xmas 1893 for Macclesfield Rd_

Meter Register.

Do. last half-year.

	£	s.	d.
Feet at 2s. 11d. ℔ 1000 cubic ft.	2	14	11
~~Meter Rent....~~			
Paid on a/c		3	4
~~Stove Rent....~~			
£	2	11	7

Notice to Gas Consumers.

This account is now due and is hereby demanded. An allowance of six-pence per 1000 feet will be made on

ALL ACCOUNTS PAID AT THE OFFICE,

TOWN HALL, MARKET STREET,

before 10 o'clock on the morning of January 20th, and three-pence per 1000 if paid between that time and 10 o'clock on the morning of the 15th February following, after which time no allowance will be made.

The Collector will not make any calls until after the 20th of January, nor will he receive accounts at his residence.

In order to prevent unnecessary crowding and delay at the last, Consumers are respectfully requested to pay their accounts as soon after delivery as possible.

Payment by Cheques on other than Leek Banks must be made 3 days before the above-mentioned dates, or the respective allowances will be forfeited.

By order of the Commissioners,

W. DISHLEY, Collector.

[SEE OTHER SIDE.

To Owners and Cultivators of Land.

SULPHATE OF AMMONIA.

The Leek Improvement Commissioners who are making Sulphate of Ammonia, wish to call the attention of Farmers and others to the opportunity they now have of obtaining this valuable fertilizing agent, in quantities of not less than one cwt. for cash, at the Leek Gas Works. Price until the end of March 13s. per cwt.

The saving effected by purchasing the Sulphate direct from the maker is one worthy of consideration by all Farmers. A competent writer on the subject asserts that by adopting this plan and carefully mixing it to suit his requirements instead of obtaining it from the dealers he has saved over 30 per cent. upon the cost, and probably another 20 to 25 per cent. in its freedom from adulteration.

Used with ordinary farm yard manure or well mixed with equal quantities of sand, fine dry earth, or super-phosphate of lime and spread not later than the month of April in moist showery weather, its beneficial effect upon Grass, Corn, Mangold Wurzel, Turnips, and Cabbages will be quickly apparent and should lead to an increased use of it.

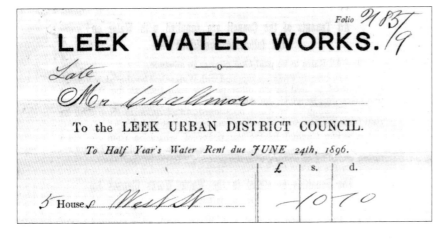

LEEK WATER WORKS.

Mʳ C Drapington

TO THE COMMISSIONERS ACTING UNDER THE LEEK IMPROVEMENT ACT, 1855.

To half a Year's Water Rent, due 29th Dec. 18 } £ 0 2 2
One Quarter in advance ....

THE ABOVE IS HEREBY DEMANDED,

William Barker,

COLLECTOR.

The Collector will be in attendance at the Public Offices, Russell Street, on the Wednesdays of the
and between the hours of 12 and 2 o'clock, P.M.,
to receive accounts which are not paid when called for ; and any Person failing to pay on or before the
latter date, their supply will be discontinued. [See other side.

Folio

LEEK WATER WORKS.

Late
Mr Challinor

To the LEEK URBAN DISTRICT COUNCIL.

To Half Year's Water Rent due JUNE 24th, 1896.

	£	s.	d.
5 House West St		10	0

Clean water is one of the first necessities and it was foremost of the many and onerous demands upon the Leek Improvement Commissioners in 1855. In the 1880s they purchased the water rights from the Earl of Macclesfield for £11,000, and from the springs at Upperhulme and a small storage reservoir at Blackshaw Moor water was piped into Leek for the first time.

The Leek Chamber of Commerce.

First Annual Report and Statement of Account.

The annexed statement shows that the Chamber has 60 members, and that there is a balance in hand of £7. 5s. 1d.

The formation of the Chamber was first publicly mooted at the Board of Commissioners, and a public meeting convened by the Chairman of the Commissioners, was held in the Town Hall, on 23rd March, 1886, and it was resolved to form a Chamber, and a Committee was appointed to frame rules and to ascertain whether sufficient support would be afforded to make the Chamber a success.

Exors of late
W. Challinor

Town Hall,
Leek.

68

Mr ~~Chas Watson~~ Pickwood

DR. TO THE

Leek Urban District Council.

1896	GAS.	£	s.	d.

May 20th	To Fittings &c for Hanarles Farm			
19 Feet of	1" Iron tube		6	9
1 "	4" Thimble		2	3
30 lbs "	Lead		3	2
3 . "	Tarred Yarn			8
1 " "	Red lead putty			8
1 . "	Paint			4
2 " "	1" Sockets			4

The Town Hall in Market Street was purchased by L.U.D.C. in 1884 from the Union Buildings Company who had built it for use as an independent gentlemens' club which proved unsuccessful. It served as the Council's headquarters until local government reorganisation in the 1970s. The large hall was in great demand for local amateur dramatic and operatic performances, dances, large social functions and public meetings

Leek & Manifold Valley Light Railway.

LEEK,

June, 1904.

OPENING CEREMONY.

Dear Sir,

I enclose Luncheon Ticket, for which perhaps you will kindly send me 2/6.

I also send a Railway Ticket.

Yours truly,

E. CHALLINOR.

The Manifold Valley Light Railway passing Brown End Farm, Waterhouses.

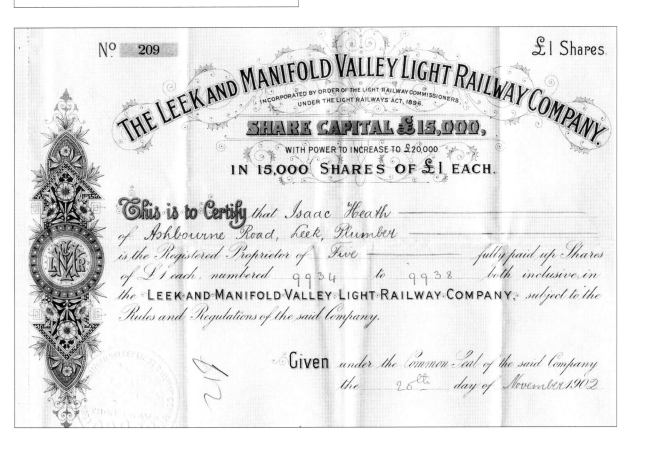

Nº 209   £1 Shares.

THE LEEK AND MANIFOLD VALLEY LIGHT RAILWAY COMPANY.

INCORPORATED BY ORDER OF THE LIGHT RAILWAY COMMISSIONERS,
UNDER THE LIGHT RAILWAYS ACT, 1896.

SHARE CAPITAL £15,000,

WITH POWER TO INCREASE TO £20,000.

IN 15,000 SHARES OF £1 EACH.

This is to Certify that *Isaac Heath* of *Ashbourne Road, Leek, Plumber* is the Registered Proprietor of *Five* fully paid up Shares of £1 each, numbered *9934* to *9938* both inclusive, in the LEEK AND MANIFOLD VALLEY LIGHT RAILWAY COMPANY, subject to the Rules and Regulations of the said Company.

Given under the Common Seal of the said Company the *25th* day of *November 1902*

Leek and Manifold Valley Light Railway Coy.

The Directors have pleasure in enclosing you a reprint of the report of the Annual General Meeting of Shareholders, held at the Town Hall, Leek, on the 23rd October last.

You will gather from this the great difficulties which your Directors have had in bringing the scheme to its present position, and now that the Contract for the actual construction has been let, and active work has been, or is about to be, commenced, they urge upon you the necessity of increasing your present holding to the extent of at least one half or one third, or to such an extent as you feel able to afford. Until the balance of the 1500 shares is taken up they cannot go to the County Council to make arrangements for receiving the loan of £10,000 which has already been granted. Moreover, the terms of the Order authorizing the line make it a condition that the 15,000 shares should be taken up by persons living in or interested in the area affected by the line. In urging that you should increase your holding, they have every confidence that when the line is in working order, dividends will be earned from the first, as for every £1 of gross receipts taken, by the N.S.R. Coy., (who have to work and maintain the line), 9s. will be handed over to the Shareholders of this Company, out of which the only payment would be a sum of £360 to the County Council in repayment of principal and interest, leaving a considerable margin for the Shareholders; the N.S.R. Co. out of their share of the gross receipts, paying all expenses incurred in the working of the line.

In addition they would urge on the present Shareholders and inhabitants of the districts affected, the great importance the line will be to themselves in providing a means of outlet and inlet for agricultural produce, coal, minerals, lime, &c., &c., at low rates.

In consequence of a contrivance for the carrying of normal gauge goods waggons, cattle trucks, &c., &c., over the 2ft. 6in. line, the Directors expect to avoid transhipment at Waterhouses, which in itself will be an obvious gain to this company. Thus a normal gauge waggon filled with coal, say at Manchester, can be delivered at any of the numerous sidings between Waterhouses and Hulme End for unloading.

Your Directors have every confidence that the further shares will be taken up, and that there will be no delay from this cause in handing over the line completed within 2½ years from this date to the N.S.R. Company for working.

If you are willing to increase your holding, will you kindly fill up and return the enclosed application form to MR. E. CHALLINOR, 10, Derby Street, Leek, THE SECRETARY.

CHARLES BILL,

CHAIRMAN.

Two envelopes
with enclosures

12 Oct 1908
C. Payne.

LEEK
Literary and Mechanics' Institution.

Leek, *Oct 12* 190 8

Dear Sir,

Referring to your letter of the 24th ult,
I have pleasure in enclosing a copy of
last years report and Balance sheet,
together with an Account of the Income
and expenditure for the half year ending
30 Sept 1908.

The loss has arisen from the
Reading Room and Library, the present
loss being at the rate of £24 per annum.

You will notice from the
Annual Report that the present total
membership is 133, whereas in the year
1906, previous to the opening of the
Billiard Room it was only 97 shewing
an increase of 36, due undoubtedly
the opening of the Billiard Room

the

The Mechanics' Institute was established in 1837 - first in the schoolroom of the Congregational Chapel, then from 1854 in Russell Street. In 1862 its new headquarters building was designed by Sugden. The Institute - an example of early adult education - included classes on many subjects: lectures, a reading room and library, art classes, and a chess club. It continued until 1929.

The Seventy-first Annual Report

OF THE

Leek Literary & Mechanics' Institution,

APRIL, 1908.

The Terms of Subscription are:—Honorary Members 21/- per annum. Ordinary Members, 3/- per quarter. Ladies 2/- per quarter. Family Tickets are also issued at the following reduced prices 21/- for 3 persons. 28/- for 4 persons. and 35/- for 5 persons.

Number of Ordinary Members, 100. Ladies, 7. Honorary Members and Family Ticket Holders, 26. Total 133.

Leek Mechanics' Institution.

THE COMMITTEE BEG TO ANNOUNCE THAT,

TWO EXHIBITIONS

OF

DISSOLVING VIEWS

FROM THE

NEW OXY-HYDROGEN APPARATUS,

BELONGING TO THE INSTITUTION,

WILL TAKE PLACE AT THE

SWAN INN ASSEMBLY ROOM;

THE FIRST,

On Thursday Evening, the 29th of December instant,

AND THE SECOND,

ON FRIDAY EVENING, THE 6th OF JANUARY NEXT.

Explanations and Pieces, illustrative of the Scenery, will be given by Mr. CHALLINOR, who will also have the assistance of several Friends, who have promised some Songs and Glees appropriate to the occasion.

The First Exhibition will consist of Views illustrating

THE ASCENT OF MONT BLANC,

In Switzerland, (which Mr. C. visited in 1851,)

AND SOME OTHER SCENERY;

The Second will consist of a few

ILLUSTRATIONS OF MECHANICS & ASTRONOMY,

Succeeded by some GENERAL VIEWS, accompanied by Recitations.

Doors open on each evening at half-past Seven, to commence at Eight precisely.

ADMISSION :—To Non-Members, on each occasion,—
Front Seats 1s., Back Seats 6d.

MEMBERS HALF-PRICE.

Tickets of Admission may be had of Mr. Nall, Mr. Hilliard, or Mr. Hallowes.
LEEK, DEC. 23rd, 1853.

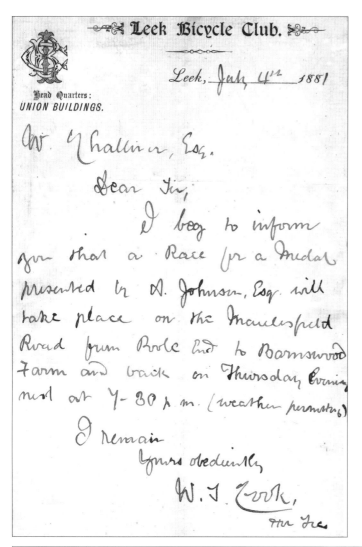

Leek Bicycle Club.

Leek, July 4th 1881

Head Quarters:
UNION BUILDINGS.

Mr. Challinor, Esq.

Dear Sir,

I beg to inform you that a Race for a Medal presented by A. Johnson, Esq. will take place on the Macclesfield Road from Poole End to Barnswood Farm and back on Thursday Evening next at 7-30 p.m. (weather permitting)

I remain
Yours obediently
W. T. Cook,
the Sec.

Established in 1876, the Leek Cycle Club was first known as the Leek and Moorlands Bicycle Club. It is probably the oldest cycling club in the country still operating today.

For a period of time in the 1980s the Club staged an annual professional racing event with the centre of the town closed off to cars.

Opposite bottom of page the Club is seen in carnival mood outside their Duke of York headquarters in Derby Street.

TEN COMMANDMENTS FOR CYCLISTS

Daily Express Correspondent.
LEEK (Staffordshire),
Tuesday.

LEEK CYCLISTS' CLUB, now celebrating their sixtieth year, have never had a serious accident to any member. They claim that this immunity is due to a model set of safety-first rules.

Their members have covered well over a million miles awheel under club auspices.

The club's "ten commandments" are:—
Never ride more than two abreast.
Never ride in groups of more than twelve.
Never disobey the Highway Code.
Never show discourtesy on the road.
Never disobey the captain's whistle.
Never ignore the captain's blast to form single file at a sign of danger.
Never fail to ride a sufficient distance apart.
Never fail to give sufficient warning when overtaking.

Never ride a machine which is not roadworthy.
Never ignore Safety First principles in the interests of speed.
A club official told me that road deaths would soon be reduced if these rules were invariably obeyed.
Motorists were right in condemning cyclists in groups of forty of fifty, he said. "Haphazard" cycling clubs were a new menace.

REPORT
OF THE
LEEK TEMPERANCE SOCIETY,

For the Year ending December 31st, 1861.

OFFICERS.

PRESIDENT :
Mr. JOHN BROUGH.

VICE-PRESIDENTS :
Mr. SUGDEN AND Mr. SILAS GIBSON.

TREASURER :
Mr. TURNOCK.

SECRETARY :
Mr. CHARLES.

COMMITTEE :

Mr. JOSEPH BARLOW,	Mr. JOSEPH HALL,
„ THOS. BROUGH,	„ RITCHIE,
„ THOS. BULL,	„ H. SIMPSON, Jun.
„ GEORGE BURTON,	„ GEORGE TIPPER,
„ HENRY G. CARR,	„ CHARLES WALKER.

The temperance movement was strongly supported in Leek, with much involvement from the churches. Many of the officers of the Leek Temperance Society listed here were prominent in the free churches of the Town.

The annual Band of Hope procession through the streets of Leek was a demonstration of the principles of the temperance movement.

During the Victorian years there was a great proliferation of learned and artistic societies in Leek. This was a reflection of the Town's standing in the Arts and Craft movement, and the influence of the Pre-Raphaelites through such personalities as William Morris and Walter Crane. Musical and dramatic presentations were performed to a high standard and involved many of the Town's leading citizens - professional men and silk manufacturers.
Thomas Wardle was involved with natural history societies and had a great interest in geology.
A branch of the British Fern Society met at Westwood Hall.

THE LEEK
Ornithological Society,
1891.

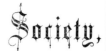

Patrons :

Rev. C. B. Maude,	W. Challinor, Esq.
John Robinson, Esq., J.P.	E. Challinor, Esq.
H. T. Hincks, Esq., M.P.	G. Wardle, Esq.
Thos. Wardle, Esq.	R. Woolliscroft, Esq.

TOWN HALL.
Leek Philothespian Club.
"The Play's the thing"

FIFTEENTH SEASON.

Wednesday Thursday (Fashionable Night) and Friday, 13th, 14th and 15th October, 1897,

SHERIDAN'S FAMOUS COMEDY

THE RIVALS

The Leek Orchestral Society
WILL GIVE SELECTIONS.
Conductor - - - Mr. J. Gwynne,

Costumes by Mr. BURKINSHAW, of LIVERPOOL.
Wigs by Mr. W. A. HUME, of MANCHESTER.

Scenic Artists :—Messrs. H. W. Campling and A. E. Quinn.   Hon. Sec. :—Mr. H. E. Rendell. Manager :—Mr. J. Wardle. Stage Managers :—Messrs. J. P. F. Smith and J. A. Ind.

Doors open at 7-30.
To commence at 8.
Carriages at 10-30.

Admission :—Reserved Seats 2/6 ; Family Ticket to admit five 10/= ; Two front rows of Gallery 1/6 ; Second Seats 1/= ; Remainder 6d.

Plan of Hall may be seen, and seats booked at Mr. W. H. Eaton's Bookshop, Derby Street.

EATON, TYP. LEEK.

THE LEEK SPUN SILK
AND MANUFACTURING COMPANY,
LIMITED.

LEEK,
STAFFORDSHIRE.

TELEGRAMS:
" SPUN CO., LEEK."

Sept-1st 18 96

Dear Sir,

I beg to enclose Cheque for dividend, at the rate of 5% per annum, as declared at the Annual Meeting of Shareholders held on August 4th last.

Yours truly,

J. D. JACKMAN,
Secretary.

London Mills, London Street was the address of Leek Spun Silk in 1896. They later (by 1904) moved to a new single-storey factory in Barngate Street.

BELOW: Miss Jean Cormack operated as an agent for the laundry and traded as a haberdasher at 20 Derby Street for many years. Shoppers would find it more convenient to collect their cleaning from Derby Street, rather than making the long walk down to Macclesfield Road.

1882.

The Old Original Leek Brass Band.

To the Inhabitants and Friends of Leek and the surrounding District—

We beg to tender our hearty thanks for the support accorded to us during the past thirty-five years and respectfully solicit a renewal of your favours at this festive season.

Our friends will please bear in mind that we shall play this year, from a carefully selected list of Music, on /8th and days of December instant.

The undermentioned Members of the Band particularly request that no subscriptions on their behalf be given to any person *except to those who produce a book with the above name of Band attached thereto*, as some unscrupulous persons have from year to year used our circulars, and by those means obtained the subscriptions intended for our band.

Please see that our initials are at the foot of the circular produced to you, and then you will not be deceived.

Wishing you a Merry Christmas and a Happy New Year.

J. MELLOR, *Collector.*
J. SHENTON, *Band Master.*

Glees, Choruses and Anthems to be played.

Loud the Mighty Host proclaim	Compassion
But in the Last Days	Ainsworth
Hear the Call	Innocence
Four Christmas Hymns	Hail Messiah
Old Christmas	Christians Awake
The Star Journal	Diadem
Angelic Voices	Royalty
Refuge	King of Kings
Glad Tidings	Miriam
Acclamation	The Merry Bells

NAMES OF THE BAND.

J. SHENTON	J. BIRCH	T. DANIELS
G. BALL	G. DANIELS	M. BALL
J. DANIELS	J. MELLOR	W. BALL

N.B.—Any of the above Selections will be played on the same being asked for.

Leek Sanitary Steam Laundry,
MACCLESFIELD ROAD.

FROM

Wm. PARTINGTON,
Proprietor.

To *Miss Challinor Blackwood*

☞ Post Cards to the Works or Messages to Miss CORMACK'S, 20, Derby Street, will have immediate attention. Orders called for and Delivered Promptly.

January 8th 1896.

Leek Silk Twist Manufacturing Society - later C.W.S. - were at Park Mills, a factory in Nelson Street.

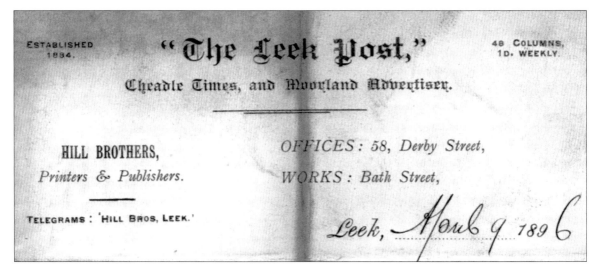

Hill Bros (Leek) Ltd were the proprietors of the local newspaper, the 'Leek Post' and also of the 'Post Press' - part of the business which undertook commercial printing for trade and private customers.

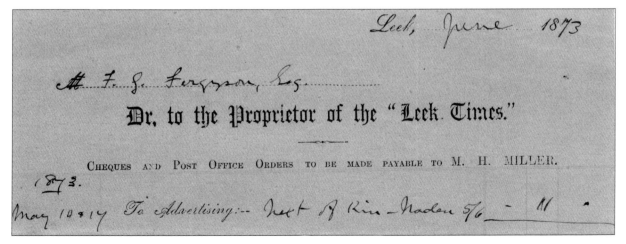

The 'Leek Times' was a local newspaper in competition with the 'Leek Post'. Political differences separated the two - the 'Post' being Conservative and the 'Times' favouring the Liberal cause.

Telegrams : "Times," Leek.   Leek Times Office.   Estd. 1870.
Telephone : 6 x.

Leek, *Apl 7* 1914

Staffs.

M Exor. of Mr C. Robinson

Dr. to THE LEEK TIMES.

Prompt Settlement of Accounts is requested.   Monthly Accounts.   All Cheques payable to Miller Bros., Proprietors.

To Advertising :

Dec 20   *On Sheet Almanac*   5/-

Telegrams. Times. Leek.   **The Leek Times.**   Estd. 1870.
Telephone, No. 14.

From   To

M. H. Miller,

Proprietor,   *Mr Robinson*

LEEK, Staffordshire.

The Oldest, Biggest, & Best Newspaper Printed in Leek or within Ten Miles.

Oct. 25 1898.

Dear Sir,

The matter referred to in yours of this morning has been amicably settled by the parties concerned.

Faithfully yours,

M H Miller

This memo carries the signature of M.H.Miller, the editor of the Leek Times.

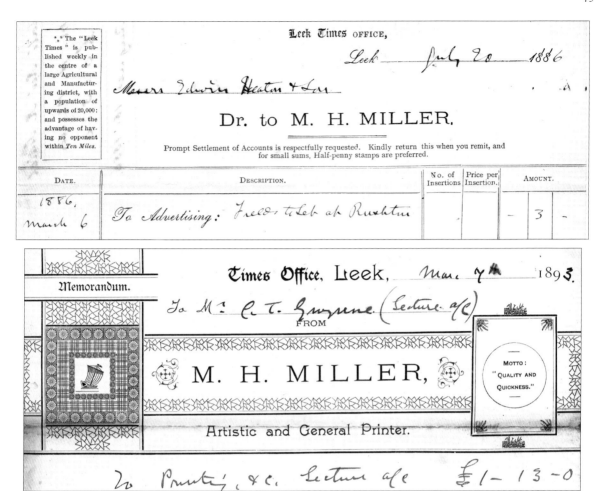

Leek Times OFFICE,

Leek ___ July 20 ___ 1886

. The "Leek Times" is published weekly in the centre of a large Agricultural and Manufacturing district, with a population of upwards of 20,000: and possesses the advantage of having no opponent within *Ten Miles*.

Messrs Edwin Heaton & Son

Dr. to M. H. MILLER.

Prompt Settlement of Accounts is respectfully requested. Kindly return this when you remit, and for small sums, Half-penny stamps are preferred.

DATE.	DESCRIPTION.	No. of Insertions	Price per Insertion.	AMOUNT.
1886, March 6	To Advertising: Field to Let at Rushton			— 3 —

Memorandum.

Times Office, Leek, Mar. 7th 1893.

To Mr C. T. Gwynne (Lecture a/c) FROM

M. H. MILLER,

Artistic and General Printer.

MOTTO: "QUALITY AND QUICKNESS."

To Printing, &c. Lecture a/c £1 – 13 – 0

Matthew Henry Miller was a great influence on Victorian Leek. Born in Birmingham 7th February 1843, he came to Leek in 1864 to manage Robert Nall's printing business in Stanley Street. He was the local correspondent for the Birmingham Daily Post and the Staffordshire Advertiser, and was on the outside staff of the Sentinel. On 26th September 1870 he married Annie Lovatt, daughter of John Lovatt, silk manufacturer, of Leek.

On 30th July 1870 he commenced the weekly publication of the Leek Times using a partly printed London sheet of national and international news, and adding two pages of Leek news. His problem was to persuade local businesses to advertise in the new journal, but this he achieved and the modest paper was a success.

M.H.Miller's editorial policy displayed fearless criticism of local, county and national affairs. Politically he was a Liberal but the columns of his newspaper were open to all political persuasions. A Nonconformist, he was a generous supporter of local charitable causes amongst which was the Cruso Nursing Fund.

The Leek Comet was another of Miller's ventures. This paper, published each Wednesday, was aimed at the farming community, but it ceased after only a few months.

John Sleigh, whose *History of the Ancient Parish of Leek* was published in a second edition in 1883, was a great influence in fostering Miller's interest in local history. It was largely from material supplied by Sleigh that Miller was able to publish his little book Leek Fifty Years Ago in 1887. As the title suggests, it was a miscellaneous collection of news items from 1837 - the year of Queen Victoria's accession to the crown. The response to this book led Miller to publish his Olde Leeke in 1891, and so warm was the welcome it received that a second volume followed in 1900. A number of other publications also bear M.H. Miller's name.

In his leisure time he took part in amateur entertainments as a humourist and elocutionist. He often performed in 'Penny Readings' at the old Temperance Hall. He died in October 1909.

63.   **Leek Times** *Office. Market Street,*

Messrs Challinors & Shaw   **LEEK,** *Dec 31*   189**4**

Dr. to M. H. MILLER,

Legal, Commercial, and General Printer.

TELEGRAMS, TIMES, LEEK.   TELEPHONE, No. 14.

TRADE MOTTO: QUALITY AND QUICKNESS.

Nov 29.   100 reprints – Ipstones   3 .. 0

Matthew Henry Miller

This building in Market Street, the
offices of the Leek Times, is now the
Central Liberal Club.

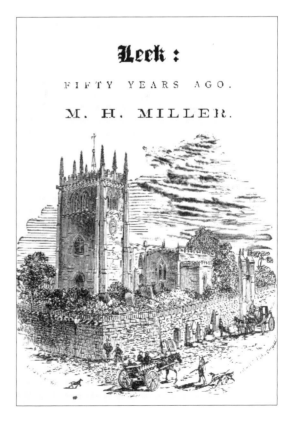

Leek:

FIFTY YEARS AGO.

M. H. MILLER.

The Leek Steam Sanitary Laundry,
William Partington, Proprietor,
Macclesfield Road.

The modern steam laundry is essentially a product of the 19th century, its genesis being directly traceable to the demands of the age for labour economisation in every shape and form. Hardly a town of any pretensions to the go-ahead spirit of the age but has such an establishment, and in this respect Leek is not a whit behind the times. The steam laundry which has just been opened by Mr. William Partington, can hardly fail to prove a success. Its proprietor is a capable man of business, its situation is in many respects most advantageous, its equipment of plant and machinery perfect, and all the working accessories are of the newest type. The laundry possesses an ample supply of water, while the spacious drying grounds fully meet every requirement. Every precaution is taken to prevent loss or damage happening to any of the articles entrusted temporarily to Mr. Partington to be cleaned. To ensure the punctual collection of goods and the subsequent delivery of the same at the residences of customers, the messengers connected with the establishment call at given intervals, or otherwise as requested, so that patrons can rely on a total absence of inconvenience, while reaping a maximum of the benefits which the operations of a steam laundry confer over and above the slower old fashioned method of hand washing. It may be mentioned in conclusion that all messages and business communications for the laundry manager if left at Cormack's, 20, Derby Street, Leek, will receive immediate attention. The following list will show that charges rule extremely moderate.

Macclesfield Road and Mill Street became something of a 'growth area' in the late 19th century. In addition to high-density housing in terraced houses along Mill Street, industry began to intensify along the Macclesfield Road. Following the early silk dyers along the River Churnet came larger mills including Wardle's Hencroft Dye Works (later Sir T & A Wardle), Davenport Adams and Brough, Nicholson & Hall's dye works. The Churnet was an important factor in this development

LADIES' DEPARTMENT.

Chemises	... ... each	2d.
Drawers	... ... ,,	2d.
Night Dresses	... ,,	3d.
Pocket Handkerchiefs	,,	½d.
Collars	... per doz.	9d.
Cuffs	... per pair	1d.
Slip Bodices	... ... each	1½d.
Petticoats	... ... ,,	4d.
Flannel Petticoats	... ,,	2d.
Stockings	... per pair	1d.
Muslin Dresses according to work.		
Blouses	... 4d. upwards.	

GENTLEMEN'S DEPARTMENT.

Dress Shirts	... ... each	4d.
Fronts	... ... ,,	1½d.
Night Shirts	... ... ,,	2d.
Collars	... ... ,,	1d.
Cuffs	... per pair	1d.
Drawers	... ... each	2d.
Singlets	... ,,	2d.
Socks	... per pair	1d.
Handkerchiefs	.. each	½d.
Silk Handkerchiefs	... ,,	1d.
White Ties	... ,,	1d.
White Waistcoats	... ,,	4d.

SERVANTS' DEPARTMENT.

Cotton Gowns ..	... each	4d.
Aprons	... ... ,,	1d.
Caps	... ... ,,	1d.
Collars	... per doz.	6d.
Cuffs	... per pair	1d.
Chemises	... each	1½d.
Night Dresses	... ,,	2d.
Drawers	... ... ,,	1½d.
Stockings	... per pair	1d.
White Petticoats (plain) each		3d.

HOUSEHOLD DEPARTMENT.

Table Cloths	... ... each	3d.
,, Kitchen	... ,,	2d.
Table Napkins	... ,,	1d.
D'Oyleys	... ... ,,	1d.
Tray Cloths	... ... ,,	2d.
Towels	... ... ,,	1d.
Kitchen Cloths and		
Dusters	... per doz.	9d.
Sheets	... per pair	4d.
Pillow Cases	... each	1d.
Bolster Slips	... ,,	1½d.
Toilet Covers	... ,,	1½d.
Counterpanes according to size.		
Curtains ,,		
Blankets 6d. per pair upwards.		

CHILDREN'S DEPARTMENT.

About 1s. per dozen, which does not include Frocks and Petticoats.

Special terms are quoted to hotels, families, and schools. No chemicals are used, and nothing under any circumstances but pure water, ordinary washing soap, and common soda.

Three views of Mill Street showing some of the great number of terraced houses, shops, pubs and factories which lined the street in Victorian days

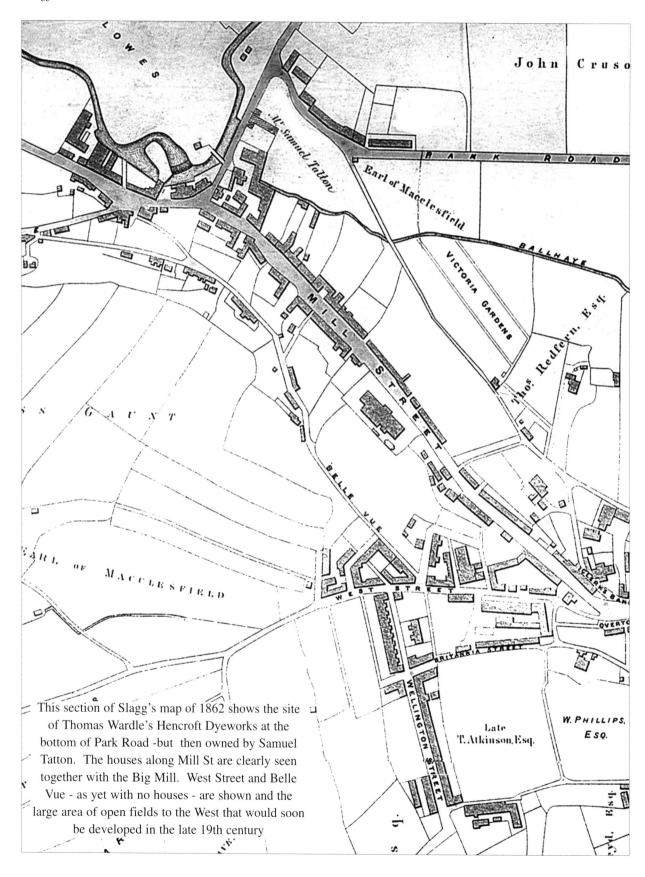

This section of Slagg's map of 1862 shows the site of Thomas Wardle's Hencroft Dyeworks at the bottom of Park Road -but then owned by Samuel Tatton. The houses along Mill St are clearly seen together with the Big Mill. West Street and Belle Vue - as yet with no houses - are shown and the large area of open fields to the West that would soon be developed in the late 19th century

The Market Place in the 1880s showing a block of property at the left hand corner occupied by Robert West, watch and clockmaker. He erected the large public clock on the wall in 1883 - which created a lot of interest at the time.

The little shops below the Red Lion are where the Buttermarket was erected in 1895. One of these was a saddler - well situated next to the Red Lion coaching inn.

By the early 20th century the Market Place looked much as it does now although the block of property at the top left hand corner was not demolished until about 1930 when Church Street was widened for the first time.

Leek Town Hall, demolished in 1982, is seen front centre in Market Street. The Leek & Moorlands Building Society buildings, seen centre back in Stockwell Street became the Council headquarters. Later still, in the late 1980s, the present Staffordshire Moorlands District Council headquarters were built to the left, just off Stockwell Street, where a row of old Leek shops is seen in 1956.

The Leek Savings Bank was based in the old Town Hall at the bottom of the Market Place which was demolished in 1872. It opened in January 1823 with Richard Badnall and Richard Gaunt as treasurers. By 1876 it held £68,000 for 1694 depositors and had moved to new offices at the top of Russell Street (now The Halifax).

The old Leek General Post Office which was fine example of Leek's Victorian architecture. Demolished in the 1960s and replaced by a modern post and telephone complex.

Outside the old Golden Lion in Church Street. Church Street disappeared about 1970 with the removal of the George, the Golden Lion and all the shops to widen the road for cars and lorries. The road shown below is in fact the main thoroughfare that leads into Stockwell Street.

Thomas William Lightfoot's business was at The Grapes in Spout Street (St Edward Street) when it was usually known as 'Lightfoot's Vaults'.

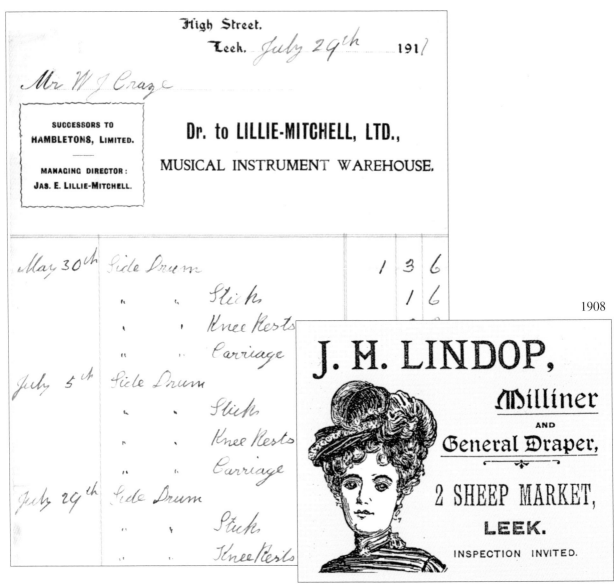

High Street,
Leek, *July 29th* 191*1*

Mr W J Craze

SUCCESSORS TO
HAMBLETONS, LIMITED.

MANAGING DIRECTOR:
JAS. E. LILLIE-MITCHELL.

Dr. to LILLIE-MITCHELL, LTD.,

MUSICAL INSTRUMENT WAREHOUSE.

May 30th	*Side Drum*	1	3	6
"	" *Sticks*		1	6
'	' *Knee Rests*			
"	" *Carriage*			
July 5th	*Side Drum*			
"	" *Sticks*			
"	" *Knee Rests*			
"	" *Carriage*			
July 29th	*Side Drum*			
"	' *Sticks*			
"	' *Knee Rests*			

1908

J. H. LINDOP,

Milliner

AND

General Draper,

2 SHEEP MARKET,

LEEK.

INSPECTION INVITED.

This map of 1862 was before High Street was built. The road was cut through in 1900 opposite Sheep Market removing the old Globe Yard and Fallon's poultry and game shop.

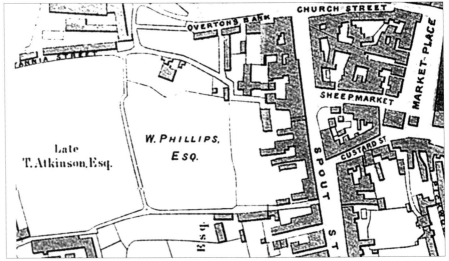

LONDON HOUSE,

Sheep Market, Leek,

May 15th 1903

Messrs Heath & Lowe

Bought of T. LOCKETT,

DRAPER, HOSIER, &c.

TERMS: CASH.

Painting outside			
House in Newcastle Rd.	4	5	0
Covering Sewerage Tank	3	19	3
Steps into Garden	1	0	0
£	8	4	3

London House was No 17 Sheepmarket.

5 and 7, BATH STREET

(LATE OF HAYWOOD STREET).

G. LOVENBURY,

Carriage Builder & General Smith,

WITH 27 YEARS EXPERIENCE IN THE TRADE.

ALL KINDS OF CART IRONWORK TO SUIT WHEELWRIGHTS. ALSO SPRINGS AND AXLES.

Lancewood Shafts of the best quality kept in stock.

Also Ready-dressed Spokes and Naves kept in stock.

Any requirements to the trade got on the shortest notice at the lowest possible price

NOTE THE ADDRESS:—

G. LOVENBURY, 5 & 7, Bath St., Leek.

7 Bath Street

~~CATTLE MARKET,~~

LEEK, *Xmas* 1892

Mr T Robinson

To G. LOVENBURY,

CARRIAGE BUILDER and GENERAL SMITH.

1892		£	s	d
	To a/c rendered Midsummer	2	6	11
July 14	1 New Shaft & fitting on	.	8	.
15	1 Staple 2 Cotters to Cart &			
	Taking down to Nabhill	.	1	.
		£		

Wheels Repaired and Re-Tyred.

****

Lancewood and Hickory Shafts, Wings, Naves, Spokes, Felloes, and New Wheels always in stock.

****
*

5 & 7, **Bath Street**,

Leek, ... *Xmas* .... 190 8 ..

Messrs Challinors & Shaw   *Solrs*

To G. LOVENBURY,

Carriage Builder & General Smith.

WRINGING & WASHING MACHINES REPAIRED.

New Rollers fitted to any class of Machine at Lowest Prices.

All kinds of Plain, Ornamental and Carriage Ironwork.

****

Springs made on the Premises.

****

Grates & Ranges repaired. All kinds of New Range or Grate Fittings kept in stock.

1908		£	s	d
Sept 9	New Stud End on strap stud to			
	double doors. Time on same. 2 hrs + app 2 hrs 4 lbs.	.	2	8
	To taking railing down in Yard			
12	Setting running bars			
	5 New Upright Bars 15 lbs.			
	Fixing same + Setting other Bars			
	Time on same. 8 hrs, man 1 hr + app 6 hrs	.	10	8
		.	13	4

G. Lovenbury was based in an old-fashioned smithy in Bath Street. His son, Almora Lovenbury, was small in stature for a smith. He provided a wide range of services both industrial and domestic as the billhead suggests. Such one man businesses were very versatile and in much demand.   The agricultural and textile needs in the Leek area created considerable demand for the varied services of blacksmiths.

| NEW WHEELS
KEPT IN STOCK
OR TO ORDER.
——
CARRIAGE IRONWORK
MADE TO ORDER. | 5 & 7, BATH STREET,

LEEK, *Feb* 1906 | ORNAMENTAL
GATES AND RAILINGS
MADE TO
ANY DESIGN. |

M? S. Robinson

To G. LOVENBURY,
CARRIAGE BUILDER AND GENERAL SMITH.

1906	To Bill delivered M.S.	£	s	d
		1	3	2

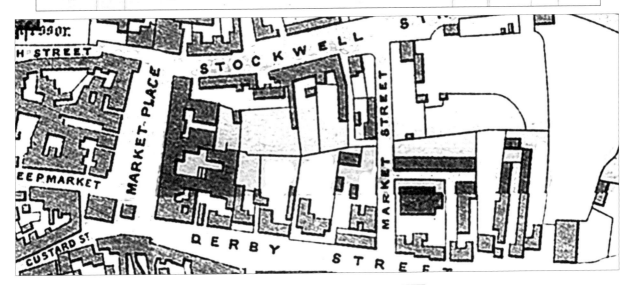

Slagg's map of 1862 above was drawn before Bath Street was constructed. The Public Baths, and Getliffe's Yard to the left, stand isolated with fields behind.

By the time of the 1879 Ordnance Survey map (left), construction was complete.

~~CUSTARD STREET AND SPOUT STREET,~~

W. Phillips Esq.   **Leek,** _____ 186

Bought of William Lowe,

WINE AND SPIRIT STORES,

DEALER IN DUBLIN PORTER IN CASK AND BOTTLE, BASS & Co's. BURTON ALES.

Families supplied.   Country Orders attended to.   Dealer in British Wines.

				£	s	d
1860					1	2
Aug 26	2 doz Pints Ale	at 4/3			8	6
Sept 3	2 doz	Do	Do		8	6
					17	0
Nov 22	2 doz Pints Ale	4/3			8	6

Leek, _____ 188   *Staffordshire.*

Mrs Plant.

To W. Lowe, Dr.

	1884		£	s	d
June 4	1 Bot Port			3	.
	1 — Sherry			2	.
	2 — Raisin Wine			3	0
				8	0

William Lowe was at 11-13 Stanley Street (Custard Street) and 11 Church Street (Spout Street). The Church Street property was the King William IV public house, and by 1892 William Lowe had taken over Lightfoot's business at The Grapes in St Edward Street. The main shop for wines and spirits was the double-fronted shop in Stanley Street, where the business was founded in 1861. Mr Lowe was the agent for most of the leading breweries including Fremlin's Maidstone Ale. The business continued at Stanley Street into the 1970s.

Market Place, **Leek** . 18

W. Challiner Esq
Pickwood

Bought of William Lowe.

Importer of and Dealer in Foreign Wines and Spirits

ALLSOPP & SONS' INDIA PALE & MILD BURTON ALES.   D'ARCY & SONS' DUBLIN STOUT.

			£		
1871			£	1	0
Jan 21	1 doz Stout 2/. ½ gall: Brandy 12/.		14	—	
Feb 1	1 doz Stout 2/. March 2			2	.
March 3	3 bottles Brandy at 4/2		12	6	
"	3 Do. Rum at 2/10		8	6	
	1 doz Stout	— — —		2	.
April 6	2 doz. Stout at 2/.		4	.	
14	2 Firkins Ale at 21/.		2	2	

---

11 and 13. Stanley Street. **Leek** STAFFORDSHIRE. Mar. 14th 1892.

M The Executors of the late Miss Mellor

Bought of William Lowe.

Importer of and Dealer in Foreign Wines and Spirits.

ALLSOPP & SONS' AND THOMPSON'S PALE & MILD BURTON ALES IN CASK.

BASS'S AND ALLSOPP'S BURTON, AND FREMLIN'S CELEBRATED MAIDSTONE ALES IN BOTTLE.

FREMLIN'S ALES IN CASK.   GUINNESS'S DOUBLE STOUT IN CASK & BOTTLE.

Feb. 8.	1 Brandy 5/. 11th 1 Do. 4/10. 15th 1 Do. 4/10 1 Soda 6d	15	2
20	1 Brandy 4/10 1 Soda 6d 24th 1 Brandy 4/10	10	2
26	1 Do. 4/10 27th 1 Do. 4/10 29th 1 Do. 4/10 1 Soda 6d	15	"
Mar. 1	1 Do. 4/10 4th 1 Do. 4/10. 5th 1 quart Do. 2 bot. 7/10	17	6
11	1 bot. Do. 4/10 14th 1 Do. 4/10.	9	8

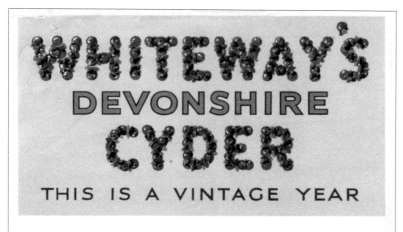

WHITEWAY'S DEVONSHIRE CYDER

THIS IS A VINTAGE YEAR

Miss Shaw,   6/7/ 193

BOUGHT OF
WILLIAM LOWE
STANLEY STREET, LEEK

13/6/3	½ Little Silk	-	6	6
	1 Flash Jerry	-	9	0
	1 Small Haunt		2	3
			11	9

It became a common custom during this period for national companies to supply invoices on which the local trader could have his name and address printed, or even use a rubber stamp to save money. Of course the national company's advert dominated the billhead.

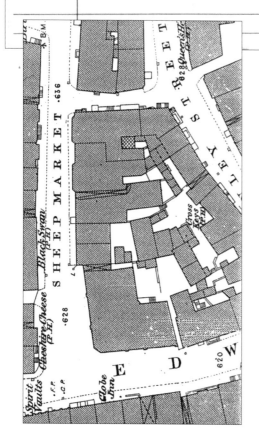

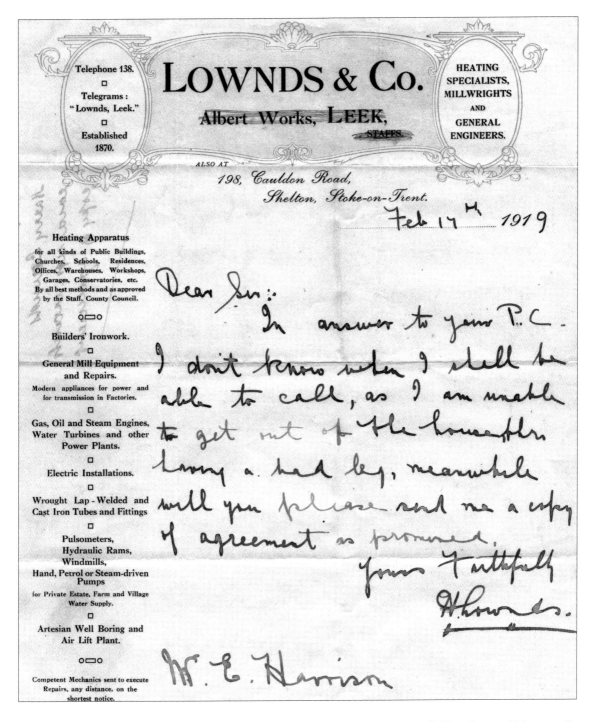

LOWNDS & Co.

Telephone 138.

Telegrams : "Lownds, Leek."

Established 1870.

Albert Works, LEEK, STAFFS.

HEATING SPECIALISTS, MILLWRIGHTS AND GENERAL ENGINEERS.

ALSO AT

198, Cauldon Road, Shelton, Stoke-on-Trent.

Feb 17ᵗʰ 1919

Heating Apparatus
for all kinds of Public Buildings, Churches, Schools, Residences, Offices, Warehouses, Workshops, Garages, Conservatories, etc. By all best methods and as approved by the Staff. County Council.

Builders' Ironwork.

General Mill Equipment and Repairs.
Modern appliances for power and for transmission in Factories.

Gas, Oil and Steam Engines, Water Turbines and other Power Plants.

Electric Installations.

Wrought Lap - Welded and Cast Iron Tubes and Fittings

Pulsometers, Hydraulic Rams, Windmills, Hand, Petrol or Steam-driven Pumps
for Private Estate, Farm and Village Water Supply.

Artesian Well Boring and Air Lift Plant.

Competent Mechanics sent to execute Repairs, any distance, on the shortest notice.

Dear Sir :-

In answer to your P.C. I don't know when I shall be able to call, as I am unable to get out of the house after having a bad leg, meanwhile will you please send me a copy of agreement as promised,

yours Faithfully

H. Lownds.

W. E. Harrison

The firm of Lownds and Co, founded in 1870, was situated in Albert Street off West Street. This versatile little firm offered a range of services to local industry, including electrical work and heating installations which they also maintained. A report in the 'Leek times' of October 1st 1881, records that Edwin Lownds was called upon by Robert Farrow, Leek's Sanitary Inspector, to supervise the installation of an ingenious anti-smoke pollution device at the factory of Clowes and Stafford, Dyers, Brook Street, following complaints about the nuisance caused by the dense black smoke. The device, which was simple and not costly, was the invention of a Mr Ireland of Macclesfield.

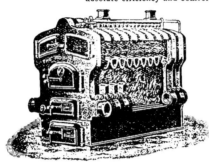
This housing development took its name from the builder - Lowther Place.

19, FORD STREET,

LEEK, *Midsummer* 1895

Mr W. B. Badnall Esqre —

Dr. to THOMAS MACKRELL,

JOINER, BUILDER AND CONTRACTOR.

1895			£	s	d
April 20	3 hours 2/- at house in Stockwell			2	0
	occupied by Mrs Hawksworth			"	"
22	9½ hours 6/4 Taking out old			6	4
	window & making new one			"	"
	5ft × 9 × 3 2/1 for Lintol			2	1
23	9½ hours 6/4 21ft 6" × 3 × 2¼ 2/8			9	0
	10ft 6" × 2 × 2 2ft × 3 × 2¼			1	1
	16ft × 2 × 1 13ft × 1½ × 1/2			"	11
	1 Casement fastener 1 Casement stay			"	9
	1 pr of 2½ Butts & screws			"	6
Do 26	1 hour 1ft 6 × 11 × 2 for foot			1	3
	path front of house occupied			"	"
	by Mr Fallon			"	"
			£	1 · 3	11

Feb 5th 1896

Thomas Mackrell was by 1906 (Kelly's Directory) operating from 13 Ball Haye Street and 19 Ford Street, but does not appear in the 1904 directory. The firm was one of the many local builders contracted by the Leek architects, Sugden & Son. Records show that they were one of the firms who worked on the Nicholson Institute. Mackrell is not a local name.

17, DERBY STREET, AND 18, RUSSELL ST. **LEEK.** 1888
Staffordshire.

Mr. W. C. G. Smith, King St

Bot. of John Magnier.

Confectioner,

Wholesale Corn & Flour Merchant.

SACKS CHARGED 1/6 EACH, AND ALLOWED FOR IF RETURNED IN GOOD CONDITION WITHIN ONE MONTH.
5 Per Cent Interest Charged On Overdue Accounts.

TERMS CASH.

1881			
July 20	3 lb Oats 4½ Bran 3 Midd Meal Oatmeal 3	1	1½
„ 25	Oats 9 Scotch Meal 1/4	2	1
Aug 3	Oats 9½ Bran 5	1	0½
17	Oats 9 Bran 9	1	6
Sep 6	Bran 9 Oats 7½. 23rd Oats 9 Bran 9	2	8½
Oct 17	½ ct Super Flour 1/6 Bran 8. 27th Oats 9	13	11
Nov 13	50 lb Oats 4 – 50 lb Bran 3 – 2 4 9	10	0
Dec 16	1 ct Flour 1/8	1	8
1882			
Feb 2	4 ct Oats 6 . 14th Oats 6	1	0
May 2	Wheat Barley &c 3rd 20 lb Corn 14	2	2
„ 3	20 lb Wheat 1/0 20 lb Barley 1/8	3	6
		£ 2 1 8½

The Magniers were direct descendents of Pierre Louis Magnier, a French prisoner from the Napoleonic Wars who was sent to Leek on parole in 1809. He afterwards settled in Leek and married a local girl, Ann Thompson. Pierre died in 1874 aged 93. Pierre's son, Peter, leased his shop in Derby street from William Condlyffe, where he traded as a baker and confectioner, and later as a corn merchant and provision dealer. Peter's son, John, carried on the business when his father retired and continued to do so after his death. However he only survived his father by 8 years and the business passed to his son, Harry Reginald Magnier. The Derby Street premises were sold to the Midland Bank in 1927.

The billhead above incorporates a nice impression of John's shop at No 17 Derby Street. The building is the work of Sugden - built in 1868 and altered in 1885

17, DERBY STREET, & 18, RUSSELL STREET,

L E E K,_____ 188

STAFFORDSHIRE.

Mrs Gibson

Bought of JOHN MAGNIER,

CONFECTIONER,

WHOLESALE CORN AND FLOUR MERCHANT.

Sacks charged 1/6 each, and allowed for if returned in good condition within one month.

TERMS—*Five per Cent. Interest charged on Overdue Accounts.*

Oct 15	2 Score Sharps	2/4
	Paid J. C.	
Oct 18	2 Score Sharps	2 4
	1/2 Score Ind Meal	7½
		2/11½
	Paid J. C.	
Oct 20	2 Score Bean Flour	8/—
	Paid J. C.	
22	2 Score Sharps	2 4
	1/2 " Ind Meal	7½
		2/11½
	Paid J. C.	
28	2 Score Sharps	2 4
	1/2 Score Bean	4½
	Ind Meal	7½
	Paid J Clowes	8 3½

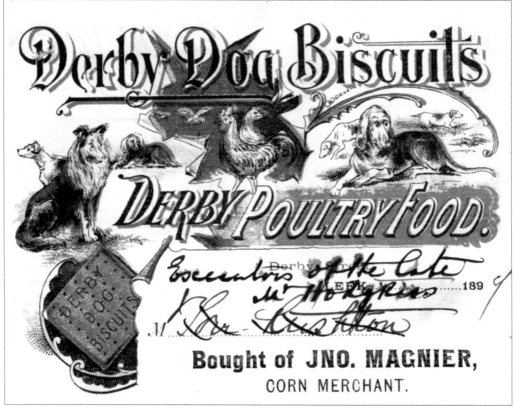

Magnier's original shop, seen here, was rebuilt by Sugden in 1868 and altered in 1885. (see page 96)

Nᵒ 6.

H. R. MAGNIER,

CYCLE & MOTOR DEPOT,

Ball Haye Street,

Garage SILK STREET. . . LEEK, STAFFS.

CARS FOR HIRE.

Telegrams:—"Magnier, Leek." Telephone, No. 72.

Dunlop, Michelin, and Continental Motor Tyres stocked.

DISTRICT AGENT FOR
Darracq, Humber & Rover Cars.
Royal Enfield, Sunbeam, Rover Cycles, etc.

For Mr Roland Taylor.

Oct 1908	Re enamelling & Plating Cycle	
	New Palmer Cover fitted	
	New Pedals Rubber Chain	
	Blocks & Shoes, Handles,	
	Overhauling etc	£3 . 3 . 6
	1 Lucas Bell 2/6 New Brake Springs	3 . 0
		2 . 9
Ap 09	New Carrier fitted	
	New shoes & Block for Brake & Adj.	1 6
		£3 . 10 9

Paid June 16th /09
F. Magnier

ONE PENNY

LEEK, STAFFORDSHIRE.

VACANT POSSESSION.

VALUABLE EXTENSIVE

FREEHOLD PROPERTY

FOR SALE BY AUCTION, BY

J. OAKES ASH AND SON,

AT THE

Red Lion Hotel, Leek, on Thursday, 3rd March, 1927,

At 6-30 p.m. subject to Conditions to be then read.

THE ATTRACTIVE CENTRALLY SITUATED

BUSINESS PREMISES

No. 17, DERBY STREET

— AND —

SILK STREET GARAGE, LEEK,

Having a frontage to Derby Street of 25ft. 9in. with private domestic entrance, and a depth of about 150 feet, extending to a total area of 4,700 SQUARE FEET, or thereabouts, comprising the business establishment of a Motor and Cycle Agent and Engineer, having ample accommodation for display, storage and repair, as now occupied by Mr. H. R. Magnier who will give

VACANT POSSESSION ON COMPLETION.

The business premises are conveniently arranged, well lighted and commodious, and comprise attractive double-fronted Shop (22ft. by 18ft. 9in.) and Office with Storage Cellar and Petrol Tank beneath, Garage (55ft. by 42ft.), with Storage and Repair Lofts and having Central Heating and direct access to Silk Street, Petrol Store, Cycle Shed, (18ft. by 16ft.) and usual Conveniences.

The Domestic Accommodation, adjoining the above but having separate approaches, comprises Entrance Hall, Dining and Drawing Rooms, Kitchen, Cellar-Kitchen and Store Cellar, five Principal Bedrooms, Bath Room and Lavatory, two Servants' Rooms and Box Room, with Yard and usual Out-Offices.

The property occupies a central position in the main thoroughfare, and comprises one of the finest Business premises in the town of Leek. The whole is in excellent repair and might easily be converted into suitable premises for any class of Retail business.

TO VIEW. apply on the Premises. and for further particulars and to inspect plan to the Auctioneers, 43. St. Edward Street. Leek; or

MESSRS. BISHTONS, SOLICITORS, LEEK.

The headings on the opposite page suggest that by 1910 H.R. Magnier's business was centred at 17 Derby Street, with his garage in nearby Silk Street.

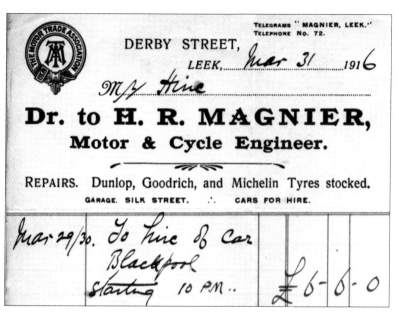

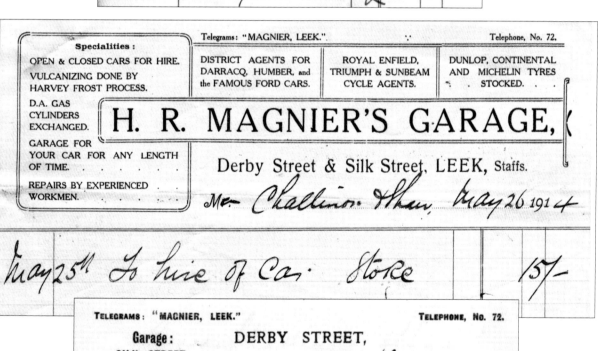

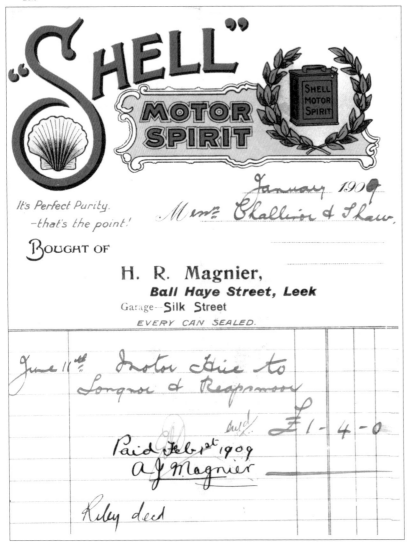

"SHELL" MOTOR SPIRIT

It's Perfect Purity.
—that's the point!

BOUGHT OF

January 1909
Messrs Challinor & Shaw.

H. R. Magnier,
Ball Haye Street, Leek
Garage—Silk Street
EVERY CAN SEALED.

June 11th   Motor Hire to
Longnor & Reapsmoor

Paid Feb 1st 1909   £1 - 4 - 0
A J Magnier

Riley deed

H.R. Magnier was a cycle and motor
dealer with a shop in Ball Haye
Street and a workshop in Silk street.
He was one of the pioneers of the
motor trade in Leek.

Locals in a charabanc
about 1925

The Management of the
" MAJESTIC "
wish all their patrons
A Merry Christmas and
a Happy New Year
and beg to announce the following
COMING ATTRACTIONS.
....

JEW SÜSS CONRAD VEIDT

The House of Rothschild
GEORGE ARLISS

BELLA DONNA

WONDER BAR AL JOLSON

BULLDOG DRUMMOND STRIKES BACK
RONALD COLMAN

DANNY BOY

NELL GWYN, ANNA NEAGLE

The Last Gentleman, GEORGE ARLISS

FLYING DOWN TO RIO

Cockeyed Cavaliers WHEELER and WOOLSEY

ARE YOU A MASON ?

Some fine old films and stars are shown on this Leek cinema advert from the 1930s.
The Majestic Cinema stood in Union Street. It was formerly the Temperance Hall,
when it was used for musical and dramatic performances, and the traditional 'Penny
Readings' on Saturday evenings*. It was later used by the Salvation Army before
they acquired their own premises in Salisbury Street, and has also been a skating rink.
It was destroyed by a fire in 1961.

* Oscar Wilde gave a lecture here in 1884.

◢LONGNOR,
NEAR BUXTON,

August 1ᵗʰ 1900

Mʀ. ....

Bought of R. H. MALKIN,

❋ TAILOR and GENERAL DRAPER. ❋

Dear Sir

I enclose you £ s d
1. 4. 6
in Postal Orders for one
Quarters Rent Due on the
First Day of August
as I want to know if the
2. Cottages are on Sale
as we want some repairs
doing badly as the Grate
Back is out Please Let
me know if on Sale
and what You want for
Them

Yours Etc

R. H. Malkin

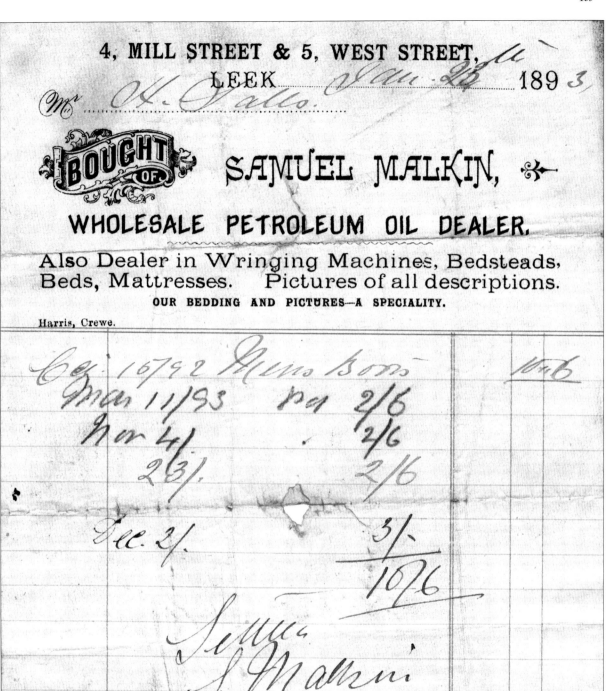

4, MILL STREET & 5, WEST STREET,
LEEK _____ *Jan. 25* 189 *3*

Mr *H. Salls*

BOUGHT OF SAMUEL MALKIN,

WHOLESALE PETROLEUM OIL DEALER.

Also Dealer in Wringing Machines, Bedsteads, Beds, Mattresses.   Pictures of all descriptions.
OUR BEDDING AND PICTURES—A SPECIALITY.

Harris, Crewe.

In Victorian times, traders often had many aspects to their business. Here Samuel Malkin offers petrol, bedsteads, wringing machines.... and pictures of all description.

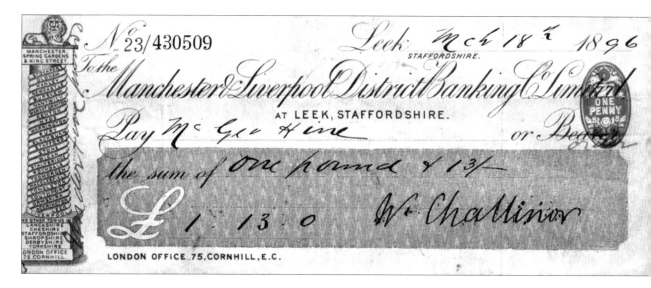

In 1829 an effort was made to get a branch of the Manchester and Liverpool District Bank established in Leek. A meeting presided over by Thomas Carr appointed a committee consisting of Mr Carr, Mr William Challinor Senr and Mr Samuel Bower Whittles, a grocer in the Market Place, but it was another 4 years before a branch arrived. It was a sub-branch to Hanley and at first only opened for a few hours on Wednesdays. In the following year a full branch was established in Sheepmarket with about 20 accounts, most of them silk manufacturers.

When the lease of these premises expired after 7 years the business moved to a room in one of the old houses at the top of the Market Place. In 1855 the bank again opened a daily branch this time in Stanley Street. Six years later it moved again to a house in Derby Street previously occupied by Mr Anthony Ward. In 1881 the building and adjoining premises were demolished and a fine new building was erected - now the Nat West Bank.

The building is regarded as one of the finest by Sugden and Son, displaying many of the hallmarks of their architectural style. The builders were Massey of Alderley Edge and the ornate relief work between the Venetian windows and on the gable is by Stephen Webb. The windows contain some fine stained glass incorporating the Bank's monogram and the Leek halfpenny. The interior is superb with some splendid woodwork and ceilings.

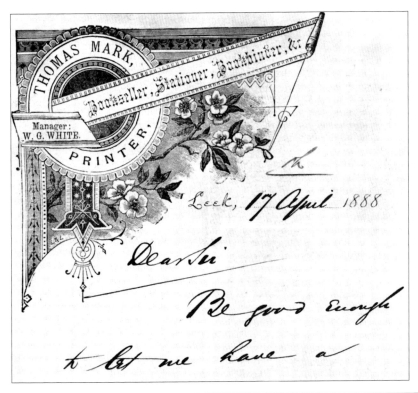

THOMAS MARK,
Bookseller, Stationer, Bookbinder, &c.

Manager:
W. G. WHITE.

PRINTER.

Leek, 17 April 1888

Dear Sir

Be good enough

to let me have a

The Leek Printing Offices
and Stationery Warehouse,

6 DERBY STREET,
Aug 19 1892

FROM

THOMAS MARK,

Printer, Lithographer, and Account Book Manufacturer,

PATTERN CARD MAKER, GOLD BLOCKER, AND MACHINE RULER.

To E Challinor Esq.

In reply to your enquiry of *to-day* I have pleasure in submitting my Estimate and shall be glad to be favoured with your orders.

Yours respectfully,

P. D. Glover

PLEASE REFER TO

ESTIMATE.

Ptg 100 Posters 2½ sheet Dble Demy
in black ink as your
pattern £1.7.6

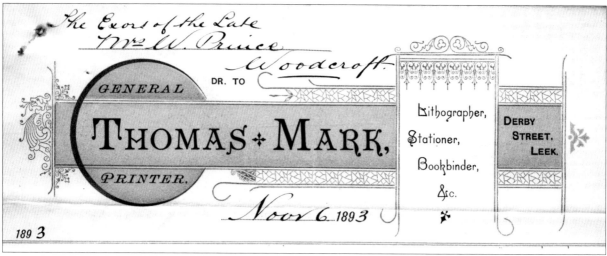

The Exors of the Late
Wm W. Prince
Woodcroft

DR. TO

GENERAL

THOMAS ✦ MARK,

PRINTER.

Lithographer,
Stationer,
Bookbinder,
&c.

DERBY STREET, LEEK.

Novr 6 1893

189 3

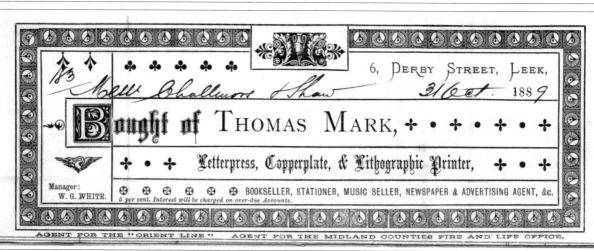

6, DERBY STREET, LEEK,

Messrs Challinors & Shaw　31 Oct. 1889

Bought of THOMAS MARK, ✦ • ✦ • ✦ • ✦

Letterpress, Copperplate, & Lithographic Printer, ✦ • ✦

Manager:
W. G. WHITE.

BOOKSELLER, STATIONER, MUSIC SELLER, NEWSPAPER & ADVERTISING AGENT, &c.

5 per cent. Interest will be charged on over-due Accounts.

AGENT FOR THE "ORIENT LINE"　AGENT FOR THE MIDLAND COUNTIES FIRE AND LIFE OFFICE.

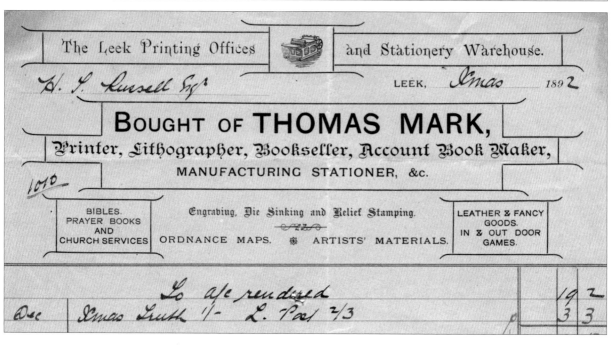

The Leek Printing Offices　and Stationery Warehouse.

H. S. Russell Esqr　LEEK, Xmas　189 2

BOUGHT OF THOMAS MARK,

Printer, Lithographer, Bookseller, Account Book Maker,

MANUFACTURING STATIONER, &c.

1070

BIBLES. PRAYER BOOKS AND CHURCH SERVICES	Engraving, Die Sinking and Relief Stamping. ORDNANCE MAPS. ❀ ARTISTS' MATERIALS.	LEATHER & FANCY GOODS. IN & OUT DOOR GAMES.

	To a/c rendered		19	2
Dec	Xmas Truth 1/- L. Post 2/3		3	3

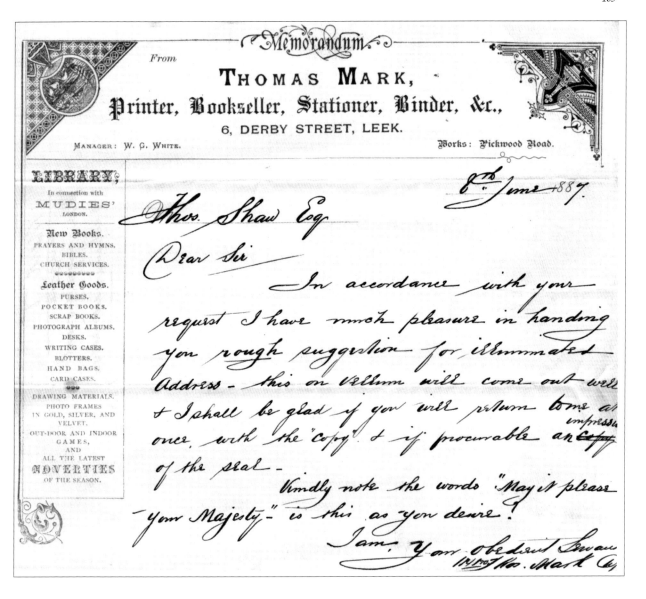

Like most printers Thomas Mark's headings were fine examples of the art of the engraver. The widest range of stationery items was stocked, from pins and pen nibs to cash safes, and from sealing wax and inks to ledgers and journals. Thomas Mark's printing services were very comprehensive, offering printed books and booklets as well as general jobbing work. Mark's Almanac was a regular annual publication in the late Victorian years. This included a diary for the coming year in the manner of Old Moore's Almanac, bound in with the main section which contained local information, dates and events and a comprehensive commercial directory of the town.

Books printed included a list of books in the Nicholson Institute and a Register of Voters.

The business operated at 6 Derby Street between 1846 and 1892.

This plan shows Thomas Mark's shop fronting on Derby Street and his print workshops at the rear, at the top of Pickwood Road.

Surrounding the property to the left (west) is Bull's the grocer and the Black's Head. To the right (east) are the offices of Challinors solicitors. Further down Pickwood Road stand a row of terraced cottages so typical of the courts that were around the Town centre.

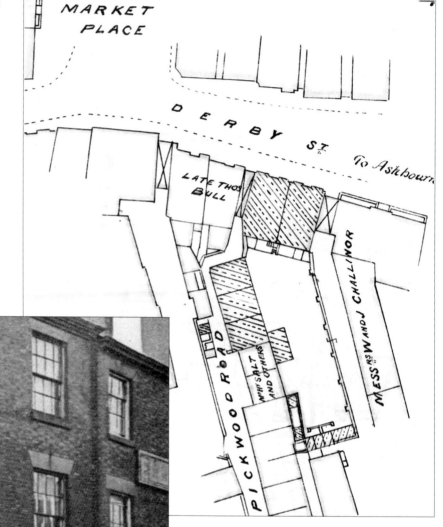

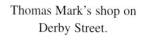

Thomas Mark's shop on Derby Street.

STANLEY STREET,

Leek, *Nov 13th* _____ 186 9

Trustees of the Alms Houses Leek

To W. Marsden, Dr.

Painter, Plumber and Gas Fitter.

DEALER IN CUT AND MOULDED GLASS.

			£	s	d
1869					
Jany 14	To Repg Water Tap J. Shenton 1hr Washerve				9
May 25	To Painting outside Walls & Doors &c. Alms House Comhton as per Contract		5	5	0
June 18	Extra colouring Gable &c			4	3
23	3-0 Stone col for House occupied Mrs Lovatt			1	6
	4 pieces of Wall paper ½-4 of Flour ¼ lb Glue			4	5
	Hordern 1 day			4	6
25	¾ lb White pt 1-8 Stone col pt Hulme 1 day			4	1½
July 13	1-8 Stone col C. Robinson ½ day			1	9
26	Miss Wain's House 4-8 Stone col 1-8 White			3	0
	Sharratt ¾ day			2	3
27	Mrs Lovatts & Miss Wains Houses Painting Sharratt ½ day			1	6
	Settled Jany 14 1870	£	6	13	0 ½

William Marsden

STANLEY STREET,

Leek, _____ Xmas _____ 1871

Messrs Challinor & Co

To W. MARSDEN, Dr.

PAINTER, PLUMBER & GAS-FITTER.

DEALER IN CUT AND MOULDED GLASS.

1872

Jany 25	1-½" Gas main cock ²/⁻ N. Robinson 3hrs ⁴/5½ Office Derby Street	—	3	5½
July 3	Derby St office 2 Sqrs of glass & Frosted 14 ³/₈ + 10 ⁵/₈ Sharratt		2	6
Sept. 7	To Gas in Mr Challinor's office Man ¼ day		1	2½
Oct. 4	To Repg Gas Office Derby St Man ¼ day		1	2½
		£ —	8	4½

Settled Jany 9th 1872
William Marsden

Marsden's bills are a further example of how some traders were willing to render their accounts at the end of the year, for annual settlement. Kelly's directory of 1888 lists Mrs Elizabeth Marsden, glass dealer, No 1 Stanley Street. Stanley Street was formerly Custard Street and the change had not long been made in 1871.

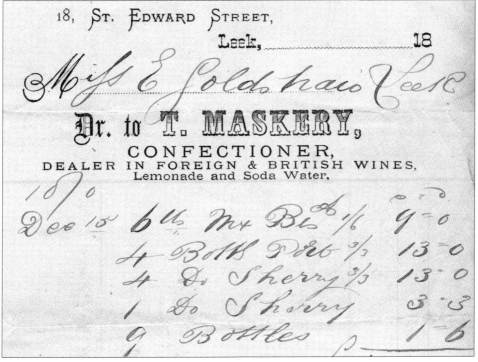

1876

Maskery's business was established in 1795. Owned by Francis Maskery (Slater's Directory 1862) the business moved to 58 St Edward Street soon after 1880. The site was formerly occupied by an inn, the Holly Bush, which was demolished when the shop was built. Maskery's had a high reputation for the quality of their pork pies and gingerbread. All their bakery and confectionery products were highly regarded by Leek people and they also supplied wines and spirits from the attractive bay-windowed shop in St Edward Street where the business remained through two world wars.

ESTABLISHED 1796.

T. MASKERY,

CONFECTIONER, ETC.,

58, ST. EDWARD STREET, LEEK.

BRIDE CAKES, CELEBRATED GINGERBREAD,

RICH CURRANT BREAD, BON BONS,

COSSAQUES IN VARIETY.

Established 1831.   10, SHEEP MARKET,

Leek, _____ Dec _____ 1883

The Ex⁰ˢ late Mr H. Goldshaw
Wetley Rocks,

Dr. to C. H. & W. Massey,

Wholesale Confectioners and Biscuit Manufacturers.

Packages not allowed for until received and in good condition.

1880				
Jan 2ⁿᵈ	1 ᵗʰ Maccaroons		2	0
	2 ᵗʰ Savoy Bᵗˢ	1/4	2	8
	2 Currant Loaves	1/4	2	8
	2 Seed do	1/4	2	8

ESTABLISHED 1831.
Sheep Market.

Leek, Feb 1880

To The Exor of the late Mr Henry Goldshaw
Wetley Rocks

and to

To George H Massey Dr

Wholesale Confectioner & Biscuit Baker.

ALL PACKAGES TO BE PAID FOR WITH THE GOODS AND THE SAME
PRICE ALLOWED IF RETURNED FREE WITHIN 4 MONTHS.

1879			
Oct 22ⁿᵈ	1 doz Wakes Cakes	2	0
25	Currant Loaf 1/ Buns 6	1	6
1880	Tea Cakes 2½ Pork Pie 2/-	2	2½
Jan 2	1 ᵗʰ Maccaroons	2	0
	2 ᵗʰ Savoy Bᵗˢ 1/4	2	8
	2 Currant Loaves 1/4	2	8
	2 Seed do 1/4	2	8

George Henry and William Massey were bakers and confectioners. They traded from Sheepmarket where Brassington's shop was located later, and where we now find Country Cuisine and the Primo Piano restaurant.

£300

BUXTON ROAD,
Leek: June 11th 1862

Jas Alsop Esq

Bought of John Mathews,

Builder and Timber Merchant,

Dealer in Slates, Fire Bricks, Chimney Pots, Cement, Plaster, Drain Pipes, Sanitary Traps, Ridges,
Floor Bricks, Quarries, &c., &c.

To Traps, fitting in &c & Making good
the property in the Road & New St

May 24	13	9 in Earthenware Traps		4/9	3	1	9
	12	9 in Iron Grids to Do		9/		9	0
	4	4 in Straight Sockets pipes		7/2		2	6
	1	4 in Bend Do					11
	1	Barrow Mortar 1º Cement 3				1	1
	20	Blue Dust Bricks		5/		1	0
		Excavator 4¼ Days		2/10		12	0½
		Carting away Rubbish	1 Hr	8/			8
					4	8	11½
Cr By		5 Grid Stones & Old Iron Grids				2	9
					£4	6	2½

Received November 29th 1862

C Slagg   John Mathews

June 20/62

This series of headings for J. and J. Mathews represents the activities of an old-established family business which undertook work for business and private clients. On a number of occasions they worked with the Leek architects, William and Larner Sugden.

60, BUXTON ROAD,

LEEK, *December 6th 1883*

Wr. B Badnall Esqr

→ Dr. to J. and J. MATHEWS,

JOINERS, BUILDERS AND TIMBER MERCHANTS,

SPOOL TURNING AND SAWING MILLS, &c.

PINE, RED & WHITE DEALS, BATTENS, BOARDS, MOULDINGS, LATHS, &c.

Interest charged on Overdue Accounts.

1883		£	o	d
Sept 25	*1 Load Firewood + Logs to Thorpe*		8	0

Messrs Exors late John Brealey   Nov. 26.   19

Dr. to J. & J. MATHEWS,

Steam Saw Mills and Joinery Works,

English and Foreign Timber Merchants,

SPOOL MANUFACTURERS,

21, & 60, BUXTON ROAD, LEEK.

PINE, RED AND WHITE DEALS, BATTENS, BOARDS, MOULDINGS. LATHS, &c.

OAK AND ASH PLANKS, CART FELLOES, SHAFTS, ETC.

709

1901				
May 24	*1 pair new rollers Turned & fitted To mangle*		13.	
Sep - 14	*26.0 of 4½ × 3 red deal Spout to Stone Row 3d*		6	
	12 Iron Spout Stays @ 6/- Screws + nails 6d		6	
	Joiner working new spouting & fixing same &			
	repairing old Spouts, new pails + pales to Gardens 20 hrs		13	
	13.0 of 3 × 2 rail ½ 9 pales 2 - 0 Long 2½ × 3/4 ½		2	
" 28	*2 lbs wire nes d paint 6d Joiner to Garden Rails +c. 14 Hrs 8d*		10	
	To Best Polished oak Coffin for late John Brealey,			
	lined, Brass furniture, Engraved Brass Plate,			
	Shroud, + attendance, + arranging		6	10

John and Jabez Mathews also offered a spool and bobbin-making service to the local textile industry. They were used in great volumes in the local factories.

645

60, BUXTON ROAD, LEEK, *March. 1.* 18 9 9

Messrs Trustees late Dr Turnock

Dr. to J. & J. MATHEWS,

JOINERS, BUILDERS, & TIMBER MERCHANTS.

SPOOL TURNING AND SAWING MILLS, &C.

PINE, RED AND WHITE DEALS, BATTENS, BOARDS, MOULDINGS, LATHS, &c.

OAK AND ASH PLANKS, CART FELLOES, SHAFTS, &c.

1898	Globe Yard wall to Mrs Cheethams & boundary wall between Garden & Mrs Whittles, Drain Mr Fallows Stable & opening & unstoping Drain Globe Yard			
Oct 6	200 Common Bricks 8/- Carting Same 1/-	9	0	
	8 Barrows Water houses Lime 8/- 3 Loads Sand 3/-	11	·	
	Carting Sand 3/- 5-4 Drain pipes 2/11	5	11	
	100 Slates to top of wall 20×10½ 12/6 1-6 Gully & Grid 4/-	16	6	
	Man opening & unstoping Drain & putting in Gully & pipes to Mr Fallows Stable 30 Hrs 6	15	·	
	Bricklayer taking top courses off wall in Globe Yard & rebuilding same 43 Hrs 9d	1	12	3
	Labourer 49 Hrs 6d £1/4/6 Labourer dressing Bricks 35 Hrs 17/6	2	2	0
	Carting one load dirt to tip	1	·	
8	Bricklayer Building wall 34½ Hrs 9d	1	5	10
	Labourer 20 Hrs 6d 10/- Labourer dressing Bricks 43 Hrs 17/11 50	1	4	11
	4 Loads Sand & carting 1/9 7/- carting 2 loads dirt to tip 2/-	9	·	
15	Bricklayer Building wall & pointing Same 33½ 9d	1	5	1
	Labourer do 22 Hrs 6d	11	·	
	1 Load Mortar 7/- Carting Same 1/-	8	·	
22	Bricklayer to wall in Garden 31 Hrs 9d	1	3	3
	Labourer do 11 Hrs 5d	4	7	
	1 Load Mortar 7/- Carting Same 1/- 2 loads to tip 2/-	10	·	
		£ 13	17	4

Settled

May 6 1899.

J & J Mathews

Bill 1

39

Residence 31 Portland St. South

50, REGENT STREET,

LEEK, *Xmas*   191*1*

M *To the Trustees of the late H. Goostry*

Dr. to WILLIAM MATTHEWS,

BUILDER AND CONTRACTOR,

General Property Repairer and Dealer in Building Materials.

1911

		£	s	d
	To a/c rendered	3	8	1½
Nov 28	To providing & fixing new clay pot, bedroom grate & clay tile As agreement	1	2	6
		£ 4	10	7½

£4 .. 8 : 0

Rec*d* with thanks May 8/12

W Matthews

Bill 2

50, REGENT STREET,

Leek, *Sept qtr*   1908

M *To the Trustees Late R. Gurnock*

Dr. to WILLIAM MATTHEWS,

BUILDER & CONTRACTOR,

General Property Repairer and Dealer in Building Materials.

1908

			s	d
July 10 & 11	Bricklayer & Labourer 10 Hrs		12	6
	58 Red & blue 6" Quarries 3/4. 1 Barrow mortar 1/.		4	4
	2 Com. bks 1". 1 Sq. clay pot 3/3. 1 Pk cement 1/.		4	4
Aug 14	Bricklayer & Labourer 6 Hrs		7	6
	1 Sq. clay pot 3/3. 1 Pk cement 1/. 6 Roof tiles 4½		4	7
	3/4 Barrow mortar 9. 6 Com. bks 3. 3½ lbs plaster 3½		1	2½
	1 Damper & frame 9d. 1 Iron bar 12" long 2			9
		£ 1	15	3

Repairs Victoria Street

Rec*d* with thanks
Oct 2/08

FRANK MAYFIELD

PRACTICAL

Umbrella . . . .

Manufacturer,

18 ST. EDWARD STREET

LEEK.

RE-COVERS and REPAIRS at the Shortest
Notice, at Reasonable Prices.

St Edward Street was formerly named Spout Street because an open drain flowed down its length. It was a street of great social contrasts with the large houses on the left occupied by several of the Town's gentry, including Hugh Sleigh and Thomas Wardle. Joshua Strangman lived here and the lawyers Hacker and Allen were based in a building that also served as the County Court. In contrast, on the opposite side of the street, several courts, or alleys, led off the street and opened out into groups of silk workers cottages. Thus there was a cross-section of the social strata of Leek within a stone's throw of each other.

This view of St. Edward Street shows the Tudor style Victoria Buildings on the left (architect James Gosling Smith), with the gable of Richard Norman Shaw's Spout Hall above, on the left.

A tree-lined St. Edward Street at the turn of the 20th century with one of Leek's old gas lamps on the right.

The top of Mill St leading into Church St, shows Overton Bank on the right and Clerk Bank on the left, and the parish church of St Edward dominating the scene. Horsedrawn carts are very evident.

Butchers often enhanced their headings with pictures of prime livestock. The family business of Meakin is still trading as butchers in Queen Street today.

LONDON ROAD, LEEK,

Xmas 190**1**

M Executors of the Late John Brealey Esq

Dr. to JOHN MEAKIN,

Wheelwright, Shoeing & General Smith
IN ALL ITS BRANCHES.

1901

		£	s	d
July 2	to 1 new fork & rod to 1 Pump. 4/ hooping bucket to 0/9		4	9
"	to 1 Plate & cotter & repairing handle 1/9 3 holdfasts 9		2	6
4	to Pesing & repairing 1 pump bucket drawer			9
		£	8	0

Settled May 27 / 1902

John Meakin

These attractive headings illustrate various aspects of the blacksmith's craft. The smithy was on Ashbourne Road, opposite Moorhouse Street (now part of the Leek Health Centre car park)

M Trustee's of The Late Cuthbert Robinson   Xmas   1913

Dr. to ———

JOHN J. MEAKIN,

𝔚𝔥𝔢𝔢𝔩𝔴𝔯𝔦𝔤𝔥𝔱,

SHOEING AND GENERAL SMITH,

Waggon, Cart and Prize Float Builder,

ASHBOURNE ROAD, LEEK.

Repairing neatly and expeditiously executed with
well seasoned materials, best workmanship,
and at moderate charges.

HORSES CAREFULLY SHOD.

1913

		£	s	d
July 5	to drilling & plating 1 cistern lever		1	0
28	to 2 new drive in spout stays with risers		1	6
Aug 29	to 20 drive in spout stays with spurs risers		14	2
		£	16	8

Private Address :
57, BARNGATE ST. LEEK.

Whitfield Gardens, JUNCTION ROAD,

LEEK, *Oct 28* 192

Bought of R. MEAKIN,

Nurseryman & Florist.

WREATHS, CROSSES & BOUQUETS A SPECIALITY.

A Large Selection of Plants for Decorative Purposes always on hand

All Kinds of Gardening done by Experienced Men.

LANDSCAPE GARDENING.

Mr Brealey Land Agent

The Grave

June 12	4 Doz Best Antirrhinum		4	
" "	4 " Lobelia		3	6
" "	8 straightening Rose trees & grass		3	6
			11	.

This business was located near the Cemetery, offering wreaths and flowers, care of graves, and gardening services. The name of Whitfield Gardens is now preserved in the name of Whitfield Street off Junction Road.

FOR Good Value IN Household Furniture, Bedsteads, Spring and Wool Mattresses, JAMES MEAKIN, 45, Queen Street, Washing and Wringing Machines, Wringing Machines Repaired. New Roller & Wheels Fitted to any make of Machine. AGENT FOR JONES' SEWING MACHINES.

HATS, IES,
COLLARS,
A SPECIALITY.

Sanders' Buildings, 74, Derby Street,

Leek, *Dec 21st* 190 0

Mrs *Smith*

Bought of W. MEARS,

Gentlemen's Outfitter and Clothier.

		£	s	d
June 3rd 1899	Loom Suit	1	2	6
"	Tie 6½ Shirt 1/9 Hankchf 4½		2	8
June 15th	Cap 1/- Hank. 4½		1	4½
June 24th	Loom Suit		16	11
"	Ties		2	0
July 4th	Cap 1/- Stockings 9d½		1	9½
"	Stocking 10½ Socks 8½		1	7
" 8th	Shirt		1	6
"	Shirt		1	9½
"	Loomtrs		6	11
"	Loom vest		3	6
12th	Do & Collars		1	1
15th	2 Collars 1/1 tie 1/-		2	1
18th	Blouse		2	11
"	2 Mrs Dress length 1/8		3	4
22nd	Jockey cap	X		6½
25th	Loom Blouse		2	11
29th	Loom Cap		1	0
"	Jacket & Vest		9	0
	Carried forward	4	5	5

Sanders Buildings - a fine Sugden building - stands at the corner of Derby Street with Haywood Street.
The business later became Mears' greengrocery shop, and part of the building remained a greengrocery
business under different ownership until 2000.

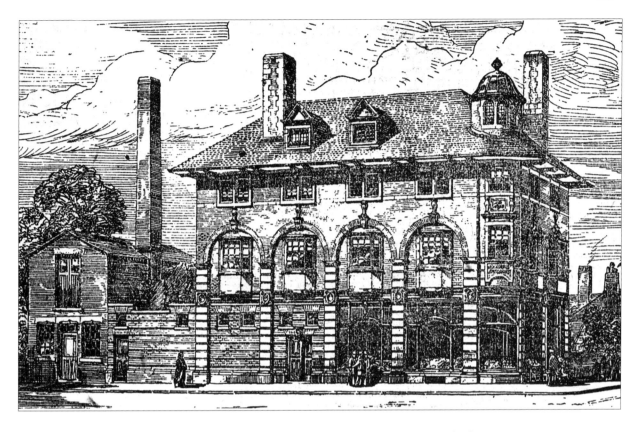

Mr. Sanders' new business premises—now being roofed in—will constitute a salient feature in the Cattle Market, and by the courtesy of the architect, we are enabled to illustrate their finished appearance. The drawing from which our block is reduced is in the Picture Exhibition at the Nicholson Institute. Mr. Sanders is to be congratulated on the combination of art with

economy; as the phœnix arising from the ashes of the " shanty," whilst a very " eyeable " structure, is not comparatively more costly than the ordinary builders' terrors which " eclipse the gaiety " of our streets. The boldly projecting cornice and oriels give a character to the design : and it now only remains for the Improvement Commissioners to convert the arid Cattle Market

into a smiling town garden, with trees, fountain and band kiosque, to complete the picture, finishing the vista of Derby street by something more alluring than a weigh-machine-cum-cobblers-shop. Messrs. W. Sugden and Son are the architects of the building, and Mr. Grace and Mr. Isaac Heath the contractors. *Floreat porrum.*

Above, a busy Edwardian scene at Mear's corner, and below the Leek Battery set out to war in 1914.

NURSERY, BROAD STREET,

LEEK, *Midsmr* 1884

M͞ *W. B. Badnall, Esqr*

BOUGHT OF MATTHEW MELLOR,

NURSERYMAN, FLORIST AND SEEDSMAN.

DUTCH BULBS ANNUALLY IMPORTED.

1884		£	s	d
Feby 12	1 Thujaopsis Borealus 1/6 & 1 Do Do 2/.	"	3	6
	1 Bay Leaf Holly 3/. & 1 Rhododendron 2/.	"	5	"
	3 Berberrys 2/. & 12 English Laurels 10/.	"	12	"
	6 Limes 18/. & 1 striped Sycamore 7/.	1	5	"
	2 Sedums 4 & 3.5.0 strawberry Plants 8/9 2/ Spirea 2	"	9	3
	18 half std Roses 18/. & 24 Dwf Do 18/. & 1 Potentilla 3	1	16	3
	1 Christmas Rose 6 & 12 Double Wallflowers 1/6 & 18 Single Do 1/2	"	3	2
	6 Colombines 1/. & 4 Veronicas 8 & 4 Deeibers 10	"	2	6
	1 Campanula 3 & 1 Aster 6 & 12 Polyanthus 1/.	"	1	9
	1 Evening Primrose 6 & 50 Narcissus 3/.	"	3	6
	1 Clump Yellow Aster	"	"	6
	50 Lent Lilys 3/. & 50 Daffodils 2/6 & 50 Narcissus 3/.	"	8	6
	4 Pinks Fimbriata Alba Major 1/. & 4 White Pinks 4	"	1	4
	2 White Cloves Glorie De Nancy 1/. & 6 Red Do 2/.	"	3	"
	4 Laced Pinks 8 & 6 Days 21/. & Train Fare 1/9 & Lodgings 2/6	1	5	3
14	1 pt Broad Beans 3½ & 1 pt Early Peas 6 Parsnip 2 Postage 6	"	1	5½
16	6 Days	1	1	"
18	3 Dwf 2rd Plums 2/6 ch 7/6 & 1 Do Do Do 3/6	"	11	"
	3 Do Peass @ 1/6 ch 4/6 & 2 Honeysuckles 2/. & Wire 1/.	"	7	6
23	6 Days 21/. Trainfare 1/9 & Lodgings 2/6	1	5	3
April 12	2 qrts Peas 2/. & 1 pt Broad Beans 3½ & Radish 3	"	2	6½
	1 z Onion 4 Lettuce 2 Leeks 2½ Carrot 3 Parsley 6	"	"	10
	HorseRadish 1/6 & 1 pt Sc Runners 6 Turnip 1	"	2	1
		£10	12	2

341

→* NURSERY, BROAD STREET, *←

LEEK *Mids* 1893

Mrs W Prince

Dr. to MATTHEW MELLOR,
NURSERYMAN, FLORIST, AND SEEDSMAN.
DUTCH BULBS ANNUALLY IMPORTED.

				£	s	d
Jany	24	1 pot Lily of the Valley		"	1	"
March	10	1 Wreath & Box		"	10	6
April	24	4 Tea Roses		"	1	"
		15 1/2 hrs at 5½		"	6	5¼
	18	1 Wreath & Box		"	8	"
May	30	2 Maiden Hair Fern 2/. Pennyroyal 2		"	2	2
June	16	1 Cross flowers 6/. carriage to Bucknall 6		"	6	6
				£ 1	15	7½

Settled Dec 13/93
G W Jno
Matthew Mellor

Looking up Broad Street in the early 20th century.

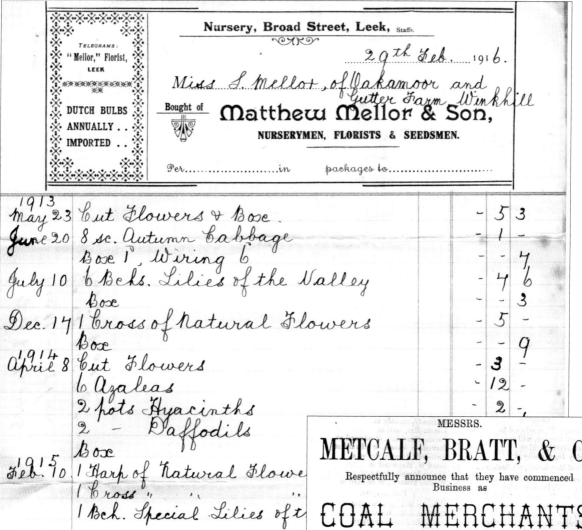

Nursery, Broad Street, Leek, Staffs.

TELEGRAMS:
"Mellor," Florist,
LEEK

DUTCH BULBS
ANNUALLY ..
IMPORTED ..

29th Feb. 1916.

Miss S. Mellor, of Oakamoor and Gutter Farm Winkhill

Bought of

Matthew Mellor & Son,

NURSERYMEN, FLORISTS & SEEDSMEN.

Per.....................in   packages to.........................

1913				
May 23	Cut Flowers & Box.	-	5	3
June 20	8 sc. Autumn Cabbage	-	1	-
	Box 1, Wiring 6	-	-	7
July 10	6 Bchs. Lilies of the Valley	-	4	6
	Box	-	-	3
Dec. 17	1 Cross of Natural Flowers	-	5	
	Box	-	-	9
1914				
April 8	Cut Flowers	-	3	
	6 Azaleas	-	12	-
	2 pots Hyacinths	-	2	-
	2 - Daffodils			
	Box			
1915				
Feb. 10	1 Harp of Natural Flowe			
	1 Cross " " "			
	1 Bch. Special Lilies of t			

TELEGRAMS: "MELLOR. FLORIST. BROAD ST., LEEK."

The Nurseries, Broad Street,

Mr. Dakeyne,

LEEK,   October   193 0.

STAFFS.

Stockwell St., Leek.

Bought of

WILLIAM MELLOR & SON

High-class Florists, Seedsmen,

& Market Gardeners.

SELECTED
SEEDS, BULBS,
HERBACEOUS
AND
ROCKERY
PLANTS.

WREATHS,
CROSSES AND
BOQUETS
ON THE
SHORTEST
NOTICE.

Per .... in Packages to ....

Date	Item		£	s	d
Sept 27	2 lbs Brusselsprouts 6; 2 lbs Runner Beans 8		"	1	2
	20 lbs Potatoes 1/8; 8 lbs Swede Turnips 8		"	2	4
	1 lb Tomatoes 10		"	"	10
Oct 4	2 lbs Brusselsprouts 6; 3 lbs Beet 1/-		"	1	6
	2 lbs Runner Beans 8; 8 lbs Swede Turnips 8		"	1	4
	20 lbs Potatoes 1/8		"	1	8
	10" Cut Michlemas Daisies		"	"	4
11"	2 lbs Brusselsprouts 6; 12 lbs Swede Turnips 1/-		"	1	6
	20 lbs Potatoes 1/8; 3 lbs Parsnips 6		"	2	2
19"	2 lbs Brusselsprouts 6; 12 lbs Swede Turnips 1/-		"	1	6
	20 lbs Potatoes 1/8; 3 lbs Parsnips 6		"	2	2
25"	2 lbs Brusselsprouts 6; 12 lbs Swede Turnips 1/-		"	1	6
	20 lbs Potatoes 1/8; 3 lbs Parsnips 6		"	2	2
Nov 1st	20 lbs Potatoes		"	1	8
		£	1	1	10

SELECTED
SEEDS, BULBS
HERBACEOUS
AND
ROCKERY PLANTS

Telegrams : "Mellor, Florist, Broad Street, Leek"
THE NURSERIES, BROAD STREET,
LEEK _____ Jany. ____ 193 2.

WREATHS,
CROSSES and
BOUQUETS
on the
Shortest Notice

Mrs. Dakeyne ; Stockwell St, Leek.

Bt. of WILLIAM MELLOR & SON
—— HIGH CLASS ——
Florists, Seedmen & Market Gardeners

Per _____ in Packages to

Jany 2nd	20 lbs Potatoes 2/6°; 2 lbs Brusselspts 6		„	3	„
	4 lbs Carrots		„	4	8
9th	20 lbs Potatoes 2/6°; Savoys 6		„	3	„
	6 lbs Carrots 1/-; 6 lbs Parsnips 1/-		„	2	„
16th	20 lbs Potatoes 2/6°; 6 lbs Carrots 1/-		„	3	6
	6 lbs Parsnips 1/-; 2 lbs Brusselspts 6		„	1	6
	Savoys 6		„	„	6
23rd	20 lbs Potatoes 2/6°; Savoys 8		„	3	2
30th	20 lbs. Potatoes 2/6°; 3 lbs. Brusselspts 9		„	3	3

Residence, :-Market Street.   **Yard & Works :--Earl Street. LEEK, Staffs.**

Mr C. Robinson   Plumber & c.

DR. TO T. MESSHAM,
PLAIN AND ORNAMENTAL PLASTERER,
AND   GENERAL   PROPERTY   REPAIRER.

Vases and Pedestals, Trusses. Shields Pediments, Letters, Door and Window Heads, &c., in Artificial Stone.
Ceilings, Cornices, Centre Flowers, Doorheads, Capitals, Trusses, Slabs. Partition Blocks, &c., in Improved Fibrous Plaster.
Centre Flowers for Ventilating Purposes. Plaster, Cements, Pytho Adamant, &c., kept in stock.

	Patching Wall Inside				
	& over Hospital				
1913	for Painters				
Oct 12th	Jm 3 hours	?		2	3
	Kins Cement & ct			2	6
		By Contra		4/9	

Memorandum.

From *W. H. Middleton,* Grocer & Tea Dealer. *Leek,* STAFFORDSHIRE.

To *Messrs Challinor & Shaw.*

June 20 1892.

8 King St.

Gentlemen,

I enclose cheque to balance Messrs Nixon's a/c. Mr W. Nixon owes me for goods since Xmas £2.4.7, Mr John £3.6.11 & Messrs W & J. for goods since last October 1.18.7. Total £7-10-1. Deduct from £15.7.5 leaves £7.17.4 owing. Cheque for £7.17-0 enclosed. Yours truly, W H Middleton.

MIDDLETON,

Wholesale and Retail

Grocer, Tea and Coffee Dealer,

Tobacconist, &c.

MARKET PLACE, LEEK.

Fine Fresh Roasted Coffee, Cocoa, Chocolate, Fruit and Spices.

This elaborate advert with its exotic impression of the East, appeared on an advertising calendar. Such calendars promoting local businesses were very popular in the late Victorian period.

Joseph Mien was a grandson of Jean Baptiste Francois Mien, a French prisoner from the Napoleonic Wars who was sent to Leek on parole on 1st October 1804, and later married and settled in Leek. Joseph Mien died in 1902 and the fact that this receipt dated 1917 is signed 'P. Mien' suggests that his wife Phoebe continued the business after his death.

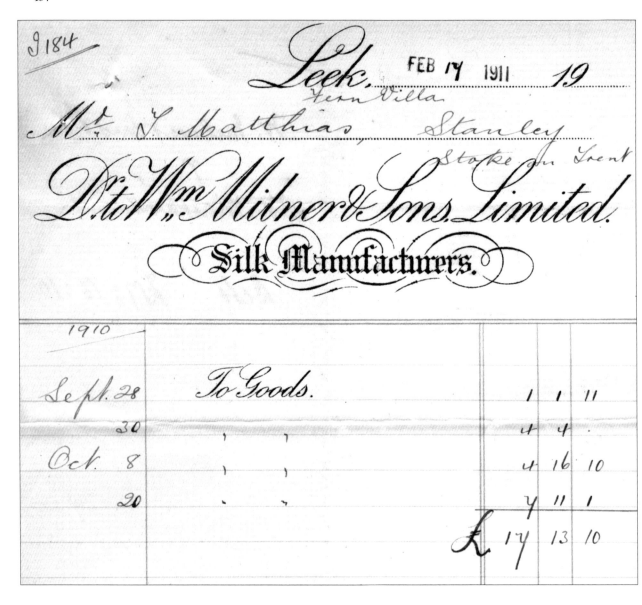

9184

Leek, FEB 14 1911 19

Fern Villa

Mr T Matthias, Stanley

(Stoke on Trent

Dr to Wm Milner & Sons Limited.

Silk Manufacturers.

1910

		£	s	d
Sept. 28	To Goods.	1	1	11
30	" "	4	4	.
Oct. 8	" "	4	16	10
20	" "	4	11	1
		£14	13	10

The head of the firm William Milner & Sons for many years, Robert Schofield Milner was a man who made his mark on Leek in many ways. Born in 1847 and educated at the Old Leek Grammar School, he joined his father in the family firm when he completed his education. He was elected a Leek Improvement Commissioner in 1873, and later served on the Leek Urban District Council until 1914. His many other public duties included serving as trustee and secretary to the Cottage Hospital. His father, William Milner, was a founder-member of Leek cricket Club and Robert Milner was a very able cricketer, playing his first match for Leek against Ashbourne in 1863 and later serving as captain for about 20 years. He died February 4th 1925.

The name of Milner was perpetuated in Leek in several ways:

1. The Milner Bequest: an educational grant
2. Milner School: the old Council School for Girls was renamed Milner Girls' School
3. Milner Terrace: a road on the new housing scheme of the 1920s
4. Milner was one of the four 'houses' in the old Leek High School

TELEGRAMS:
MILNERS, LEEK.

N.B. This includes both Frances &
Winifred's Bills –

W. Milner & Sons.
Silk Manufacturers.
Leek, Staffordshire. July 13ᵗʰ 1907

MEDALS,
VIENNA, 1873.
PHILADELPHIA, 1876.
SYDNEY, 1879.
BARCELONA, 1888.
—
DIPLOMA,
MELBOURNE, 1880.

March 07	Brockhill H.	4 – 3	✓
May	Benbow	3 – 6	✓
Feby	Hill A J	5 .	✓
Jany	Hall & H	3 . 11	✓
July 07	Hallidie	2 . 2 . 0	✓
Jany	Hall Geo H	4 . 4 . 9	✓ 9/
"	International Stores	3 . 5	✓
March	Kenward H	3 . 1 . 4	✓ 4/
	Metcalf & Kirkpatrick	7 . 0 . 5	✓
Jany	Miles W	2 .	✓
Feby	Neve Hⁿ	4 . 3	✓
	Philpot Son (as rendered 8/11 not sent)	1 . 8 . 5	✓
Jany	Palmer J G	5 . 10	
"	Pickett Son	6 . 6	✓
Jany	Plummer Roddis Ltᵈ	29 . 0 . 8¼	Miss ✓ Francis
3 Decr items included 8/11	do do	19 . 18 . 3	Miss ✓ Winifred
		£ 68 . 14 . 6¼	

189

Mr Joseph Shufflebotham

Dr. to JOSHUA MILLWARD,
AUCTIONEER AND VALUER.

◆

Longnor near Buxton; and at the Red Lion Hotel, Leek.

1897			
June 2	Brandy Lee Farm Rushton		
	To making tenant right Valuation upon the above farm.		
	Meeting the umpire upon the said farm and at Macclesfield, including journies postage &c on my part.	7 . 7 . =	
	Copy of Mr Turners Bill		
Apl 27.	charges for award.	4 . 4 – 0	
	Stamps & expenses.	16 – 0	

JOSHUA MILLWARD,
Auctioneer & Appraiser,

AUCTION & VALUATION OFFICES:

CHESHIRE CHEESE INN, LONGNOR,

AND

RED LION HOTEL, LEEK,

ON WEDNESDAYS.

◆

All orders will receive prompt attention with moderate
charges.

1876

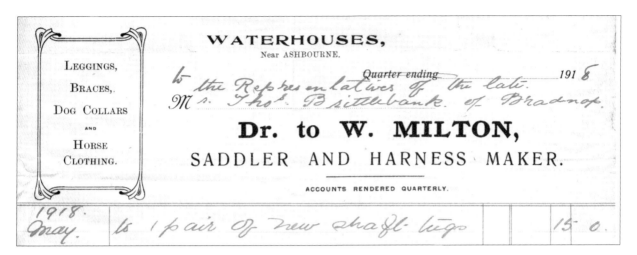

WATERHOUSES,
Near ASHBOURNE.

LEGGINGS,
BRACES,
DOG COLLARS
AND
HORSE
CLOTHING.

Quarter ending _____ 191 8

to the Representatives of the late
M^r. Thos. Brittlebank of Bradnop.

Dr. to W. MILTON,
SADDLER AND HARNESS MAKER.

ACCOUNTS RENDERED QUARTERLY.

1918.			
May.	to 1 pair of new shaft tugs	15	0

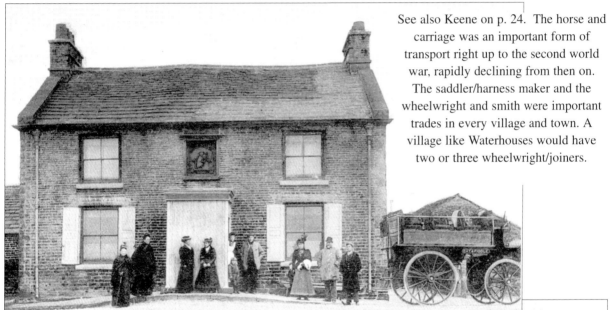

See also Keene on p. 24. The horse and carriage was an important form of transport right up to the second world war, rapidly declining from then on. The saddler/harness maker and the wheelwright and smith were important trades in every village and town. A village like Waterhouses would have two or three wheelwright/joiners.

A hostelry like the Cat and Fiddle on Axe Edge was very dependent on the horse and carriage for its trade - although by the 1930s (right) transport was changing for certain.

C.E Mitchell was a grocer at 23 Market Street. Soap was a great commodity for hygiene-conscious Victorians and many famous brands, like Hudsons, Pears and Sunlight vied with each other through many forms of advertising.

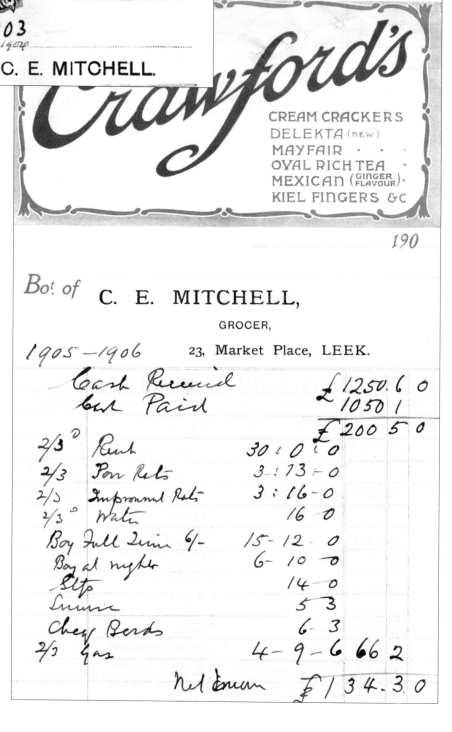

Depot S.P.C.K.
„ Religious Tract Society.
Agent for Oxford University Press.
„ Cambridge Warehouse.
„ Ordnance Survey.

The Moorlands Press and Leek Stationery Warehouse.

Leek, _Octr 18_ 1915

Messrs. Challinors & Shaw

Dr. to W. H. Eaton,

Artistic Printer, Lithographer, Bookseller, Account Book Maker,

Manufacturing Stationer, &c., &c.

Engraving, Die Sinking & Relief Stamping.   Artists' Materials.   Cricket, Golf & Lawn Tennis Goods.

ptg 1/300 Receipt Books "Tithes"   6 6

p° W H Eaton
Oct 18 1915

William Eaton was printer at 6 Derby Street (Mark's old premises) who published many local and some national books under the name of The Moorland Press. *In the Highlands of Staffordshire* was a successful title. The Moorlands Press continued until the 1960s, in later years under new ownership. See also Eaton in Volume I.

W.H. NITHSDALE
TAX INSPECTOR, PHOTOGRAPHER, AUTHOR

W.H.Nithsdale was a Scotsman who was based in Leek as the agent of the Inland Revenue between 1904 and 1909. During that short time he developed a great love for the Town and the Moorland area, and was able to record his impressions in his book *In the Highlands of Staffordshire* 1906 (a reprint of which is still available from Churnet Valley Books).

His other talent was photography which enabled him to capture many aspects of the local scene in a series of fine photographs, some of which were used as picture postcards.

In the HIGHLANDS OF STAFFORDSHIRE

W H NITHSDALE

W H EATON
THE MOORLAND PRESS
LEEK 1906

EVERY DESCRIPTION OF

Electrical
Work ...

UNDERTAKEN BY

The "Moorland" Electrical

.. AND ..

General Engineering Works,

LONDON MILLS,

— LEEK.

Lighting and Bells, Repairs
to Dynamos, etc.

COMPLETE INSTALLATIONS.

Experts sent out to any distance to
quote for FITTING-UP, or for REPAIRS.

This "Moorland" Electrical advert is from 1926. Leek had its own Local Authority run direct current generating station in Station Street. There are still houses in Leek with the brass conducting bars set under their hallway floors.

G. MORRIS,

(late the Misses Stonehewer).

....

HIGH-CLASS
CONFECTIONERY.

PASTRIES SWEETS	GENOA and Other CAKES
BRIDE CAKES	BIRTHDAY CAKES
GINGER-BREAD	BISCUITS

PLAIN MILK, and FANCY BREAD.

COMFORTABLE CAFE,
open all day
Teas & Refreshments at
Reasonable Charges.

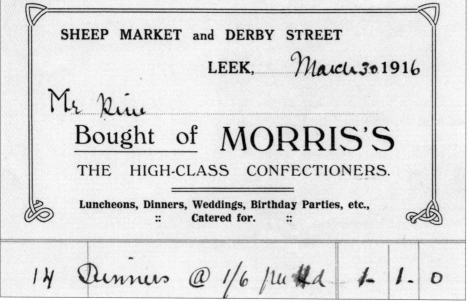

SHEEP MARKET and DERBY STREET

LEEK, *March 30 1916*

Mr Pirr

Bought of MORRIS'S

THE HIGH-CLASS CONFECTIONERS.

Luncheons, Dinners, Weddings, Birthday Parties, etc.,
:: Catered for. ::

14 Dinners @ 1/6 .... 1 . 1 . 0

The gentility of Victorian and Edwardian Leek is reflected in the number of tea rooms and cafes which flourished at the time.

ST. EDWARD STREET,

LEEK, *Aug* 1895

Mr *J Morris*

Bought of W. MORRIS,

BOOT & SHOE MANUFACTURER.

1 pair	Lace	" 7 " 9
1 pair	Soleing heeling	" 1 " 9
		9 " 6

Settled
E Morris
Thanks

The address of William Morris, shoedealer, at this time was 67 St Edward Street. In 1904 he was still in business at 51 St Edward Street.

TELEPHONE No. 55.

"EAGLE" PRINTING WORKS,

LONDON STREET, LEEK, *Nov 6* 1908
STAFFS.

Mess Challinors & Shaw *Leek*

Bought of DAVID MORRIS & Co.,

LITHOGRAPHIC AND LETTERPRESS PRINTERS,

✢ BOOKBINDERS AND PATTERN CARD MANUFACTURERS. ✢

Supplying 8 Reams Note Paper ½	9/6 £	2 12 "
paid by Mr. L Challinor		1 6 :
	£	1 6 :

Mar 15/09
Recd

Morris & Co
W S Darby

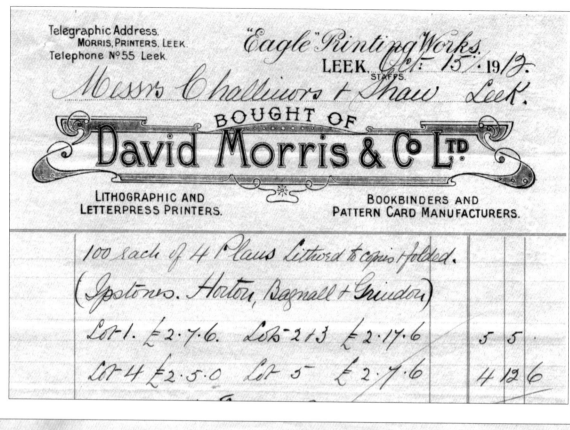

Telegraphic Address.
MORRIS, PRINTERS, LEEK.
Telephone Nº 55 Leek.

"Eagle" Printing Works,
LEEK. *Oct. 15. 1912.*
STAFFS.

Messrs Challinors + Shaw Leek.

BOUGHT OF

David Morris & Cº Lᵀᴰ

LITHOGRAPHIC AND
LETTERPRESS PRINTERS.

BOOKBINDERS AND
PATTERN CARD MANUFACTURERS.

100 each of 4 Plans Lettered to copies + folded.		
(Ipstones. Horton, Bagnall + Grindon)		
Lot 1. £2.7.6 Lot 2 + 3 £2.17.6	5	5 .
Lot 4 £2.5.0 Lot 5 £2.7.6	4	12 6

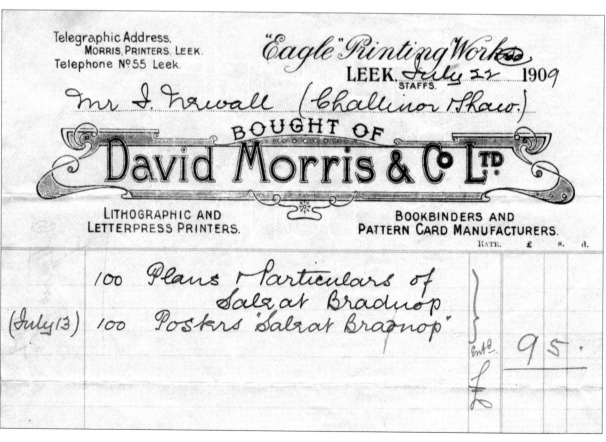

Telegraphic Address.
MORRIS, PRINTERS, LEEK.
Telephone Nº 55 Leek.

"Eagle" Printing Works,
LEEK. *July 22* 1909
STAFFS.

Mr I Nuvall (Challinor + Shaw.)

BOUGHT OF

David Morris & Cº Lᵀᴰ

LITHOGRAPHIC AND
LETTERPRESS PRINTERS.

BOOKBINDERS AND
PATTERN CARD MANUFACTURERS.

		RATE.	£	s.	d.
	100 Plans + Particulars of Sale at Bradnop				
(July 13)	100 Posters "Sale at Bradnop"			9	5 .

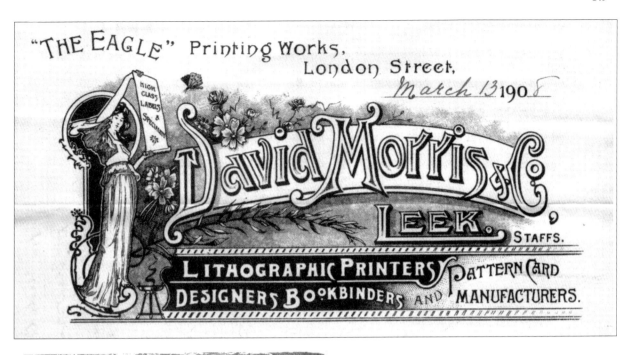

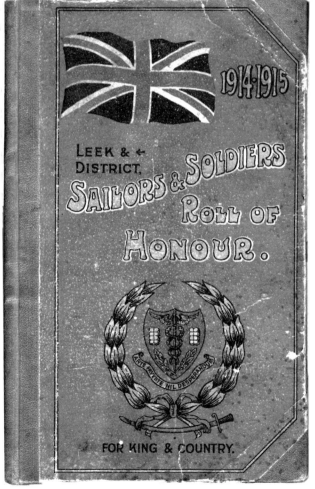

There is more than a hint of the Art and Craft movement in the billheads of David Morris & Co. This ornate, elaborately decorated, style was the hallmark of much of their printing work, reflecting perhaps the influence at the time of his more famous namesake.

One of the books produced by the firm was a highly treasured little hardback volume, listing the full names on the roll of honour of all the 1,550 soldiers and sailors from Leek and District who were serving during the first year of the Great War, 1914-15. This included photographs of a number of the local men, interspersed with poems, some by local poets.

LITHOGRAPHIC MACHINE ROOM

ARTISTS DEPARTMENT

LITHOGRAPHIC TRANSFERS

PATTERN CARD AND BOOKBINDING ROOM

MESSRS DAVID MORRIS AND COMPANY, LEEK - PRINTERS AND LITHOGRAPHERS

Morris & Co employed a large staff at their London Street works. A photograph taken by W.H.Nithsdale for his *Leek Past and Present* (another of Morris's publications) shows four men in the artists' department and at least 10 men and women in the pattern card and book-binding room, plus machinists, typesetters and lithographers.

236

Telephone No. 55.
Telegrams:
"Morris, Printers, Leek."

"Eagle" Printing Works,
LONDON STREET,
Leek, *May 3rd* 191

DAVID MORRIS & Co., Ltd.,
Lithographic & Letterpress PRINTERS.

BOOKBINDERS AND
ACCOUNT BOOK MANUFACTURERS

ESTIMATE

H. Watson Esq.

Dear Sir,

Your esteemed enquiry has received our careful attention and below we have much pleasure in quoting our price.

We trust in due course to be favoured with your orders.

Yours faithfully,

For David Morris & Co., Limited,

Established 1864.

6, St. GEORGE STREET,
LEEK, *July 24th* 1897.

Mr. J. F. Marsh Frekwell St Leek

Dr. to Joseph Morrow,

· INSURANCE, · ADVERTISING · AND · COMMISSION · AGENT, ·

1897		£	s	d
January to December	To 2¼ inch by 2¼ inch Space, taken for 12 months in *Right words* magazine for Business advt. subject to a quarterly change in the matter of such advertisement if desired		1	5

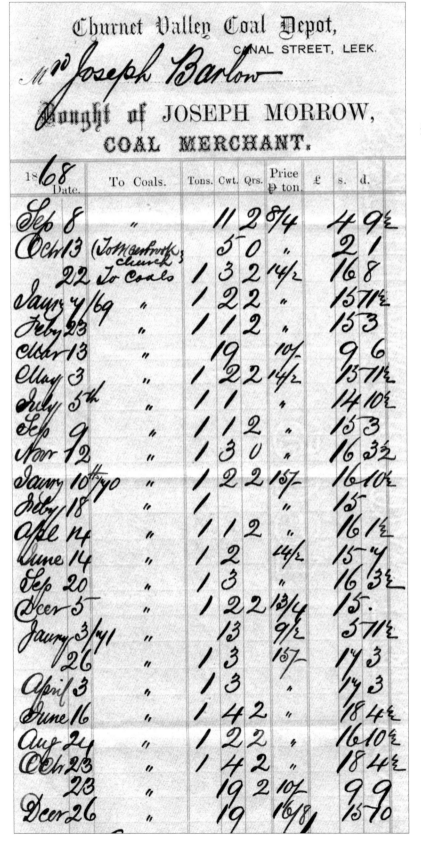

Astonishingly, this bill represents over 3 years' supply of coal to this customer.

Of course at this time coal was king and every house and factory in Leek used solid fuel. The pall of smoke can be imagined although Leek had nothing on the Potteries where as late as the 1950s people describe many areas as being in a semi-twilight from the potbank and blast furnace smoke.

The better houses at this time would have a fire in every room - a comfortable town house could easily have a dozen open fires - no wonder they needed house servants to service and clean after them all.

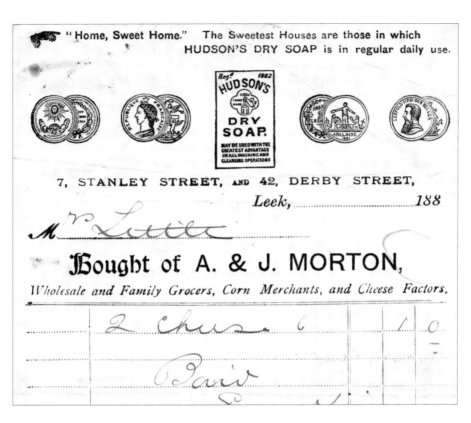

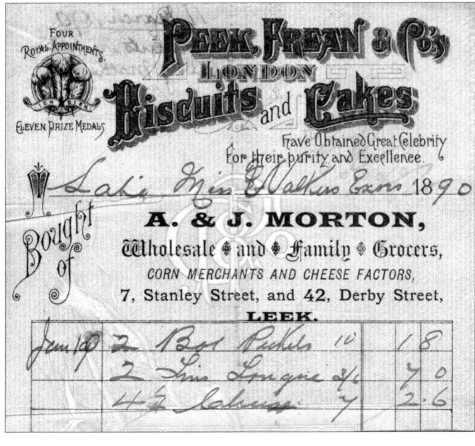

The names of Andrew and James Morton figure very prominently in the story of Methodism in Cheddleton. James left Cheddleton in 1867 and went to live in Leek. Andrew was a Leek Improvement Commissioner and later served on the Leek Urban District Council. He left a bequest to provide a house for the resident Methodist Minister in Cheddleton - Morton House, built in 1925.

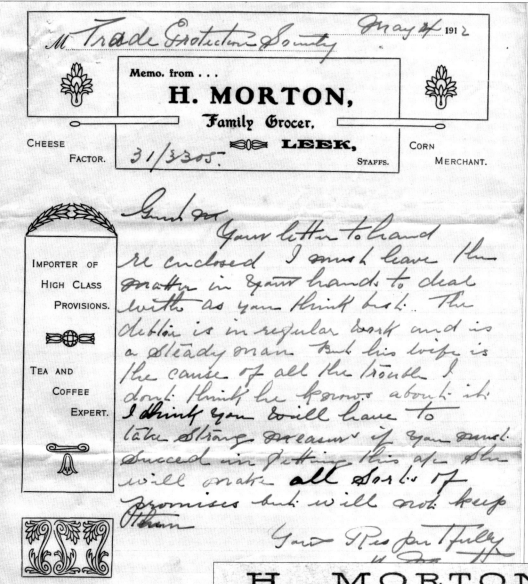

The grocery shop of H. Morton (formerly A. and J. Morton) was next door to J.R. Morton's jewellery shop.

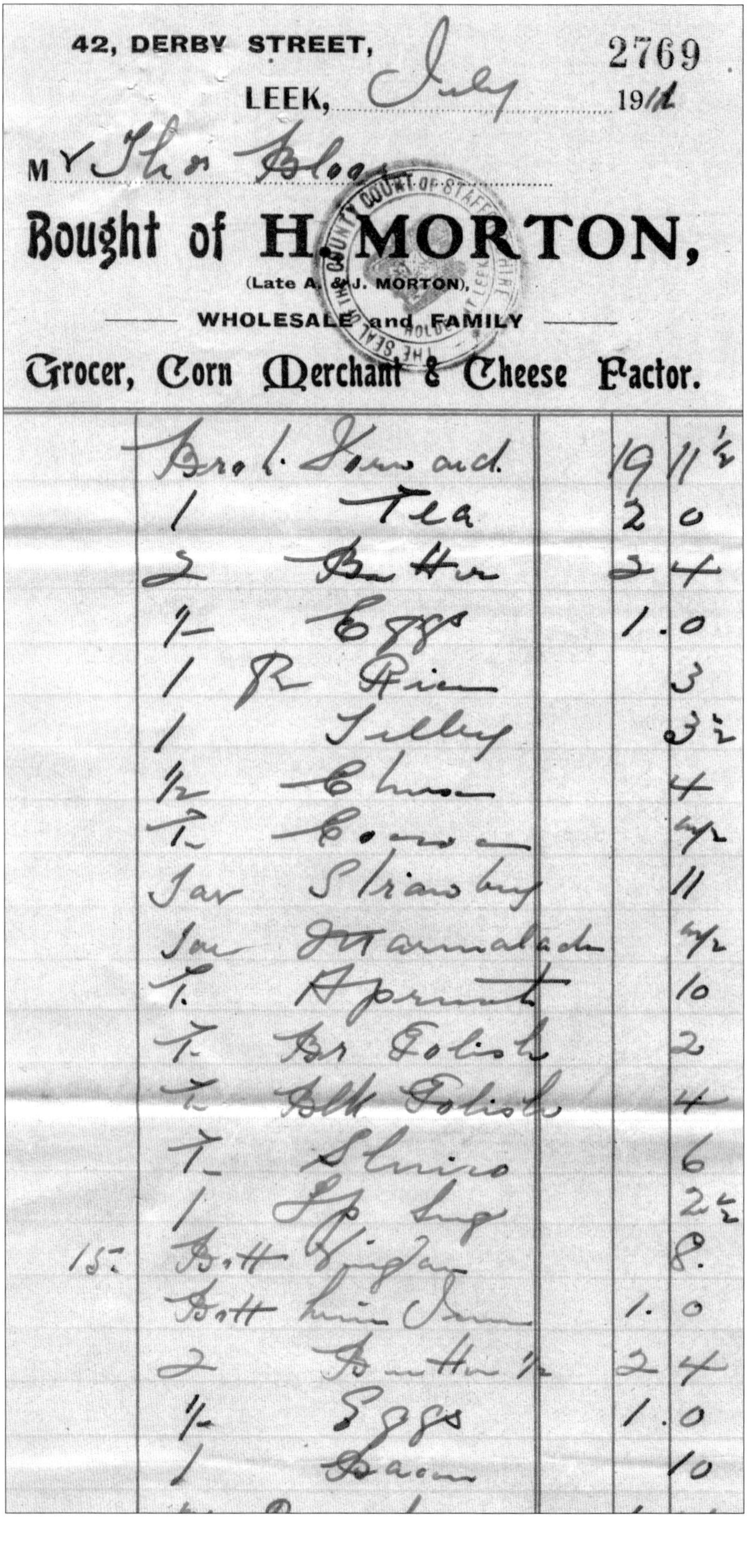

42, DERBY STREET,

LEEK, *July* 19__

No. 2769

Mᵣ *Thos Bloor*

Bought of H. MORTON,

(Late A. & J. MORTON),

—— WHOLESALE and FAMILY ——

Grocer, Corn Merchant & Cheese Factor.

		£ s	d
Bro.t forward		19	11½
1	Tea	2	0
2	Butter	2	4
½	Eggs	1	0
1	R. Rice		3
1	Jelly		3½
½	Cheese		4
½	Cocoa		4½
Jar	Strawbry		11
Jar	Marmalade		4½
½	Apricots		10
½	Bs Polish		2
½	Blk Polish		4
½	Shinio		6
1	Lp Sup		2½
15	Bott Ginger		8
Bott Lime Juice		1	0
2	Butter ½	2	4
½	Eggs	1	0
1	Bacon		10

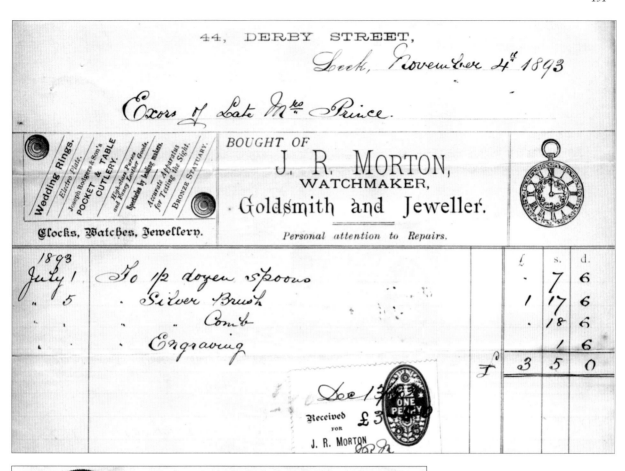

44, DERBY STREET,

Leek, November 4th 1893

Exors of Late Mrs Prince.

Wedding Rings. *Electro Plate.* Joseph Rodgers & Son's **POCKET & TABLE CUTLERY.** *High-class Purses and Fancy Leather Goods.* Spectacles by leading makers. *Accurate Apparatus for Testing the Sight.* BRONZE STATUARY.

Clocks, Watches, Jewellery.

BOUGHT OF

J. R. MORTON,
WATCHMAKER,
Goldsmith and Jeweller.

Personal attention to Repairs.

1893		£	s.	d.
July 1	To ½ dozen spoons	·	7	6
" 5	" Silver Brush	1	17	6
"	" " Comb	·	18	6
"	" Engraving		1	6
		£ 3	5	0

Dec 13

ONE PENNY

Received £3

FOR

J. R. MORTON

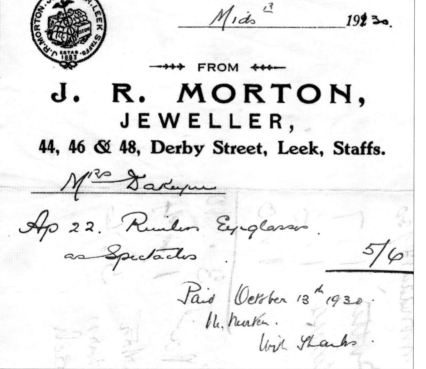

J. R. MORTON · JEWELLER · LEEK · STAFS · ESTAD 1893

Mids 13 1930.

→→ FROM ←←

J. R. MORTON,
JEWELLER,
44, 46 & 48, Derby Street, Leek, Staffs.

Mrs Tarppe

Ap 22. Rimless Eyeglasses.
as Spectacles . 5/6

Paid October 13th 1930.
th. Morton.
With Thanks

John Richard Morton, established 1887, is first listed in Kelly's Directory of 1888, and the shop changed very little over the years, to the mid-20th century. Later the business was operated by J.R. Morton's two daughters, the Misses Mollie and Fanny Morton, who kept the business on strictly traditional lines. Jewellery items were sumptuously displayed in velvet-lined display cases and trays. Silver cutlery and tableware were housed in solid glass display cases. Clocks and watches were stored with loving care and the entire ambience reflected a bygone age - a veritable time capsule in the 1950s.

BELOW: The row of shops on the right, No 2, 4, 6 and 8 Derby Street, were Salt's (clothing), Eaton (printer), Ellerton (draper) and Bull (grocer) remembered by Leek folk as: "SALT'S EATON ELLERTON'S BULL"

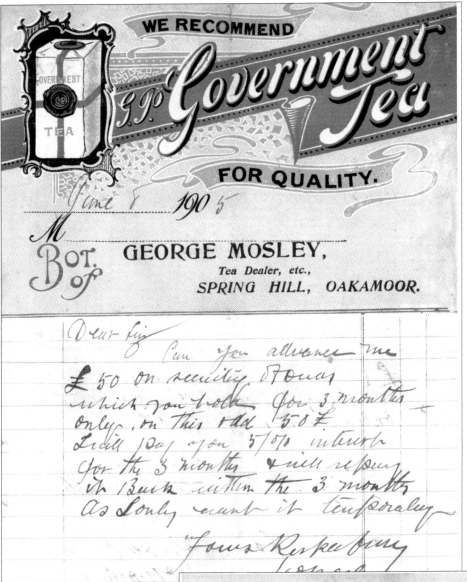

WE RECOMMEND

G.P. **Government Tea**

FOR QUALITY.

June 1 190*5*

M

B OT. of

GEORGE MOSLEY,

Tea Dealer, etc.,

SPRING HILL, OAKAMOOR.

Dear Sir Can you advance me £50 on security of Tomas which you took for 3 months only, on this add 50£ I will pay you 5/0/0 interest for the 3 months & will repay it Back within the 3 months As I only want it temporaly

Yours Respectfully

☞ **Use Glovers Borax and Glycerine Dry Soap Powder.**

PRIZE MEDALS
Awarded
PARIS 1878;
BRADFORD, 1882;
YORKSHIRE
JUBILEE, 1887

SPRING HILL,
OAKAMOOR, Staffs.

Nov 15 190*5*

M

Bought of GEO. MOSLEY,

Family Grocer, Italian Warehouseman, Corn and Provision Merchant.

AWARDED GOLD AND OTHER MEDALS AND DIPLOMAS AT THE LONDON EXHIBITION.
ESTABLISHED 1834.

MEMORANDUM.

FROM

A. J. MOSS.

Builder & Contractor,

LONGSDON,

STOKE-ON-TRENT.

WALL GRANGE STATION, N.S.R.

March 30th 1904

To J. T. Brealey Esq.

Architect

Hanley

Dear Sir

My price for "Additions to Portland Mills" Leek for the trustees of the late P. J. Worthington according to the plans & quantities prepared by you would be £. 153 0.

Trusting to be favoured with the work

ROYAL OAK INN

RUSHTON, *Oct 17* 1902

To the Exors of the Late Miss Kent

Dr. To WILLIAM MOSS,

1902		Bar. Kil. Fir. Terms Cash 3 Months.			
Oct 17	To 6 Bottles of Whisky 4/6		1	7	0
	To 4 Syphons Soda			2	0
	To Drinks & Cigars			3	8
Dec 17	To Luncheons for Auctioneer & Men			5/	0
			1	17	8

Longsdon has been for a long time a prosperous village on the outskirts of Leek and has changed little in character over the past 100 years. The New Inn on the main road through Longsdon from Leek to the Potteries is seen in this 1930s picture much as it is today.

The Village has a fine church, churchyard and vicarage. Built in 1908, its architect was Gerald Horsley and the main contractors were Thomas Grace & Sons (Vol. I). On the following page is the schedule of payments for the building of the church.

Payments.

PURCHASE OF HOUSE AND LAND.

Mr. Wilfred H. H. Eaton and his Mother, Purchase Money for Yew Tree House, Longsdon, and Land 1000 0 0

INTEREST ON TEMPORARY LOANS, BANK COMMISSION, &c. 100 9 11

FIRE INSURANCE.

Premiums paid 5 7 3

LEGAL AND OTHER EXPENSES.

Solicitors,' Surveyors' and other expenses and payments in connection with the purchase of the property, transfer to the Ecclesiastical Commissioners, Diocesan Registrars' and other Fees, Stamps and payments, and assignment of Ecclesiastical District 180 3 11

BURIAL GROUND.

Contractors and others for work in laying out, Draining and Planting Burial Ground, &c. 502 12 5

YEW TREE HOUSE IMPROVEMENTS.

Joiners, Plumbers, &c., for work done, 1900 to 1904 ... ... 116 2 5

BUILDING OF CHURCH & ADDITIONS TO VICARAGE, &c.

Thomas Grace & Sons, Builders 11,022 10 4

Note.—The original Contract for the Church was £6990/0/0, and the work at the Parsonage was according to a Schedule of Prices as arranged with the Architect, and the balance is for extras.

Fire Proof Safe for Vestry 40 0 0

Planting and laying out Land, &c., &c. 74 0 2

Furniture and Kneelers in Church, Kitchen Range in Vicarage, &c. 83 19 11

Church Bell 68 12 0

ARCHITECT.

G. C. Horsley, Esq. 605 18 6

CLERKS OF WORKS.

Messrs. Thomas Brealey & Son 105 5 3

Water Supply and Sundries 44 15 8

Balance :—

In Leek and Moorlands Building Society 37 4 2

In Manchester & Liverpool District Bank 2 18 3

40 2 5

£13,990 0 2

12th March, 1908.

We have examined the Accounts of which the foregoing is a correct abstract, and certify the same to be correct.

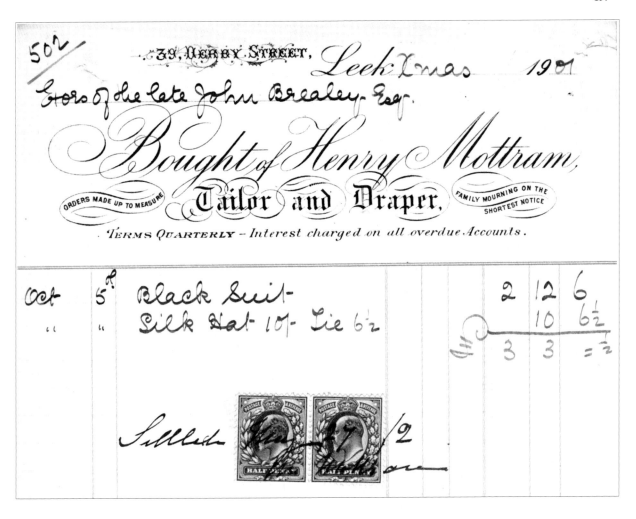

502/

39, DERBY STREET, *Leek* Xmas 19 01

Ers of the late John Brealey Esq.

Bought of Henry Mottram,

ORDERS MADE UP TO MEASURE

Tailor and Draper,

FAMILY MOURNING ON THE SHORTEST NOTICE

TERMS QUARTERLY – *Interest charged on all overdue Accounts.*

Oct	5	Black Suit		2	12	6
"	"	Silk Hat 10/- Tie 6½			10	6½
				3	3	= ½

Settled /2

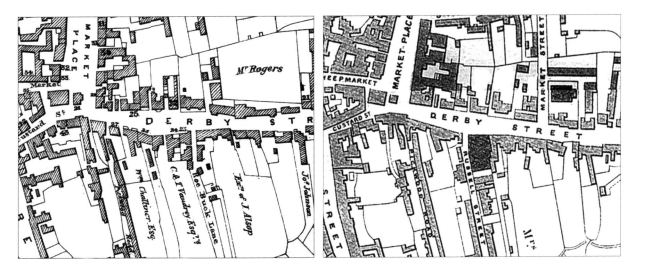

Derby Street 1838 and 1862. By 1862 Leek had a busy town centre with many shops and drinking places. From then on it was mainly a matter of rebuilding premises with the increasing wealth of the Town.

| LEEK—WEDNESDAYS.
ASHBOURNE—SATURDAYS. | | WATERHOUSES,
ASHBOURNE, |

.... 191

Messrs Challinors & Shaw,

Dr. to Samuel Mottram,

AUCTIONEER,   VALUER,   SURVEYOR,   &c.

1914	*re Ann Mellor, deced.*					
	To valuation of Real Estate for Estate at Oakamoor, Moneystone, Cotton, Cauldon Lowe & Parwich for Estate Duty			4	4	.
	To making plan of property at Parwich for sale by auction			2	2	.
	To posting sale announcements in Parwich & district				10	.
	To postage of circulars to solicitors, adjoining owners & others				3	.
	To fee for conducting sale			3	3	.
			£	10	2	.

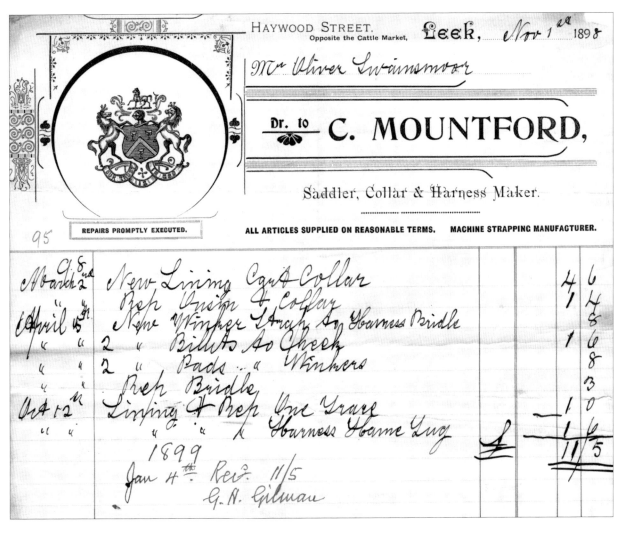

95

Mr Oliver Swainsmoor

HAYWOOD STREET.
Opposite the Cattle Market, Leek, Nov 1st 1898

Dr. to **C. MOUNTFORD,**

Saddler, Collar & Harness Maker.

REPAIRS PROMPTLY EXECUTED.　ALL ARTICLES SUPPLIED ON REASONABLE TERMS.　MACHINE STRAPPING MANUFACTURER.

Date	Description	£	s	d
March 2nd '98	New Lining Cart Collar		4	6
	Rep Union & Collar		1	4
April 5th	New Winker Strap to Harness Bridle			8
" "	2 " Billets to Cheek		1	6
" "	2 " Pads " Winkers			8
" "	Rep Bridle			3
Oct 12th	Lining & Rep One Trace		1	0
" "	" " " Harness Hame Lug		1	6
		£	11	5

1899
Jan 4th Recd 11/5
G. N. Gilman

Cornelius Mountford's address was 73 Haywood Street.

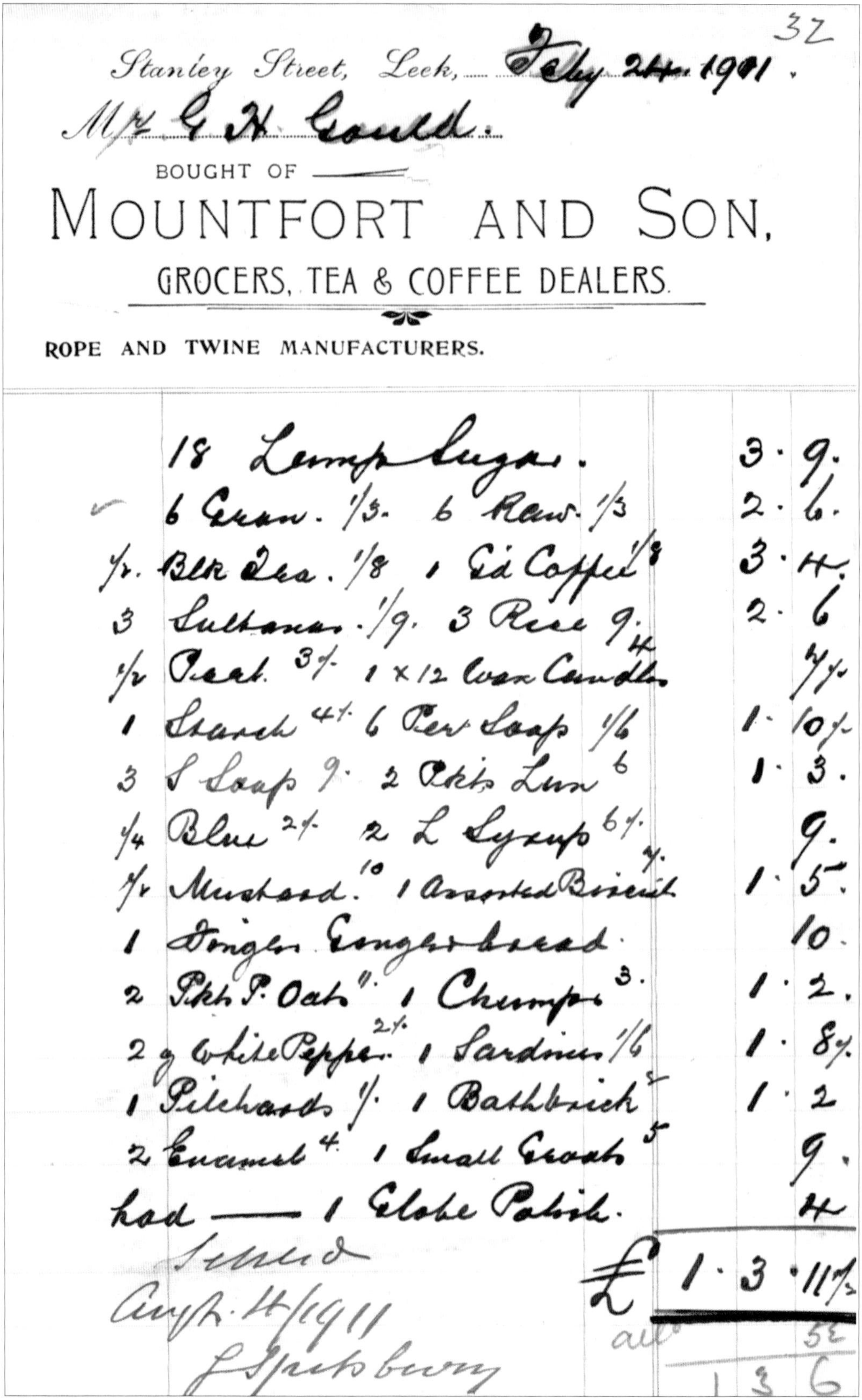

32

Stanley Street, Leek, _____ Feby 24th 1901.

Mr G. H. Gould..

BOUGHT OF _____

MOUNTFORT AND SON,

GROCERS, TEA & COFFEE DEALERS.

ROPE AND TWINE MANUFACTURERS.

18 Lump Sugar.	3 · 9.
6 Gran. 1/3. 6 Raw 1/3	2 · 6.
1/r Blk Tea. 1/8 1 Gd Coffee 1/8	3 · 4.
3 Sultanas. 1/9. 3 Rice 9.	2 · 6
1/2 Peat. 3/. 1 x 12 Wax Candles	7/.
1 Starch 4/. 6 Per Soap 1/6	1 · 10/.
3 S Soap 9. 2 Pkts Lun	1 · 3.
1/4 Blue 2/. 2 L Syrup 6/.	9.
1/r Mustard 10 1 Assorted Biscuit	1 · 5.
1 Dinglen Ginger bread.	10.
2 Pkts P. Oat 1 Chumps	1 · 2.
2 g White Pepper 1 Sardines 1/6	1 · 8/.
1 Pilchards 1/. 1 Bathbrick	1 · 2
2 Enamel 4 1 Small Groats	9.
had ____ 1 Globe Polish.	4

Settled

Augt. 4/1911

£ 1 · 3 · 11½

all 5£

1 3 6

STANLEY STREET,

LEEK, ...191

Messrs Challinor & Shaw

BOUGHT OF ∴

MOUNTFORT AND SON,

Grocers, Tea & Coffee Dealers·

ROPE AND TWINE MANUFACTURERS.

Nov 10	½ Gall Jeyes Fluid		3	6
	½ Gross Matches		1	—
	3 Soft Soap			9
29	1 Gross Matches		2	—
	1 Boy Toilet Soap		1	10
1912 Jan 22	12 Soft "		3	—
	12 Monkey "		3	—
	12 Zebra Blk Lead		1	—
			16	1

Mountforts was a popular small family grocers, typical of its kind in pre-supermarket days, offering friendly personal service and deliveries to customers. It was later owned and run by Mr and Mrs Hancock until it closed at the beginning of the 1980s.

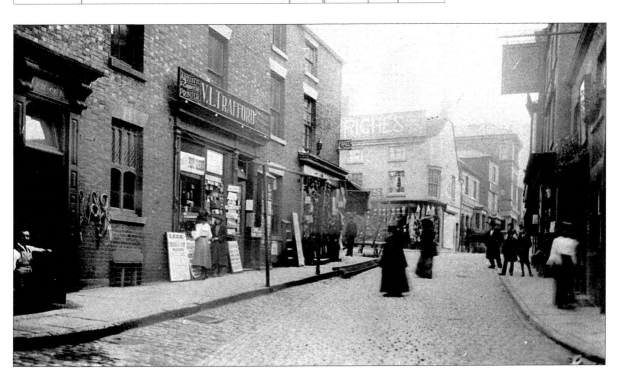

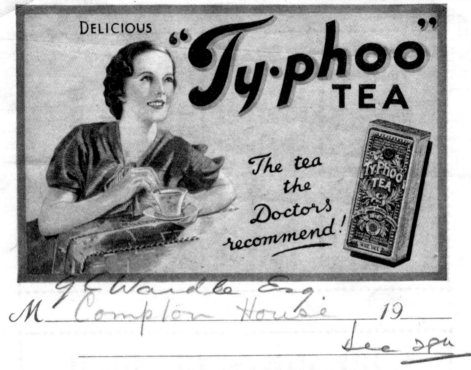

J E Wardle Esq
Mr Compton House　　　　19

Bought of **R. MOUNTFORT & SON,**

6 STANLEY STREET,

Phone **337.**　　　　　　　　　　　　**LEEK**

1197/3/39

1	✓	2 Oxtail Soup	1	4
2	✓	3 tins Raspberries	2	7½
3	✓	3 Red Currant Jelly	1	10½
4	✓	2 × 2 lbs Plum Jam	2	4
5	✓	3 tins Peas	1	10½
6	✓	2 Large Tongues	6	.
7	✓	2 Small	5	.
8		6 T. Rolls		
9	✓	1 dz Matches	1	6
10	✓	3 Borril	6	4½
11	✓	1 Bloater Paste		8½
12				
13			£1	9. 7½
14				
15				

BOLTON—Deansgate.
BLACKBURN – Darwen Street.
WIGAN—Market Place & Millgate.
LONGTON—Chancery Lane & High St.
BURSLEM—Swan Square.
HANLEY—New Street, Market Street
NEWCASTLE —Red Lion Square.
LEEK—Derby Street.
FENTON—High Street.

TELEPHONE N . 5.

MARKET STREET,

Hanley, _July 13th_ _1895_

H. T. Russell Esq. Leek R. C. C.

Bought of G. & J. MUNRO & Co.,

WINE, SPIRIT, ALE & PORTER MERCHANTS

TERMS: CASH.

Bottles must be given in exchange, or paid for on delivery, at the rate of 1s. per dozen.
Jars, 9d. per Gallon.   The amount will be allowed when they are returned.
Casks not returned in 3 months will be charged— Hogsheads, 25s. ; Barrels, 20s. ; Kilderkins, 15/-; Firkins, 10s.

70	2 Botts Gin	@ 2/-	4 - 0	
..	2 do Whisky S/F @ 3/-		3 - 0	
	3 Doz Stone Ginger 1/-		3 .. 0	
	6 do Bass P.A. 1/10		11 .. 0	
	1 case Syphone Soda	5/-	5/0	
		£	1 .. 6 .. 0	

Received Thanks
July 19) 1895
John Braddock

G. & J. MUNRO & CO.,
DERBY STREET,
LEEK.

Munros Wine Merchants had branches in many towns including Derby Street in Leek.
The last manager was Mr Grundy.

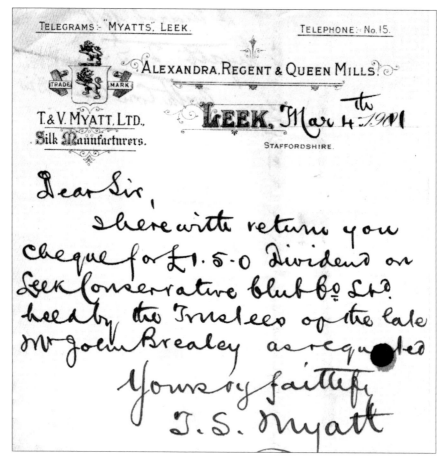

THE ALEXANDRA MILLS.

The firm of T & V. Myatt was established by John Davidson on Clerk Bank in 1845. In 1858 T. Myatt became a partner and the firm traded as Davidson and Myatt. When John Davidson retired in 1868 Mr V. Myatt joined his brother to form T. & V. Myatt Ltd. By this time the firm had moved to Alexandra Mill on Regent Street and Queen Street, a purpose-built factory to the design of William Sugden, the Leek architect.

BALL HAYE TERRACE,

Leek, _____ 188

To the Exors of the late Mrs Birch   To ——

FRANK R. NADEN,

↝ MONUMENTAL SCULPTOR, ↜

MEMORIALS IN MARBLE, GRANITE, AND STONE.

1896			£	s	d
July	To Painting 26 Doz Letters &c.			9	0
	To Engraving 6 Doz 6 Letters	6/-		7	0
	Cleaning Headstone & Kerbing.			4	4
				2	6
				16	0

Settled July 13th 1892

Harry Naden

BUXTON ROAD,

LEEK, _____ June 11th 190 8

M R. D. I. Lloyd Esqr

To FRANK R. NADEN,

Monumental Sculptor.

MEMORIALS IN MARBLE, GRANITE, AND STONE.

			£	s	d
To Examination of Stone					
Quarry. Reports &c				17	6

This Stone was sent to Mr Hurrell at his request. if you approve kindly send me a cheque for it payable to Mr Naden and I will send you the Bill receipted

Naden

There was a John Naden, monumental mason at 33 Fountain Street in 1888. In 1896 Frank R. Naden's stonemasons yard was in Buxton Road, but sometime between those dates he was at Ball Haye Terrace.

BUXTON ROAD,

LEEK, *Dec. 13*th 191**3**

M~ *To the Exors of the Late Cuthbert Robinson*

To FRANK R. NADEN,

MONUMENTAL SCULPTOR.

MEMORIALS IN MARBLE, GRANITE, AND STONE.

	£ . s . d
To Engraving & Inlaying with Lead 7 Dozen & 10 Letters 4/6 Per Dozen	1 . 15 . 3
To Regritting Marble Headstone & Stone Bases & Curbing	7 . 6
£	2 . 2 . 9

Settled in 17/14 with thanks F. R. Naden

BUXTON ROAD, LEEK,

Oct. 16 th 192**8**

M~r~s *Dakeyne Stockwell Street*

MEMORIALS IN MARBLE, GRANITE, AND STONE.

To FRANK R. NADEN,

MONUMENTAL SCULPTOR.

	£ . s . d
To Grey Granite Headstone & 1 Base With 25 feet 6in Kins of 7 x 4 Kerbing all Polished & fixed In Leek Cemetery.	
32 Bricks for 1 Clearstone flag 3.2 X 11 X 3 . Engraving & Gilding 23 Dozen & 3 Letters	
Cemetery fees 15/-	
	45 . 10 . 0
Settled Oct 18/28	75 . 11 . 0

Steam Pipe Fitting, Glazing, &c.

JOBBING WORK PROMPTLY ATTENDED TO.

BATHS, LAVATORIES, AND WATER CLOSETS FIXED ON THE MOST IMPROVED PRINCIPLES.

23, Fountain St., **Leek,** _____ Jany _____ 190 8
STAFFORDSHIRE.

Mr. Hollershed Per Mrs Turner & Co.

TERMS: QUARTERLY.
ALL CONTRACTS NETT AND DUE ON COMPLETION.
ESTIMATES FREE.

Dr. to P. NADIN, R.P.,

REGISTERED PLUMBER, AUTHORISED GAS AND WATER FITTER, PAINTER, PAPERHANGER, & HOUSE DECORATOR.

Nov. 1st		To	Weston St Property				
	1	½"	Bell Bib Tap	@	2/6	2	6
	1	½"	Joint & Hook 5				5
			Time 1½ hrs at 9 per hr			1	1½
Dec.		To	Repairing Burst pipe etc.			4	0½
	1	pc.	pipe 8°. 2 joints 8°.			1	4
			Time 1½ hrs @ 9 per hr			1	1½
			Setting Well Sink			6	6

BATHS, LAVATORIES, AND WATER CLOSETS FIXED ON THE MOST IMPROVED PRINCIPLE.

23, FOUNTAIN STREET,

Leek, _____ Aug_t _____ 1912
STAFFORDSHIRE.

R Murphy

Mr Harrison Agent

STEAM PIPE FITTING. GLAZING. &c..

JOBBING WORK PROMPTLY ATTENDED TO.

Terms: Quarterly.

ALL CONTRACTS NETT AND DUE ON COMPLETION,

ESTIMATES FREE.

Bought of R. NADIN, R.P.

REGISTERED PLUMBER, AUTHORISED GAS & WATER FITTER, PAINTER, PAPERHANGER, AND HOUSE DECORATOR.

July 10th	To	Repairing Burst pipe				
	in Ground Brunswick St.					
10 ft 6"	½" Water pipe	@ 6". 1ft			5	3
	2 Hooks 1½, 3 lbs Solder @ 1/- ll				3	1½
	Time 6 hrs @ 9". 6				4	6
	" 6 . 5 .				2	6
No. 15	1. Washer To Taps					3
					15	7

23, FOUNTAIN STREET,

LEEK, _7/ 23ʳᵈ_ 1904

Mr _Yothersten, agent to the Eate. Trustee. R. Turnoch_

❖ Dr to R. NADIN. ❖

Sanitary Plumber, Hot and Cold Water Fitter,

ESTIMATES GIVEN.   **Painter, Paperhanger, Glazier, &c.**

			£ — s — d
	To. Papering, & Painting for.		
	Mrs Burn. Victoria St		
July 25ᵗʰ 14.	rolls. Wall. Paper. @ 6ᵈ	7/.	7 — 0
1.	Gv. Size 8ᵈ Paste 6ᵈ	1/2	1 — 2
1.	Pch. Plaster 9ᵈ 1 Gv. Putty 2ᵈ	11	11
	Whiting, Lime, Lime Blue 6ᵈ	6	6
5½	Gvs. & Paint @ 6ᵈ per Gv	2/9	2 — 9
	Time 38 hrs @ 8½ hr	26/11	1 — 6 — 11
" 21ˢᵗ	To Papering House. Victoria St		
6	rolls. Wall. Paper @ 6ᵈ	3/.	3 — 0
3	Gvs. Paint @ 6ᵈ	1/6	1 — 6
	Lime, & Whiting &c. 6ᵈ	6	6
	Time 14 hrs @ 8½ per hs.	9/11	9 — 11
4. 6 ft	Egtt. Strong 4½" Beaded. Gutter	9/.	9 — 0
6	Screws & Spon. Staigs 8ᵈ ech	4/.	4 — 0
	Putty. Bolt, & Nails	8	8
2.	4½" Stop Ends @ 4ᵈ ech.	8	8
1½	Gv. Paint @ 6ᵈ	9.	9
	Time 5 hrs @ 8½ per hs	3/6½	3 — 6½
			£3 — 12 — 9½

Settled with Thanks.

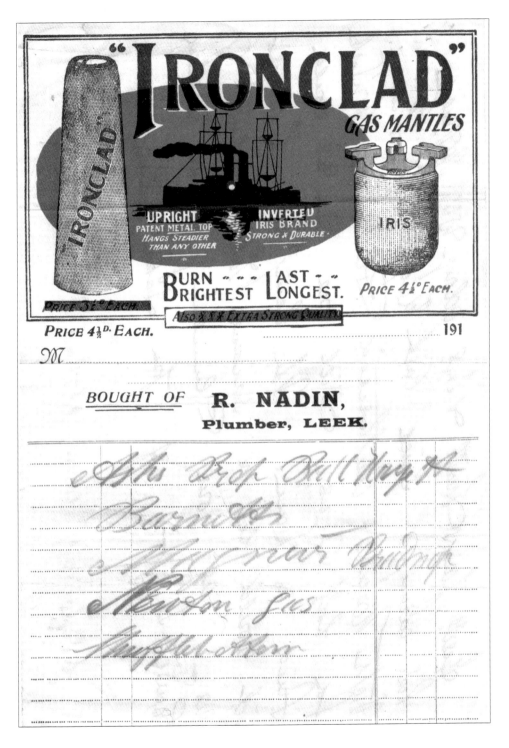

Gas mantles as featured in this heading were widely used for lighting homes, offices and
factories in the days before electric light.
They burned with a bright white light but were expendable.

MUSIC AND PAPER HANGING WAREHOUSE.

A. Ward Esqre

Stamp Office, Leek.

To Geo. Nall, Bookseller,

LETTER-PRESS AND COPPER-PLATE

PRINTER, BOOKBINDER, AND STATIONER,

SUPERIOR LEDGERS, DAYBOOKS, CASHBOOKS, &c.

RULED TO ANY PATTERN.

Superfine Water Colors, Brookman and Langdon's Black Lead Pencils, and every other Article used in Drawing.

FRENCH AND ENGLISH PRINTS.—FINE CUTLERY.

Orders for New Books, Magazines, Music, and Miscellaneous Articles executed weekly or oftener.

TORTOISE-SHELL AND OTHER COMBS.—BEAD, SILK, AND LEATHER PURSES.

ALL KINDS OF FANCY STATIONARY FOR LADIES' WORK.

(ACCOUNTS DELIVERED AT MIDSUMMER AND CHRISTMAS.)

GENUINE PATENT MEDICINES

18*30*		£	s.	d.
December 29	1 Account Book for Leek Alms houses	1	1	—

JUST PUBLISHED,

IN DEMY 12MO, PRICE 7S. 6D.

The English Party's

EXCURSION TO PARIS,

IN EASTER WEEK, 1849;

TO WHICH IS ADDED

A TRIP TO AMERICA,

&c. &c.

BY J. B. ESQ.,

BARRISTER-AT-LAW.

LONDON: LONGMAN AND Co., PATERNOSTER ROW.

LEEK: G. NALL.

These early headings of George Nall are fine examples of the engraver and illustrate the wide range of services available from this tradesman - printer, stationer, bookseller, art materials, prints, cutlery, jewellery and toys, music and paperhanging, as well as a full range of post office services.

George Nall of Bakewell was associated with Bemrose of Derby before coming to Leek about 1828 to set up his first business in Spout Street. He then moved to Sheepmarket (White's Directory 1834) before moving to Custard Street (Stanley Street) by 1846 where he also served as Postmaster (William's Directory).

About this time his son Robert joined him as a partner and it became George Nall & Son. Robert Nall printed the first edition of *Sleigh's History of Leek* in 1862, and the Nall-Bemrose association was renewed in 1883 when the Derby firm produced the second and larger edition.

Mr. Alsop.

Stockwell Street

MUSIC AND PAPER-HANGING WAREHOUSE.

Post Office, Leek.

To George Nall, Bookseller,

LETTER-PRESS AND COPPER-PLATE

PRINTER, BOOKBINDER, AND STATIONER,

DEPOSITARY FOR THE LONDON RELIGIOUS TRACT SOCIETY.

SUPERIOR LEDGERS, DAY BOOKS, CASH BOOKS, &c.
RULED TO ANY PATTERN.
Superfine Water Colors, Brookman and Langdon's Black Lead Pencils, and every other Article
used in Drawing.
FRENCH AND ENGLISH PRINTS—FINE CUTLERY—JEWELLERY—TOYS.
Orders for New Books, Magazines, Music, and Miscellaneous Articles executed weekly or oftener.
Tortoise-shell & other Combs.—Bead, Silk & Leather Purses.
ALL KINDS OF FANCY STATIONERY FOR LADIES' WORK.
HOSIERY AND SMALLWARES.—GENUINE PATENT MEDICINES.
(ACCOUNTS DELIVERED AT MIDSUMMER AND CHRISTMAS.)

LICENSED APPRAISER.

STAMP OFFICE

1847		£	s.	d.
Jan. 6	Supplement to Penny Cyclopædia, vol 2		13	.
Jun 30	Pictorial Bible, pts 4/4 4/4/4 4/6 4/7		12	6

Mr Alsop

MUSIC AND PAPER-HANGING WAREHOUSE,
CUSTARD STREET, LEEK.

TO GEORGE NALL,

LETTER-PRESS AND COPPER-PLATE PRINTER,
BOOKSELLER, BOOKBINDER, & STATIONER,

SUPERIOR LEDGERS, DAY BOOKS, CASH BOOKS, ETC., RULED TO ANY PATTERN.
ORDERS FOR NEW BOOKS, MAGAZINES ETC., EXECUTED WEEKLY OR OFTENER.
DEPOSITORY OF THE LONDON RELIGIOUS TRACT SOCIETY.   AGENT TO THE NOTTS. AND DERBYS. FIRE AND LIFE
ASSURANCE COMPANY.

POST OFFICE.

STAMP OFFICE.

Accounts delivered at Midsummer and Christmas.

HOSIERY AND SMALLWARES.—GENUINE PATENT MEDICINES.

1847		£	s.	d.
July 17	Advertising Notice to Scripholders of Thirnet & Blythe in Times		11	.

Post Office and Stamp Office, LEEK.

James Alsop Esqr.

Dr. to NALL AND SON,

BOOKSELLERS, STATIONERS, PRINTERS,

BOOKBINDERS, NEWS AGENTS, &c.

Agents for Price's Patent Case-hardened and Drill-preventive Fire-proof Safes and Deed Chests.
SOLE AGENTS FOR THE "STAFFORDSHIRE ADVERTISER."

1860		£	s.	d.
Jan. 1	Art Journal 1849 & 1850 in nos.	3	.	.
Ap. 14	Binding Art Journal 1849 & 1850			
	16 vols. in green morocco gilt edges, at 4/	5	.	.
Jan.	Rural Cyclopædia div. 16.		5	.

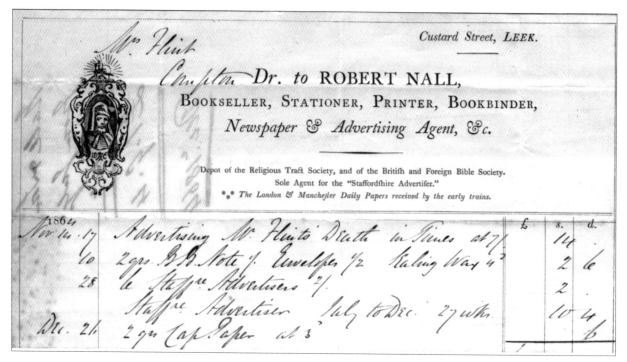

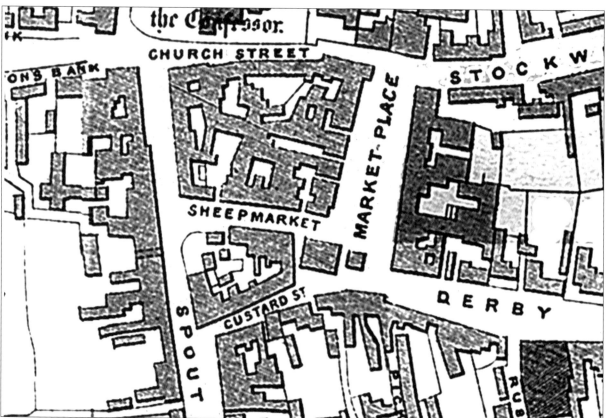

Custard Street (now Stanley Street) is clearly shown on this portion of Slagg's 1862 map. The name is believed to be derived from the costermongers (applesellers) who would have their stalls in the environs of the Market Place. The old Town Hall is shown on the corner of the Market Place and Custard Street

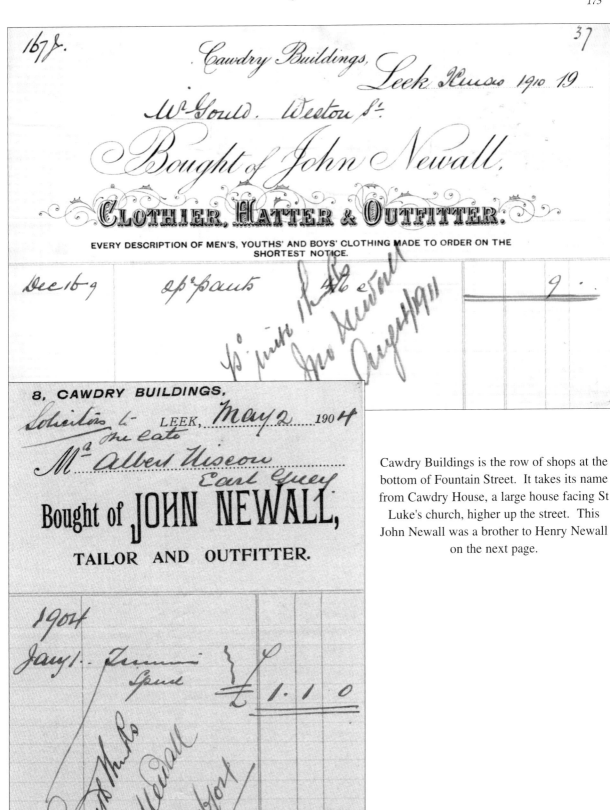

Cawdry Buildings is the row of shops at the bottom of Fountain Street. It takes its name from Cawdry House, a large house facing St Luke's church, higher up the street. This John Newall was a brother to Henry Newall on the next page.

13, Ball Haye Street, Leek,   1909

Mess Challinor + Shaw

Dr. to Hy. Newall & Sons,

CABINET and PICTURE FRAME MAKERS, UPHOLSTERERS, FRENCH POLISHERS and UNDERTAKERS.

Dealer in all kinds of Brass and Iron Bedsteads, Cots, Spring, Hair and Wool Mattresses,
Pictures and Picture Mouldings, Mounts, Glass, etc.

All kinds of Furniture Repaired, Re-Upholstered and Polished equal to new.

		£		
July 11/08	Two Awning Blinds 21/- Mr Gymne Room	£2	2	-
	Taking old blinds down + fixing new 12 hrs 8½		8	6
Oct 6	Small Box Stand + varnished. (Mr W Camp)		4	6
	New Cords to Sun Blind 1/-		1	-
	Fixing Sash Cords 2hrs 8½ 1/5 Sash cord 6		1	11
	C.V.7 £2. 14. 11	£2	14	11

Paid Mar 29/09
Newall

11 & 13, BALL HAYE STREET,

BEDSTEADS,
SPRING, HAIR, AND
WOOL MATTRESSES
—o—
CARPETS,
LINOLEUMS,
BLINDS,
UPHOLSTERY,
PICTURES.

LEEK,   June 30   1917

Mrs Tho. Bradley (Daisy Bank.)

Dr. to Hy. Newall & Sons,

CABINET AND PICTURE FRAME MAKERS,
UPHOLSTERERS, FRENCH POLISHERS & UNDERTAKERS.

1917.				
	Forward:—	40	18	.

Newall's (by then John Newall, Henry's son) undertaking business was later worked by Norman Smith, who later set up in business in his own right on Clerk Bank. His son David Smith is an undertaker in the town to this day, in Fountain Street.

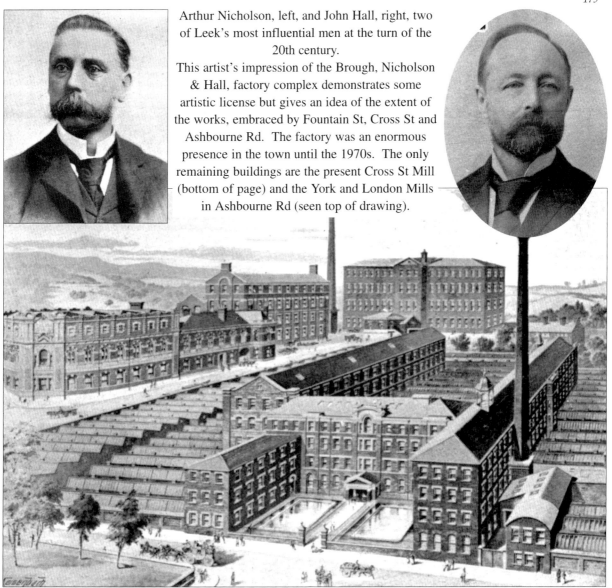

Arthur Nicholson, left, and John Hall, right, two of Leek's most influential men at the turn of the 20th century.

This artist's impression of the Brough, Nicholson & Hall, factory complex demonstrates some artistic license but gives an idea of the extent of the works, embraced by Fountain St, Cross St and Ashbourne Rd. The factory was an enormous presence in the town until the 1970s. The only remaining buildings are the present Cross St Mill (bottom of page) and the York and London Mills in Ashbourne Rd (seen top of drawing).

Left: This Sugden building was the warehouse and offices, in Cross Street.

ESTATE OFFICE,

HIGHFIELD STUD,

LEEK, Staffs.

191

Sir Arthur Nicholson's fine shire horses were renowned and King George V admired them on his Royal visit to Leek on 23rd April 1913.

The Nicholson family left its mark in many ways, perhaps the most important being the Nicholson Institute. Founded by Joshua Nicholson, the father of Sir Arthur, it opened in 1884 and the fine Sugden building housed a library, reading room, art gallery and school of art - founding principles which are still held today. In this memo heading, Kineton Parkes, the Curator and Principal of the Institute, sends a curt note to a prize donor who has not paid up!

Below: Highfield Hall, the Royal visit.

NICHOLSON INSTITUTE, LEEK.

SCHOOL OF ART, SCIENCE AND TECHNOLOGY.

May 9th 1892

Dear Sir

nothing paid yet. The amount of the prize kindly offered by your firm — £2/2/0.

Yours faithfully

Kineton Parkes

BROUGH, NICHOLSON & HALL

A WEAVING SHED, CHEADLE MILLS

MOHAIR WINDING ROOM, FOUNTAIN STREET

Above: The proclamation of George V in Leek Market Place, Wednesday 11th May 1910

The unveiling and dedication of the Nicholson War Memorial, 20th August 1925. It was given to the Town by Sir Arthur and Lady Nicholson in memory of their son Lt. Basil Lee Nicholson and other local men who were killed in the First World War.

Joshua Nicholson who founded the Nicholson Institute lived at Greystones. The 17th century house had to be preserved - so the Institute was built behind it.

Depot—Leek Wharf.   60, Picton Street,
                                                        (OFF WEST STREET),

Leek, *April 11th* 190 0

Messrs Challinor & Shaw. Leek

Dr. to **H. W. Nixon & Co.,**

COAL MERCHANTS.

1910

Jan 5	T.	C.	Q.		Price		
Jan 5	1	3	0	*Holly Lane Large Cobbles.*			

Most local coal merchants had their depot on the wharf at the basin at the Leek canal - now Barnfields Industrial Estate. There are moves afoot once more to bring the Leek branch of the Caldon Canal to a basin in the town.

GOLD & SILVER WATCHES,
ALBERTS,
WEDDING RINGS,
AND ALL KINDS OF JEWELLERY.

SMITHFIELD HOUSE,
Corner of Haywood & Leonard Sts., and 16 Haywood St.,

LEEK..1

M .... *Value of goods of the late ...... his brother* ....

Bought of **A. NOBLE & SON,**

WHOLESALE JEWELLERS.

Best Price given for Old Gold and Silver.

1 *Horse Shoe Scarf pin*	15	—
1 *Oil pencil case*	2	6
1 *— Match box*	4	—
1 *Gold Seal*	5	—
1 *15ct Scarf pin*	12	6
1 *18ct Gold Watch & 9ct Albert*	10	— —

WESTWOOD PARK ESTATE.

AN INVITATION.

May we kindly offer you a cordial invitation to visit the Westwood Park Estate. We would like you to know that we can now offer a choice selection of sites on which to erect that House you have always desired.

We are pleased to inform you that of the Sixty houses already completed, only Two Houses remain available for immediate sale.

ALL SERVICES AVAILABLE.

The Town Services are available to all parts of the estate. Several roads are completed and others are now being extended.

HOUSE PURCHASE MADE EASY.

House Purchase is made easy by the service we offer you. Deposits are as low as £30 and repayments at 2/9 per £100 weekly.

CAREFUL PLANNING.

It is our intention to make the Westwood Estate worthy of its beautiful setting. The Layout Plan can be inspected by appointment by those who are interested and who desire to see the generous way in which the whole of the estate has been planned.

New Schools will adjoin the estate and new roads giving better access, are shortly to be constructed. Shopping facilities will also be available,

We have a selection of designs showing the full Plans for Houses at prices from £540. These can be submitted for your consideration, or Houses designed to meet your particular requirements can be built at inclusive prices. Our desire will be to give you entire satisfaction.

THE EFFECT OF CAREFUL PLANNING.

For two years we have been working on this estate, and something of its finished beauty is now coming to view. We sincerely hope that with the coming of the New Year, many more discerning home lovers will take the opportunity of choosing a charming site for a new home, amidst delightful surroundings, on the Westwood Park Estate.

F. M. NORTH & Co.

The Westwood Park estate began in the 1930s as advertised in this 1935 page in Leek Illustrated.
The war intervened and the estate was not fully developed until the 1950s onwards.

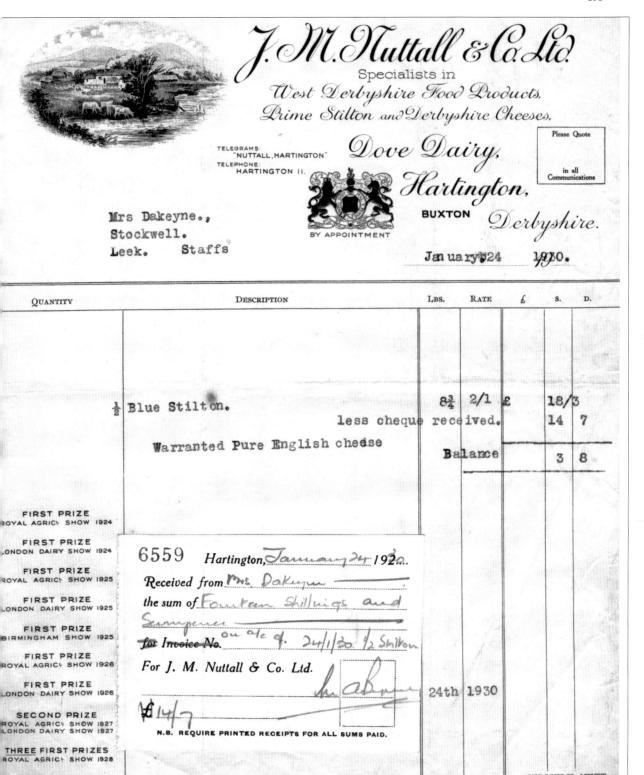

J. M. Nuttall & Co. Ltd.

Specialists in
West Derbyshire Food Products,
Prime Stilton and Derbyshire Cheeses.

TELEGRAMS:
"NUTTALL, HARTINGTON"
TELEPHONE:
HARTINGTON II.

Dove Dairy,
Hartington,
BUXTON Derbyshire.

BY APPOINTMENT

Please Quote
in all
Communications

Mrs Dakeyne.,
Stockwell.
Leek.   Staffs

January 24   1930.

QUANTITY	DESCRIPTION	LBS.	RATE	£	S.	D.
½	Blue Stilton.	8¾	2/1	£	18/3	
	less cheque received.				14	7
	Warranted Pure English cheese					
	Balance				3	8

FIRST PRIZE
ROYAL AGRIC. SHOW 1924

FIRST PRIZE
LONDON DAIRY SHOW 1924

FIRST PRIZE
ROYAL AGRIC. SHOW 1925

FIRST PRIZE
LONDON DAIRY SHOW 1925

FIRST PRIZE
BIRMINGHAM SHOW 1925

FIRST PRIZE
ROYAL AGRIC. SHOW 1926

FIRST PRIZE
LONDON DAIRY SHOW 1926

SECOND PRIZE
ROYAL AGRIC. SHOW 1927
LONDON DAIRY SHOW 1927

THREE FIRST PRIZES
ROYAL AGRIC. SHOW 1928

6559   Hartington, *January 24* 1920.
Received from Mrs Dakeyne
the sum of Fourteen Shillings and
Sixpence on a/c of 24/1/30 ½ Stilton
for Invoice No.
For J. M. Nuttall & Co. Ltd.

£14/7   24th 1930

N.B. REQUIRE PRINTED RECEIPTS FOR ALL SUMS PAID.

STRICTLY NETT

Nuttall's factory in Hartington was the first Stilton cheese factory and was built in the middle of the 19th century.
Fine Stilton is still produced there in 2005, amongst a wide range of other cheeses.

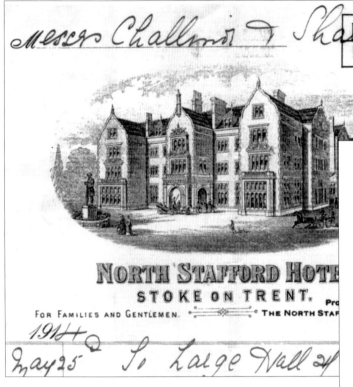

Messrs Challinor & Shaw

D.B.
L.

NORTH STAFFORD HOTEL
STOKE ON TRENT.

FOR FAMILIES AND GENTLEMEN.   THE NORTH STAF

1914
May 25   To Large Wall 24

The North Staffordshire Railway Co. were always keen to promote the visitor potential of local areas like Rudyard, the Manifold Valley and Alton Towers. They resisted the idea of a Manifold Valley Railway but when the project was finally launched - as a narrow gauge railway - the company made an effort to make the line successful. Sadly it only operated from 1904-1934. (see p. 63)

North Staffordshire Railway.

No visitor to LEEK should fail to make excursions to
RUDYARD
(the name-place of Rudyard Kipling), and the
MANIFOLD VALLEY,
which, by means of the North Staffordshire Railway, are readily accessible from that town.

RUDYARD.

Much care has been bestowed by the Company upon the extension and development of RUDYARD, which is now certainly one of the most attractive Holiday Resorts in the County. A beautiful WALK has been laid out from the NEW STATION recently opened at the North end of the Lake, leading along the margin of the water through Cliff Park. Boats may be hired on reasonable terms. The lake has been enlarged and restocked with FISH, and last Autumn heavy baskets were made by Anglers. Fishing Tickets for the day, 1/= each, may be obtained from the Stationmaster at Rudyard. **A Golf Course** (18 Holes) has been laid out quite close to Rudyard Lake Station, and is open to visitors. Tickets: Day, 2/=, may be obtained from the Rudyard Lake Stationmaster, or the Professional in charge of the Course.

WATERHOUSES and the MANIFOLD VALLEY

The New Normal Gauge Railway between LEEK and WATERHOUSES is now open, and gives a through rail connection with the MANIFOLD VALLEY "TOY" RAILWAY.

This little line, which is reminiscent of the Mountain Railways of Wales, runs from Waterhouses to Hulme End, a distance of 9 miles, through the most charming scenery of the Manifold Valley. Passengers may alight at any of the halts, and from the terminus at Hulme End a visit may be paid to the beautiful and far-famed Beresford Dale.

Further information in regard to these places and many other districts adjacent to the North Staffordshire Railway, which are celebrated for their scenery of Rock, Water, Wood and Dale, will be found in the recently published illustrated Official Guide of the Company, **"Picturesque Staffordshire,"** which may be obtained at the Stations, Price 6d. Several series of Pictorial Post-Cards have recently been issued and may be obtained upon application at a small charge.

Handbills of Excursion Facilities and any other information may be obtained at the Stations, or from

W. D. PHILLIPPS, *General Manager.*
Stoke-upon-Trent, June, 1908.

W.H.Nithsdale's photograph shows an Edwardian scene at Leek Station.

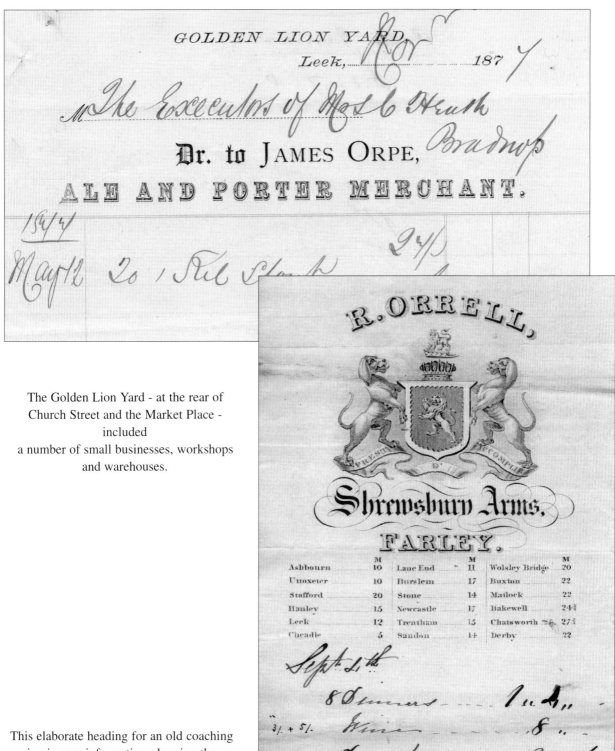

The Golden Lion Yard - at the rear of
Church Street and the Market Place -
included
a number of small businesses, workshops
and warehouses.

This elaborate heading for an old coaching
inn is very informative, showing the
mileage to various destinations.
The Inn takes its name from the Earls of
Shrewsbury whose country seat was the
nearby Alton Towers.

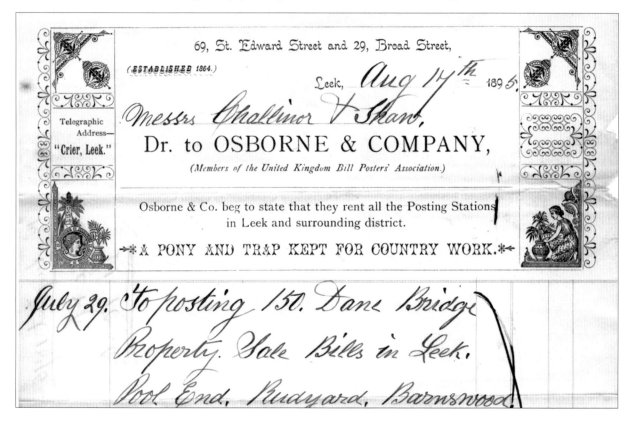

19, CANAL STREET,
LEEK, *April 2nd* 187*5*

Mrs Challinor's & Co.

Dr. to JOHN OSBORNE,

(MEMBER OF THE UNITED KINGDOM BILL POSTERS' ASSOCIATION,)

BILL POSTER, HANDBILL AND CIRCULAR DELIVERER.

J. O. begs to state that he rents all the Advertising Stations in the Town and surrounding District. All orders faithfully and expeditiously executed. A pony and trap for country work.

£ . s . d

Feb 25th ... *Dwelling houses & garden land*
bills in Leek ... 4 . .
country one day. ... 6 . .
... 12 . 0

Paid April 2th/75

John Osborne

There was a number of hoardings for the display of posters around the town, eg in Mill Street, Buxton Road, Broad Street. The bill poster would be responsible for the posting of all sorts of posters on these: sporting events, entertainment, films and circuses, auctioneers announcements, church notices, and election posters.

Printers used a specific type of paper for posters - smooth on one side, rough on the reverse side.

69, St. Edward Street and 29, Broad Street,

(ESTABLISHED 1864.)

Leek, *Aug 14th* 189*5*

Messrs Challinor & Shaw,

Dr. to OSBORNE & COMPANY,

(Members of the United Kingdom Bill Posters' Association.)

Telegraphic Address—
"Crier, Leek."

Osborne & Co. beg to state that they rent all the Posting Stations in Leek and surrounding district.

✳ A PONY AND TRAP KEPT FOR COUNTRY WORK. ✳

July 29. To posting 150. Dane Bridge
Property. Sale Bills in Leek.
Pool End, Rudyard, Barnswood

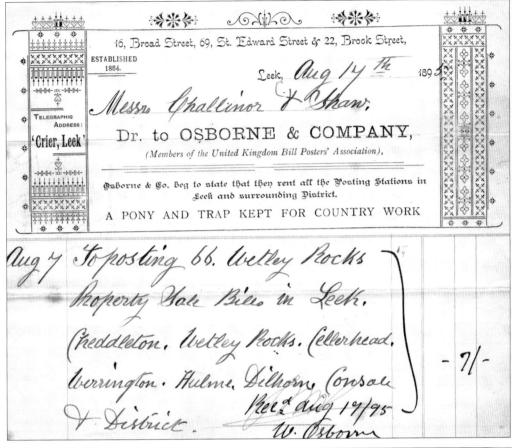

16, Broad Street, 69, St. Edward Street & 22, Brook Street,

ESTABLISHED 1884.

Leek, *Aug 14th* 189*5*

Messrs Challinor & Shaw

Dr. to OSBORNE & COMPANY,

(Members of the United Kingdom Bill Posters' Association),

TELEGRAPHIC ADDRESS:

'Crier, Leek'

Osborne & Co. beg to state that they rent all the Posting Stations in Leek and surrounding District.

A PONY AND TRAP KEPT FOR COUNTRY WORK

Aug 7 To posting 66. Wetley Rocks
Property Sale Bills in Leek.
Cheddleton. Wetley Rocks. Cellerhead.
Werrington. Hulme. Dilhorn. Consall
& District.   *Recd Aug 14/95*
                              W. Osborne

- 7/-

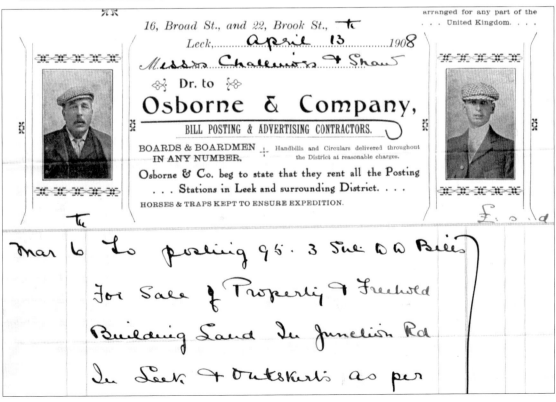

16, Broad St., and 22, Brook St.,

Leek, *April 13* 1908

Messrs Challinor & Shaw

Dr. to

Osborne & Company,

BILL POSTING & ADVERTISING CONTRACTORS.

BOARDS & BOARDMEN IN ANY NUMBER.

Handbills and Circulars delivered throughout the District at reasonable charges.

Osborne & Co. beg to state that they rent all the Posting Stations in Leek and surrounding District.

HORSES & TRAPS KEPT TO ENSURE EXPEDITION.

arranged for any part of the United Kingdom.

£ s d

Mar 6 To posting 95. 3 Sue DW Bills
For Sale of Property & Freehold
Building Land In Junction Rd
In Leek & Outskirts as per

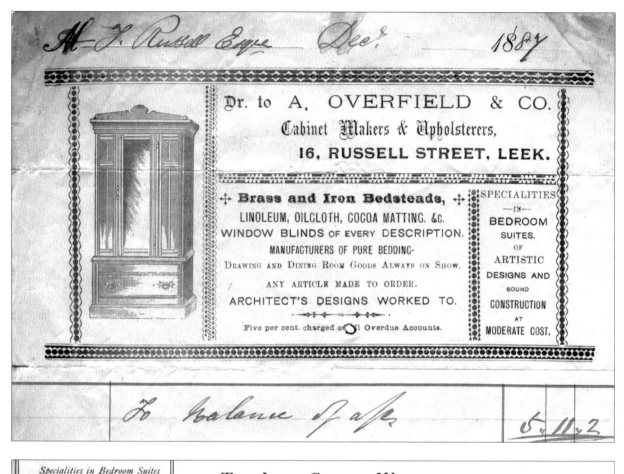

M. F. Russell Esqre   Decr   1887

Dr. to A. OVERFIELD & CO.
Cabinet Makers & Upholsterers,
16, RUSSELL STREET, LEEK.

✛ **Brass and Iron Bedsteads,** ✛

LINOLEUM, OILCLOTH, COCOA MATTING. &c.

WINDOW BLINDS OF EVERY DESCRIPTION.

MANUFACTURERS OF PURE BEDDING.

DRAWING AND DINING ROOM GOODS ALWAYS ON SHOW.

ANY ARTICLE MADE TO ORDER.

ARCHITECT'S DESIGNS WORKED TO.

Five per cent. charged on all Overdue Accounts.

SPECIALITIES
—IN—
BEDROOM
SUITES.
OF
ARTISTIC
DESIGNS AND
SOUND
CONSTRUCTION
AT
MODERATE COST.

To Balance of a/c	5 . 11 . 2

Specialities in Bedroom Suites of Artistic Design and Sound Construction at Moderate Prices.

THE LEEK CABINET WORKS,
12 to 16 Russell Street, Leek, *October* *189 3*

To the Exors of the late Mr Bunce

To A. OVERFIELD & Co.,
CABINET MAKERS AND UPHOLSTERERS.

Brass and Iron Bedsteads and Spring Mattresses, &c., Linoleums, Mattings, Window Blinds, &c.
Designs worked to.   Any Article made to Order.

5 per cent. charged on Overdue Accounts.

1893.				
Aug	16.	To 2 doz carpet nails D.L.		8 .
Sep	8	— 9½ lbs best white goose feathers @ 2/8	1 . 5 . 4
	11	— 9 red holland blinds, hemmed all round, cord, tassels &c @ 3/9 ea:	1 . 13 . 6
	20	— reprs gilt picture frame & touching up corners &c.	2 . 0
			£ 1 . 15 . 6	

Received, with thanks

Specialities in Bedroom Suites of Artistic Design & Sound Construction at Moderate Prices.

THE LEEK CABINET WORKS,

12 to 16, Russell Street, Leek, *Feb 25 / 04*

Mrs Robinson   Basford Hall

To A. OVERFIELD & Co.,

UPHOLSTERERS AND CARPET DEALERS.

Brass and Iron Bedsteads, Spring Mattresses, &c., Linoleums, Matting. Window Blinds, &c, Designs worked to. Any Article Made to Order.

FURNITURE CAREFULLY REMOVED BY ROAD OR RAIL—ESTIMATES FREE.

Terms— { Accounts rendered quarterly and 5 % Interest charged if not paid within a month from date.
NETT CASH { REMOVAL AND ALL CONTRACT ACCOUNTS DUE ON COMPLETION.

To balance of a/c rendered   £17 5 0

OVERFIELD & CO.,

THE LEEK

CABINET WORKS

AND **SHOWROOMS,**

12-16, RUSSELL STREET, LEEK.

ARTISTIC. FURNISHING. OUR. AIM.

Though we

Dont Believe

In flimsiness, we do believe in beauty. Our Furniture, while made in a thoroughly substantial fashion, is at the same time designed with a special eye to artistic effect.

Come and see it. There's no charge for admission.

UPHOLSTERERS & CARPET DEALERS

OVERFIELD & Co.

Alfred Overfield was in business in Sheepmarket in 1850. He then moved to larger premises in Russell Street, where he suffered a disastrous fire in 1866. He rebuilt on the same site and in 1896 the shop was extended by Larner Sugden. It bore many of the hallmarks of the Sugden style but brick, stone and terracotta had given way to a preponderance of wood and glass, giving the building a light, airy appearance. This large furniture emporium continued to trade until the 1920s. The building, largely unaltered, later became the offices of the Leek and Moorlands Cooperative Society, and more recently an annexe providing overspill accommodation for Leek College of Further Education.

9, ASHBOURNE ROAD,

Leek, Oct 24th 1913

Mrs Robinson London Rd.

BOUGHT OF **S. OWEN,**

DRAPER AND HOSIER.

2 Pairs Socks 8d.		1	5
1 Yd. Flannel		1	3
Frilling			3
Wht Stockings			6½
Hat Remaking & Ribbon		2	9
Blk Buckle			6½
with thanks		6 -	9

QUEEN STREET AND MARKET PLACE, LEEK.

E. J. PALMER

CABINET MAKER & UNDERTAKER

Upholstering and Polishing done. All kinds of Furniture made to order.

Brass and Iron Bedsteads, Chairs, Cots, and Beddings.

Wire and other Mattresses and all kinds of Bedhangings. Woven Wire Mattings in Stock.

Bedsteads at 12/6. Spring Mattress, 10/6
Flock Beds complete, 12/6
Bedroom Chest of Drawers, 22/-
Inclosed Wash Stands, 21/-
Wardrobe in Maple, with plate glass in door, 50/-
Carved Back Sofas, 30/-
Couches, 28/-
Dressers in Oak, 40/-
Chest of Drawers in Mahogany, 50/-
Ditto, in painted Oak, 35/-

Edwin James Palmer was based at 47 Queen Street

PARR'S BANKING COMPANY,
LIMITED.

LEEK, 4 May 18*87*

CREDIT

dup A Barber

duplicate

BILLS AND COUNTRY NOTES (AS PER LIST AT BACK).			
BANK OF ENGLAND NOTES ... ✓			
SOVS. ... ... ✓ ...	5	-	·
HALF-SOVS. ... ... ✓ ...	2		
SILVER ... ✓ ...		10	
CHEQUES ON YOURSELVES ...		6	4
	✓		
£	7	16	4

In 1855 a Mr Jennings commenced a banking business in Stockwell Street. He was formerly a clerk with a local silk manufacturer, and he became a silk broker. Jennings' bank continued for over 20 years and when Mr Jennings retired he sold out to Parr's Bank. The manager was Mr James Swindells. Eight years later the business transferred to new purpose-built premises in St Edward Street on the site of the old Plough Inn. The new bank was built several years before High Street was made. The building is still there as Bank House. Architecturally it is typical of the fine style of Leek's Victorian buildings, and reflecting the the typical imagery of the Sugdens.

5, Ballhaye Street,

Leek 190 0

Mrs E. Smith

Bought of JOHN PARR,

DRAPER, CLOTHIER,

BOOT & SHOE DEALER.

Sept 1st   1 pr boots   9   6

*E Smith   Settled with
Thanks Feb 9/1901
J Wheeldon
Pro J Parr*

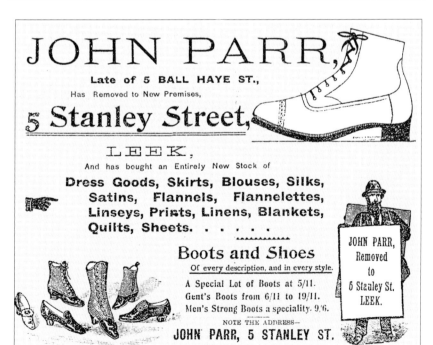

JOHN PARR,
Late of 5 BALL HAYE ST.,
Has Removed to New Premises,
5 Stanley Street,
LEEK,
And has bought an Entirely New Stock of
Dress Goods, Skirts, Blouses, Silks,
Satins, Flannels, Flannelettes,
Linseys, Prints, Linens, Blankets,
Quilts, Sheets. . . . . .
....
Boots and Shoes
Of every description, and in every style.
A Special Lot of Boots at 5/11.
Gent's Boots from 6/11 to 19/11.
Men's Strong Boots a speciality. 9/6.
NOTE THE ADDRESS—
JOHN PARR, 5 STANLEY ST.

JOHN PARR,
Removed
to
5 Stanley St.
LEEK.

15, SHEEP MARKET,

Leek, ...11th...November... 19**G**3.

The Excs. of the late Mr. C. Robinson

Dr. to H. PARTRIDGE,

Novelties in Neckwear.
Stylish Hats.
Unshrinkable Hosiery.

Best Value in . .
. Boots and Shoes.

Hatter, Hosier & Outfitter.

CLOSE AT ONE O'CLOCK ON THURSDAYS.

1913.					
Oct. 20.	To 2 prs. Gloves	3/9		7	6
" 21.	2 Silk Hats	17/6	1	15	0
" "	3 prs.	3/9		11	3

This heading incorporates a note about the traditional Leek 'half-day closing', Thursday.

THE DUKE OF YORK,

LEEK, _____ **189**

M*rs* C. Robinson

Bought of W. H. PEACH,

FAMILY WINE & SPIRIT MERCHANT.

Dealer in THOMPSON & SON'S BURTON ALES & DUBLIN STOUT in Cask & Bottle.

BRITISH WINES, VINEGAR, &c.

Oct 21	1 Bottle	Dewars		4	
	2 "	Port		4	
	2 "	Sherry		4	
				12	6

Paid With
Thanks
G Peach.

New Shop, Custard Street,

LEEK.

W. PATTINSON

Having completed his purchases of Goods, suitable for the present and approaching Season, respectfully solicits an early inspection of the leading Novelties—in

LADIES' DRESSES,

THE FASHIONABLE

EMBROIDERED TWEEDS, LLAMAS, GALAS,

and other fabrics just introduced; he also has an extensive and choice selection of NORWICH AND

SCOTCH LONG AND SQUARE SHAWLS,

WITH A LARGE ASSORTMENT OF

RIBBONS, FLOWERS, LACE AND

MUSLIN GOODS, HOSIERY, GLOVES, &c.

W. P. can confidently recommend his stock of

WOOLLEN CLOTHS,

as considerably under the present Market Value, having been bought previous to the late advance in price; consisting of

WEST OF ENGLAND AND YORKSHIRE BROADS,

DOESKINS, TWEEDS,

And the Newest Styles in

FANCY TROWSERINGS, VESTINGS, &c.

W. P. in tendering his sincere thanks to his Friends, for their kind and liberal support, begs to assure them, that he will continue to offer his Goods for the smallest remuneration possible, and hopes to be favoured with a continuance of their patronage.

He respectfully solicits an early call at the

NEW SHOP, CUSTARD STREET.

G. NALL, PRINTER, &c., LEEK.

TELEPHONE No. 46.

Cawdry Furnishing House, Leek.

Pedley's

G·WILLIAM PEDLEY.

FURNITURE
CARPETS
BEDDING
CURTAINS
ART POTTERY

CABINET MAKER AND UPHOLSTERER.

Mr Dakeyne,
Stockwell S.   Aug   193.0

July 22.	3ft Wool Mattress	1 . 5 . 0
	3ft 6: do for	1 . 3 . 6
Aug 2.	2 Flock Pillows 2/3	. 4 . 6
	£	2 . 13 . 0

The tall gentleman standing next to Mr Fred Hill (see Vol. I) is Mr George Pedley, founder of the furnishing business.

Cawdry Buildings, *March 31" 1914*

Leek, *July* 1913

M C. Robinson,

DR. TO GEO. PEDLEY & SON.

COMPLETE HOUSE FURNISHERS.

Cabinet Makers.
Upholsterers.
Picture Framers.
Undertakers, &c.

Works—Ball Haye Street.   Warehouse—Haywood Street.

Date	Description		£	s	d
Sept 14/11	2 Holland Blinds 36 in × 5 ft 6 in	2/-		4	0
	1 do 45 in			2	6
	2 Spring Rollers. complete.	@ 1/-		2	0
	1 do			1	1
	3 Cream Tassells @ 2½, Cord & Tacks 3			-	10½
	3 Knot Plates @ 1			-	3
Oct 9	Re-making Mattress, & lengthening bed etc			5	0
Nov 23	54 in Spring Roller			1	6
	man to blinds etc 1½ hrs @ 8			1	0
Ap 12/12	4 ft × 6 ft Inlaid Lino @ 4/6 yd			6	0
	6 yds Stan Baize @ 7½			3	9
Oct 14	3¼ yds Casement Cloth @ 2/4			8	5
Nov 27	Holland Blind 45 in × 5 ft 6 in			2	6
	Tassell & Cord 3, Knot Plate 1			-	4
June 12/13	Best Linen Bed Tick, bordered & piped.			16	6
	6 lbs Duck Feathers @ 1/6			9	0
	Emptying old tick & refilling			1	0
	2 yds Best 6/4 Matting @ 3/6			7	0
	Binding do			1	3
			£3	13	11½

Settled by Contra &c
April 1/1914   Geo Pedley & Son

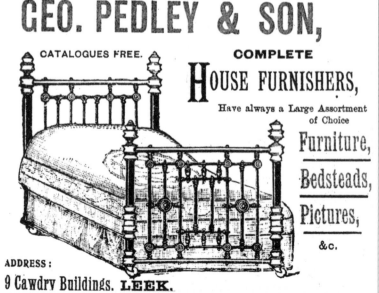

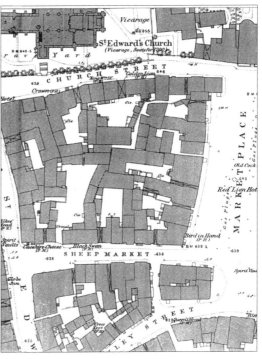

PERSEVERANCE STEAM SAW MILLS.

BUXTON ROAD, Leek Sep. 29 189 6

Mr W Howard

Dear Sir

I have own
receipt of inclosed
cheque value £8.15.0
being half years rent
of Horse Pasture

1604

LEEK, *Xmas* _____ 18

Mr *W. B. Badnall Esq*

To EDWIN PHILLIPS,

Plumber, Glazier, Painter, Paper Hanger, Gilder, Gas-Fitter, Bell Hanger, &c., &c.,

Every description of Lead and Iron Pumps, Water Closets, Baths, Spouting, &c., &c.

5 per cent. on Accounts over-due.

Mr Gailey's Nov 4	26½ lb of Sheet Lead for Top Weather plates to Casements		6	9
"	8 a Copp: Nails. 1½ lb White Paint. Man 9 hrs		7	6
12	28¾ lb Plumb: Solder 1 lb Fine Solder	1	10	1
13	To Men 34 hrs Repairing Roofs &c	1	1	3
15	Clout Nails. 3 lb Sheet Lead. 1 Slate		2	4
20	To Men 19 hrs repairing Gutter Slates &c &c on Roofs		11	10½
31	Man 2½ hrs Examining W.C. and Pipes		1	4
1881 Jun 4	Man 2 hrs Examining Soil Pipe to W.C.		1	3
May 31	Lead &c Paint Man 1 hr Painting Rails			9½
Oct 23	18' of Lead Pipe 2 Cup Joints Man 2 hrs Repairing		3	5
"	Pipe Cut by Labourer			
B. Waste "	15½' of Fall Pipe 1-2½ Shoe. Nails. Man 3 hrs		10	5
			4	14

Received by Cash

July 10th 1884

Mr Edwin Phillips

J. S.

With thanks

Stockwell Street - Phillips' shops stood on the left-hand side. Edwin Phillips' shop traded as plumbers and decorators with a showroom here until the late 1990s.

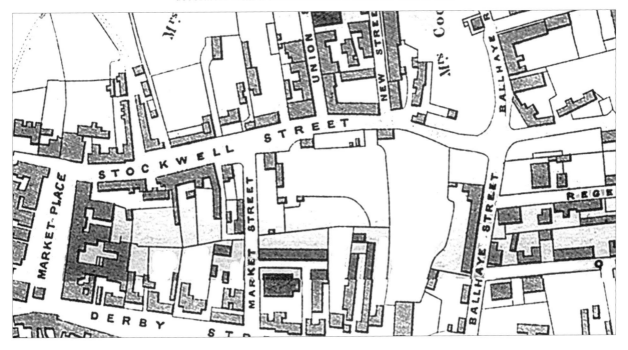

16 & 18, Stockwell St & 2, Silk St

LEEK, Dec 1905

The Exec^rs of the late Miss Flint. Stockwell Street

Dr. to EDWIN PHILLIPS,

Plumber, Hot Water & Sanitary Engineer, Decorative Painter, &c.

Gas, Bells, W.C's Lavatories, Baths, Ventilators, Pumps, Fire Extinguishing Appliances.

Artists' Materials Enamels, &c.

Glass, Lead, Oil, Paint and Varnish Depôt.

Paperhangings, Tynecastle Tapestry, Anaglypta, &c.

1905

1905				£	s	d
Aug	4	Men 6 hrs @ 8½ Cleaning windows	6/10½		4	3
	21	13¾ ℔ Stone colour paint. 2 ℔ Putty. 1 ℔ Red paint 6			7	8½
		3½ Thinners. 4 Brass hooks 2	2½		2	2½
	22	16½ ℔ Stone colour paint. Chrome & Bk Sky Umber 10	8/3		9	1
		Plaster 9. Knotting 6. 9 Walls pat distemper 3/4½			4	7½
	25	Men 8 hrs @ 9. 36½ hrs @ 8½ Stopping and	15/10	1	11	10
		painting outside walls recently cemented			.	.
		cleaning, repairing and distempering			.	.
		yard wall. w.c. v.c v.c			.	.
Sep	7	To Unstopping drain v.c			1	3
Nov	10	Men 4½ hrs @ 9. 4½ hrs @ 8½ Cleaning 3/4½ 3/2			6	6½
		windows back and front. v.c				
				£ 3	7	6

Received with thanks

31 Jany 1906

Per Pro Edwin Phillips
Sydney M. Phillips

TELEPHONE: LEEK 255.

16 & 18, Stockwell St. & 2, Silk St.
LEEK, Dec. 31st 1929

Trustees John Wm Sneyd dec. Basford Hall,

Dr. to EDWIN PHILLIPS & SONS,
Plumbers, Hot Water & Sanitary Engineers.
Decorative Painters, &c.

Gas, Bells, W, C's Lavatories, Baths, Ventilators, Pumps,
Fire· Extinguishing Appliances.

Electric Lighting,
Telephones.
Motors, &c.

Glass, Lead, Oil, Paint and Varnish Depôt.

Paperhangings,
Tynecastle Tapestry,
Anaglypta, &c.

1928				
Dec. 27 to 1929 Jan. 4	To excavating from Ram house to feed tank at pond. shoring up sides to make trench safe for working in repairing drive pipe to ram; remaking joints, securing ram & partly filling in Lead Gaskin and sheet rubber &c.	10.11		
	Plumber 35 Hrs @ 2/, Labourers 123½ Hrs @ ⅙ 3/12/11 9/5/3	12.18.2		
	Fares 11/10,	11.10		
			14.0.11	
	To amount of Estimate for remaking dam across brook as per specification April. 1929.	11.10.0		
			11.10.0	

193

STOCKWELL STREET,
LEEK, May 190 2

Messᵣₛ Heath & Lowe

Bought of JOSEPH PHILLIPS,
FURNISHING IRONMONGER AND IMPLEMENT AGENT,
OIL, PAINT AND COLOR STORES.

1900 Agent for Joseph Haywood's Celebrated "Kettle Brand" Cutlery.

July	20	1 dz 4½" rim latches, 2 dz rack pulley	17 6
		1 gro ¾" japᵈ screws, ½ dz casement fasteners	2 4
	23	1 pkt ⅞ x 3 ¼ ¼ screws, 1 cleat hook, 1 bolt	1 4½
	26	1 - 2 Keyᵈ galvᵈ pad lock	1 2
	30	1 pʳ chest handles, 1 chest lock	1 .
	31	4 - 3 x ¼" bolts & nuts	2
Aug	1	1 - 3½" cupᵈ lock, 1 hook & eye	7

SPOUT STREET,
Leek, April 4 1866

Wᵐ Phillips Esqʳ

Bought of JOHN PHILLIPS,
Linen & Woollen Draper, Silk Mercer, Haberdasher & Hosier.
IMPORTER OF IRISH AND SCOTCH LINENS,
Funerals completely Furnished, and every article in Family Mourning.

January 10ᵗʰ			
7 Mill'ᵈ Flannel	2/2	15. 2	
½ doz Towells	17/-	8.. 6	
16ᵗʰ			
½ White Calico	12½	6½	

In the 1860s St Edward Street still had its old name of Spout Street.

Telegrams
PHILLIPS IRONMONGER LEEK.

Telephone
6 Y.

12 & 14 *Stockwell St,*
Leek, Dec 1912
STAFFS.

Mess Challinors & Shaw

D.r *to Joseph Phillips,*
IRONMONGER.

1912		£	s	d	£	s	d
Oct 31	2 gal⁵ Coal hods @ 6/9				13	6
	3 hearth brushes @ 7				1	9
	1 fire shovel 11 @ 7				1	6
					16	9

STEPHENSON'S

For
Linoleum Oilcloth.
Parquetry
& Stained Flooring.

STEPHENSON BROS
SUPERIOR
FLOOR POLISH
FOR POLISHING OAK AND STAINED FLOORS
LINOLEUM OILCLOTH &&
DIRECTIONS
BRADFORD

Also
Brown Boots, Polished
& Varnished Woodwork
Motor Cars etc.

FLOOR POLISH

M.r The Executors of the late Dec 24/14 19
G H Gould Esq

Bought of JOSEPH PHILLIPS,
Telephone 6Y.   *Ironmonger,*
12 and 14 Stockwell Street, LEEK, Staffs.

1 bass broom		1	6
1 galv bucket		1	2
1 hand brush		1	3

PERCY PICKERING

GENT.'S HATTER, HOSIER & OUTFITTER,

GLOVER AND MERCER,

The latest Styles and Materials in . . .

SHIRTS, COLLARS, TIES, VESTS, PANTS, GLOVES, UMBRELLAS, &c.

AGENT FOR ——

The Celebrated "Two Steeples" Underwear.

Shirts to Measure a Specialité.

13a, Derby Street, :: LEEK.

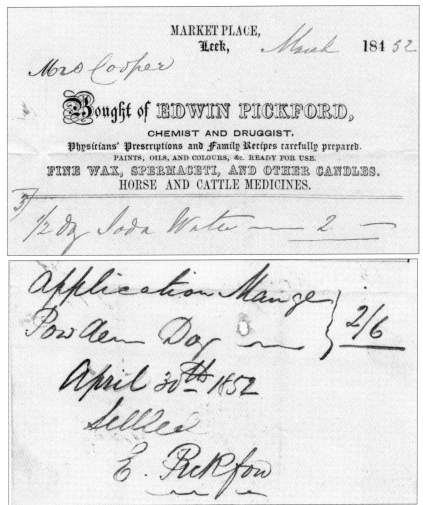

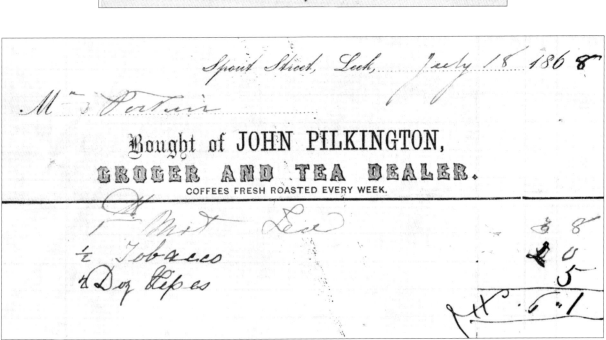

21, Mill Street,
LEEK, 191

M

Dr. to M. G. PILGRIM,
Grocer and Provision Dealer,
DRAPER, BOOT & SHOE DEALER.

Pett 31
West Bromwich

The Exors of M. G. Pilgrim
Dr to Lever Brothers

1 X 4	Comfort 4/-		10	3
2 + 4	Russo 2 20/6		10	3
			1 — 6	

No. LC 5501   18 Sept 191

Received *from* M Exors of M. G. Pilgrim

One *Pounds* I *Shillings*

and Six *Pence.*

For **Lever Brothers Ltd.** £   :10: 3
For **R. S. Hudson Ltd.** £   :10: 3   £
                          £1 :— :6   £

For Cashier

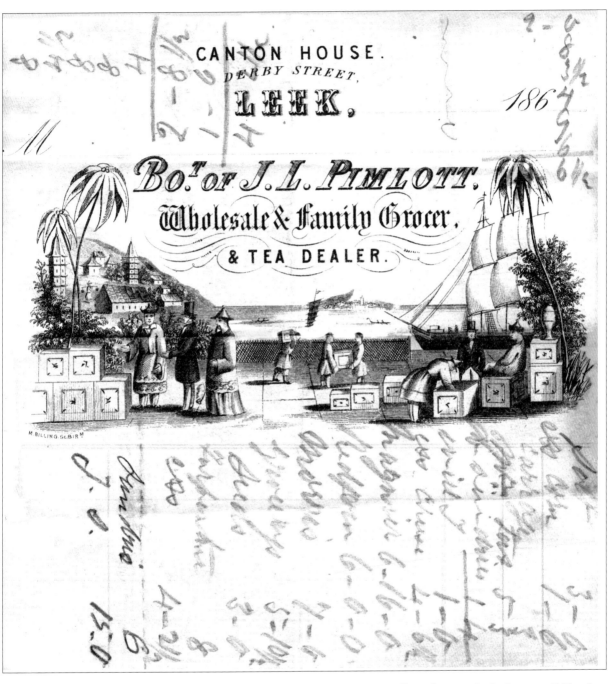

This quaint heading echoes an age of imperialism, J.L.Pimlott was a versatile tradesman: he had responsibility for the public weighing machine at the bottom of Derby Street and was the superintendent of the nearby Public Baths. He also worked as a billposter!

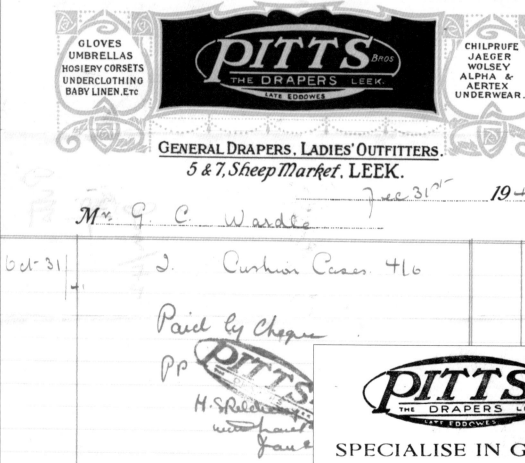

Pitts were the successors to Eddowes see volume I

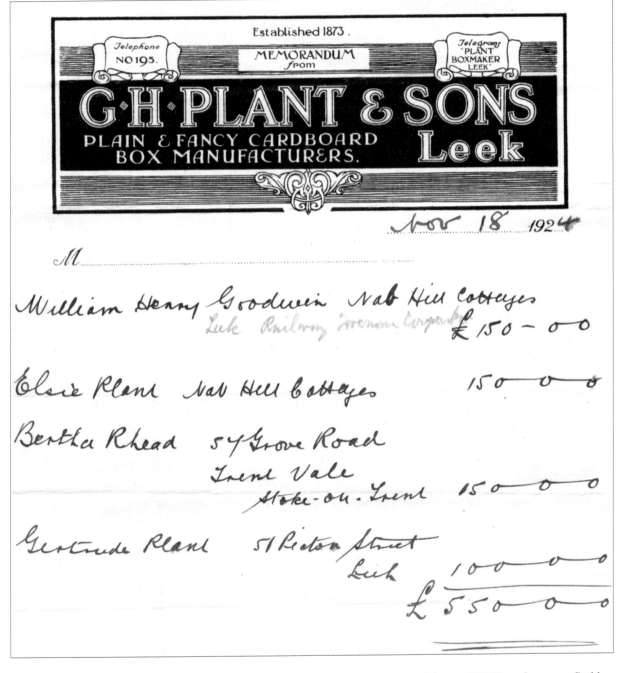

Established 1873.

Telephone NO 195.

MEMORANDUM from

Telegrams "PLANT BOXMAKER LEEK"

G·H·PLANT & SONS
PLAIN & FANCY CARDBOARD BOX MANUFACTURERS.
Leek

Nov 18 1924

M ....

William Henry Goodwin   Nab Hill Cottages

Leek Railway ironman carpenter   £ 150 − 0 0

Elsie Plant   Nab Hill Cottages   150   0   0

Bertha Rhead   54 Grove Road
Trent Vale
Stoke-on-Trent   150   0   0

Gertrude Plant   51 Picton Street
Leek   £ 100   0   0

£ 550   0   0

There were seven box makers in the 1896 Leek Commercial Directory. In addition to G.H.Plant there was Stubbs & Co, Armitt & Co, Compton, Brough & Son, Stockwell Street, L. Clowes & Co, Queen Street, F. & A. Lovatt, London Street and H. Smith of Mill Street.

George H. Plant was only six years old when he started to learn his trade. His business was originally established in Mill Street in 1873 and the works were extensive. The building was four storeys high and about 66 yards square. Many workers were employed and he held some 20 tons of cardboard at any one time, much of it imported from Holland.

In spite of being a very scattered community, the Bradnop of yesterday had all the elements of a traditional English village, as this extract from Kelly's Directory of 1860 shows. There were actually two Methodist chapels in Bradnop - one Wesleyan and one Primitive. Only the former Wesleyan chapel survives today. The Blacksmiths Arms on the main road from Leek to Ashbourne, was destroyed by fire in the 1940s when the last licensee was a Mr Plant. The village school closed about 1980 and Harold Bode was its last headmaster

BRADNOP is a hamlet and township on the main road from Leek station, distant 3 miles south-east, and 12 from Ashbourn, in North Totmonslow hundred, Leek union and county court district, and northern division of the county. In the centre of the hamlet there is a Wesleyan chapel. Ashenhurst Hall is about a mile south. The population in 1851 was 477 ; and the area is 3,344 acres 1 rood ; and the gross estimated rental, £2,972 15s. The land belongs to a number of freeholders. John Sneyd, Esq., is lord of the manor. The charities are included with Onecote, at which church, jointly with Leek, the inhabitants attend.

Richardson Rev. Harling, B.A. [perpetual curate of Onecote]
COMMERCIAL.
Bagnall Stph. farmer & miller, Gorse hill
Bailey John, farmer, Apesford
Bassett John, farmer, Gooseneck
Bassett William, farmer, Apesford
Beardmore Mary (Mrs.), farmr. Bent end
Birch Joseph, farmer, Holly bush
Booth George, farmer, Stock farm
Bott Joseph, joiner & collector of rates & taxes, Thorncliff
Bowers George, cowkeeper
Brooks John, farmer, Dirty gutter
Cantrill Richard, blacksmith
Chappell Thomas, farmer, Rootshill
Cook William, farmer, Wildgoose house
Cocke Thomas, farmer cattle dlr Lane end
Cordon George, farmer
Deaville Smith, farmer
Eardley Isaac, farmer, Ashenhurst hall
Edge Isaac, shopkeeper
Hidderley William, farmer, Holly house
Hill Enoch, farmer, Coltsmore
Hill John, farmer, Longshaw
Lees Benjamin, farmer, Lark park
Lovatt Jn, farmer & wheelwright, Ballfields
Malkin George, farmer, Well farm
Meakin Thomas, farmer, Woodhouse
Morris Joseph, farmer
Mountford William, miller
Mycock Samuel, shoemaker
Mycock William, farmer, Garstairs
Oulsman George, farmer, Stoney cliff
Phillips Williams, farmer, Ball fields
Prince Uriah, farmer, Barnfield
Robinson William, farmer
Robinson William, farmer, Pool hall
Robinson William, farmer
Sant Joseph, farmer, Middle cliff
Sigley Joseph, farmer, Wellington
Simcock John, farmer, Steelhouse
Smith John, farmer
Steers Martha (Mrs.), farmer, Herdslow
Stevenson Wm. shoemaker, Thornbank
Stubbs John, farmer, Hop meadow
Titterton George, farmer, Apesford
Titterton George, farmer, New house
Titterton John, farmer, Revedge
Torr Adam, farmer, Cliff head
Torr James, farmer, Fair fields
Torr Thomas, farmer, Hare house
Turner Jn. *Blacksmiths' Arms* blacksmith
Walwin Francis, shoemaker
Walwin Peter, farmer, Quarnford farm
Walwin Peter, *Hare & Hounds*, & frmr
Webster Thos. farmer, Lady meadows
Wheeldon Joel, farmer

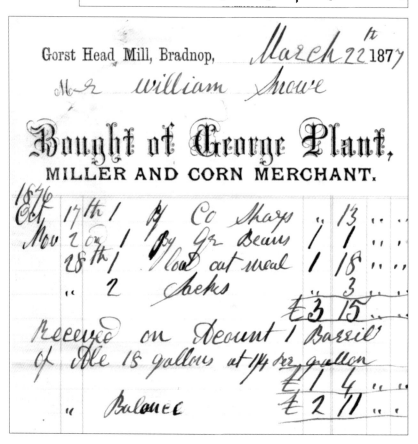

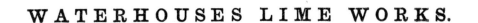

WATERHOUSES LIME WORKS.

~ 15.7 ~

Mr Hambleton Wallace

1859 DR. TO WILLIAM PLANT.

TO 71½ HORSE LOADS OF LIME, @ 9½d. ❀ LOAD. £2. 16. 7½

Decr 15 — 1859
Settled
Wm Plant

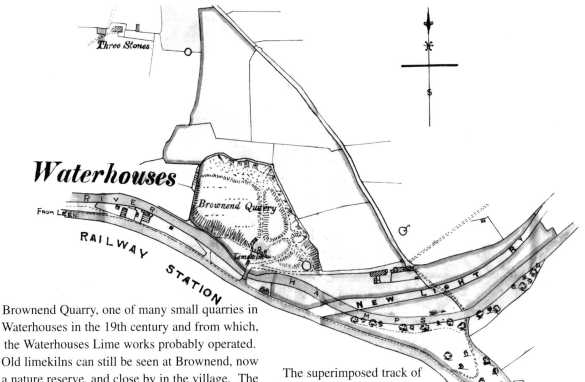

Brownend Quarry, one of many small quarries in Waterhouses in the 19th century and from which, the Waterhouses Lime works probably operated. Old limekilns can still be seen at Brownend, now a nature reserve, and close by in the village. The lime trade was an important part of the local economy - much farmland was limed to keep it 'sweet'. The quarries also provided building stone and road stone.

The superimposed track of the proposed 'new' Leek & Manifold Light Railway is seen crossing the Hamps near the quarry.

Form 16.

Works:
DRAYCOTT, SUDBURY, N.S.R
WALLGRANGE, N.S.R
FROGHALL, N.S.R.

GOLD MEDAL FOR TERRA COTTA
STAFFORDSHIRE EXHIBITION 1899.

BRAND

REGISTERED TRADE MARK
235058.

Head Office:
WALLGRANGE, Nr LEEK, STAFFS
TELEGRAMS,
PLASTIC, WALLGRANGE STATION

London Office:
11, BOSTON ST. MARYLEBONE, N.W
TELEPHONE 1882 PADDINGTON
TELEGRAMS
"SPARADRAP, LONDON"

Depôts:-
HANLEY, BIRMINGHAM AND
LONDON (ST. PANCRAS).

Manufacturers
OF
PLASTER OF PARIS,
KEENE'S, MARTIN'S
AND PARIAN CEMENTS,
ALABASTER IN BLOCKS,
GYPSUM STONE FOR ROCKERIES,
MINERAL WHITE, TERRA ALBA,
"WALLGRANGE"
FACING BRICKS, TERRA COTTA,
MOULDED BRICKS,
RIDGES, FINIALS, ETC.
MACADAM FOR HIGHWAYS,
CHIPPINGS FOR DRIVES
AND FOOTWALKS,
SPAR FOR GROTTOS, ETC.

"PYTHO" PLASTER

THE PLASTER BRICK & STONE Co. LD.

Wall Grange,
Nr Leek.
STAFFS.

Sold to Mr Stubbs   *Sep 8*   1905

Dunwood

Empty Sacks to SUDBURY, N.S.R.   Empty Terra Cotta Cases to WALL GRANGE, N.S.R.

Per .... Consigned to *Works*

Carriage .... Order No. .... Wagon No. ....

		£	s	d
2" Drain Pipes	1000		1	10

Paid December 22nd /05.
C. Redfern
Per pro Plaster, Brick & Stone Co ltd

pulling in³ 1000 Allowed for
Horrocks @ 6⁹
8
4⁶   1 . .

£ 2 10

George Stubbs

The brickworks at Wallgrange was owned by the Plaster Brick & Stone Co and there was an office and depot in Hanley. The brickworks was strategically placed for both railway and canal transportation. The firm had other works at Froghall and Draycott.

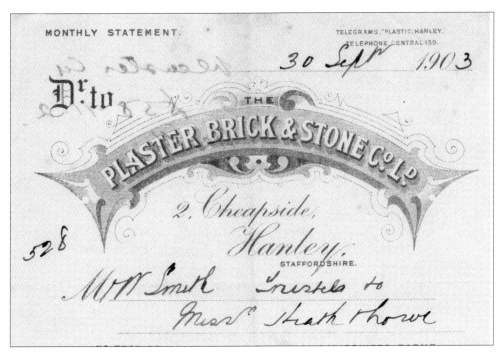

MONTHLY STATEMENT.

TELEGRAMS, "PLASTIC, HANLEY."
TELEPHONE CENTRAL 159.

30 Sep 1903

Dr. to THE

PLASTER BRICK & STONE Co. LD

2, Cheapside,
Hanley,
STAFFORDSHIRE.

528

Mr W Smith   Trustee to

Mrs Heath Howe

MONTHLY STATEMENT.

TELEGRAMS:"PLASTIC, HANLEY."
TELEPHONE 159 HANLEY.

25 Oct 1902

Dr. to The

~~Midlands~~ Plaster Brick & Stone Co. Ltd.,

2, Cheapside,

Hanley,
STAFFORDSHIRE.

Mr W. Smith (Trustee to the Estate

of Mrs. Heath Howe)

NO RECEIPT VALID UNLESS ON ONE OF OUR PRINTED FORMS.
TERMS—CASH MONTHLY.

Acc⁵ Rendered   53 7 11

up to Oct 25 Wallpaper Acc   4 10 9 £57 18 8

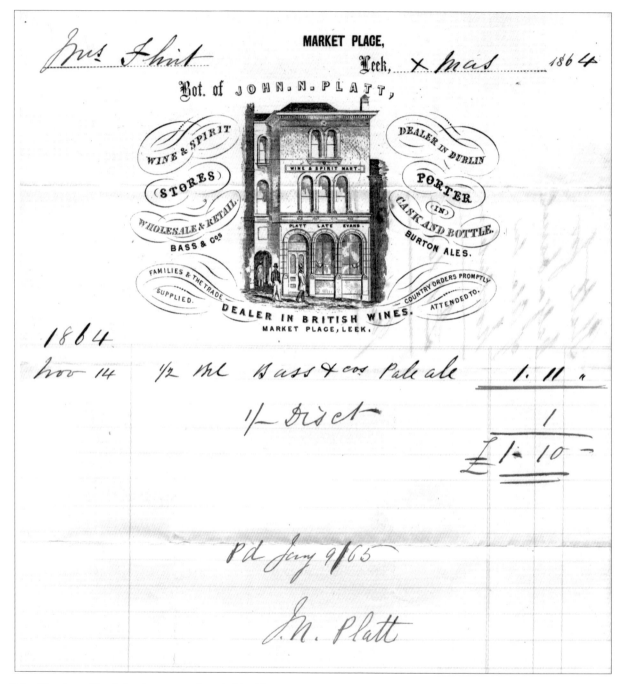

Mrs Flint

MARKET PLACE,

Leek, X mas 1864

Bot. of JOHN. N. PLATT,

WINE & SPIRIT STORES
WHOLESALE & RETAIL
BASS & Co's
FAMILIES & THE TRADE SUPPLIED.

WINE & SPIRIT MART.
PLATT LATE EVANS.
DEALER IN BRITISH WINES.
MARKET PLACE, LEEK.

DEALER IN DUBLIN PORTER (IN) CASK AND BOTTLE.
BURTON ALES.
COUNTRY ORDERS PROMPTLY ATTENDED TO.

1864

Nov 14   ½ bbl Bass & co's Pale ale   1. 11 "

     1/- Disct   1

     £ 1. 10 -

Pd Jany 9/65

J.N. Platt

John Neesham Platt's business was founded in 1847. He later became one of Leek's Improvement Commissioners. He was succeeded in his business by his son, Charles E. Platt who served as 'mine host' at the Angel Inn in addition to managing the wholesale and retail wines and spirits shop at 5 Derby Street. The building in the Market Place still bears the date 1847. William Sugden worked on substantial alterations to the building in the 1850s, soon after his arrival in Leek.

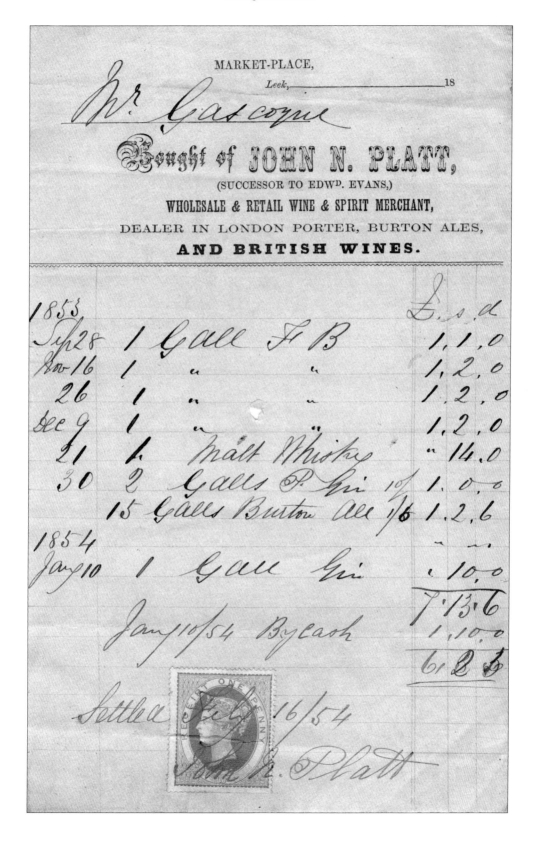

MARKET-PLACE,

Leek,_____18

Mr. Gascoyne

Bought of **JOHN N. PLATT,**

(SUCCESSOR TO EDW^D. EVANS,)

WHOLESALE & RETAIL WINE & SPIRIT MERCHANT,

DEALER IN LONDON PORTER, BURTON ALES,

AND BRITISH WINES.

1853			£ s d
Sep 28	1	Gall F B	1. 1. 0
Nov 16	1	" "	1. 2. 0
26	1	" "	1. 2. 0
Dec 9	1	" "	1. 2. 0
21	1	Malt Whiskey	" 14. 0
30	2	Galls P Gin 10/	1. 0. 0
	15	Galls Burton Ale 1/6	1. 2. 6
1854			" "
Jan 10	1	Gall Gin	. 10. 0
			7. 13. 6
		Jany 10/54 By cash	1. 10. 0
			6. 2. 6

Settled Feby 16/54

John N. Platt

MARKET PLACE,

Leek,   18

M̄ G. H. Morris , Butcher &c .

Bought of John N. Platt,

Wholesale & Retail Wine & Spirit Merchant.

DEALER IN

Bass & Cos Burton Ales, & Guinness & Cos Dublin Porter in Casks & Bottles.

BRITISH WINES, VINEGAR &c

Families and the Trade supplied.

5% ON OVERDUE A%.   A%s ½ YEARLY.

1885				
Mar. 28	2t	P. & Brandy	6	6
Apr. 13	2t	P. & Brandy	6	6
			13/	

Excors of the late MARKET PLACE,

Leek,   190

Miss Roberson   The Paddock

Bought of C. E. Platt,

Wholesale & Retail Wine & Spirit Merchant.

DEALER IN

Bass & Cos Burton Ales, & Guinness & Cos Dublin Porter in Casks & Bottles.

BRITISH WINES, VINEGAR &c

Families and the Trade supplied.

5% ON OVERDUE A%s.   A%s ½ YEARLY.

1908					
May 27	1	Firkin	Ale	10	6
	3	b.th.	Port Wine	6	6
	3	"	Sherry	6	6
29	1	b.th.	V. O. Whisky	3	6
			£1 . 7 . 0		

5, DERBY STREET,
AND 11, MARKET PLACE, Leek, Nov. 11 19 13

M. Robinson Ashbourne Rd.

Bought of Platt & Co.

Wholesale & Retail Wine & Spirit Merchants,

DEALERS IN

Bass & Co. Burton Ales, & Guinness & Co. Dublin Porter in Casks & Bottles.

BRITISH WINES, VINEGAR &c.

Families and the Trade supplied.

1 Cask Mild Ale £	-	5	3

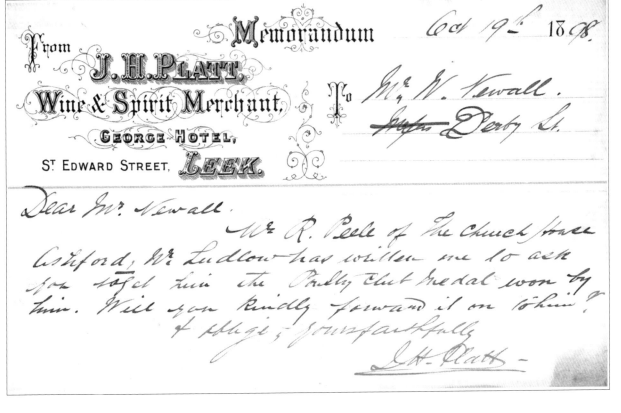

Memorandum Oct 19th 1898

From **J. H. PLATT,**

Wine & Spirit Merchant,

GEORGE HOTEL,

ST EDWARD STREET, **LEEK.**

To M. W. Newall.

~~~~ Derby St.

Dear Mr. Newall.

M. R. Peele of The Church House Ashford, M. Ludlow has written me to ask you to get him the Poultry Club Medal won by him. Will you kindly forward it on to him? & oblige; Yours faithfully

J. H. Platt —

16)

31, St. Edward Street,
LEEK
Xmas 1886

Mr Jeff Smith King St

Bought of J. H. Platt.

WINE AND SPIRIT MERCHANT.

AGENT FOR WORTHINGTON & Co's. PALE AND BURTON ALE.

FAMILIES AND THE TRADE SUPPLIED.

5 PER CENT ON OVER DUE ACCOUNTS.   ACCOUNTS HALF-YEARLY.

86					
July	19	Dos Pts Cider	"	3	"
	26	Dos Cider	.	3	"
	27	Dos ½ Sodas " Dos ½ Lemons "	"	4	"
Sep	25	2 dos ½ Pts Pale ale	.	4	6
	28	Dos Pale ale "3. Dos Stout "	"	4	3
Oct	2	Dos Stout " Dos Pale ale ⅔	"	4	3
	5	Dos Stout " Dos Pale ale ⅔	"	4	3
	9	2 Dos Dinner ale	"	3	"
	14	½ Dos D ale 9⁴ ½ Dos Stout /	.	1	9
	18	Dos Stout " Dos D ale "6	"	3	6
	26	½ Dos D ale 9⁴ ½ Dos Stout /	"	1	9
Dec	14	bot F Brandy	.	4	6
	"	½ W Rum	.	1	1½
	29	Dos Dinner ale	"	1	6
			£	2 4	4½

Mr. Charles E. Platt,
Wholesale and Retail Wine and Spirit Merchant, and Bottler of Ales and Stouts, The Angel Inn, Market Place, and 5, Derby Street.

Mr. Platt's business was founded in 1847, and taken over in 1851 by the late Mr. John N. Platt (in his day one of Leek's most respected townsmen), and has for many years past been carried on by his son, Mr. Charles E. Platt, well known locally both as a man of business and "mine host" of the Angel Inn. Mr. Platt's principal premises front directly on the Market Place, the accommodation here including a compact order office and sales' department, with stores to the rear and commodious cellars and bottling stores beneath. A large amount of space is available, the premises extending behind several adjoining shops, and running through to the wholesale department at 5, Derby Street. A very considerable stock is kept on hand both in the cellars and in bond, the chief items embracing ports, sherries, clarets, Burgundies, Chateau wines, still and sparkling hocks, champagnes, etc. Carefully matured spirits—gins, rums, brandies, and Irish and Scotch whiskies from the best distilleries—are also largely stocked, together with British and foreign liqueurs, minerals, and cigars. Mr. Platt acts as agent in Leek for Bass's, the Anglo-Bavarian ales, Guinness's stout, which are bottled on the premises by means of improved machinery. He is likewise agent for Burgoyne's cele-

THE ANGEL INN.   5, DERBY STREET.

brated Australian wines, and the equally famous "Uam Var" blend of Scotch whisky. A flourishing family and general trade is done, extending throughout Leek and the surrounding districts. The Angel Inn in the Market Place is a fully licensed house, and has been conducted by Mr. Platt since 1891, since the death of his father, Mr. John N. Platt. It contains the usual bars, smoke-room, and offices, all of which have been comfortably fitted up. On market days especially its resources are taxed to the fullest limit as a general resort.

Perhaps halfway between the Potteries (? Burslem) and Leek, or even Rudyard.

The fine bay windows and the very large mural sign enhance the frontage of the Plough Hotel. The mural is a splendid work of art in its own right and is probably the largest inn sign in the Country.

HALF WAY HOUSE,

The Plough Hotel,

Endon Sept. 24.th 1883.

PROPRIETOR,
H. PLATT,
LATE OF
RUDYARD LAKE HOTEL.

STOKE ON TRENT.

ENDON, LONGSDEN, AND STANLEY.   No 7

Parish of Leek, the 11 day of *March* 1866

Received of Mr. *Joseph Stubbs* the sum of

_____ Pounds 7 Shillings and 6 Pence,

in respect of the Cattle Rate of the above Parish, viz.:

January   £. s. d.

Rate made on the 18th day of April, 1866, on £ 90 0 0

Assessment, at _____ 1 _____ Pence in the

Pound .. ..   7 - 6

Arrear of former Rate .. ..

Total £ _____

(Signed)   W. Hale

Bath Street, Leek,   Mar 12   1912

M A H Shaw Esq.

Bought of **T. PORTER & Co.,**

Undertakers
Funerals
Completely
Furnished.

CABINET MAKERS & UPHOLSTERERS
Complete House Furnishers
and Antique Dealers.

Dealers in New & Secondhand Furniture.   Furniture Removed and Stored.

Mar 9	To Painted Cupboard		1	0	0
	" 15¾ Sq ft timber x 1"	5¼		6	11
	" 14 hours time	9		10	6
	" Painting & Varnishing				0 0

Bought of THOMAS PORTER,

CABINET MAKER, FURNITURE BROKER,

AND DEALER IN ANTIQUITIES.

Bedroom Pair		4	5	0
2 Cane seated Chairs 3/			6	2

TELEGRAMS: "PORTERS, LEEK."
TELEPHONE No. 78.

BATH STREET, LEEK,

Oct   1924

Dr. to   *Porter & Co*

CABINET MAKERS,
UPHOLSTERERS, ::
COMPLETE HOUSE FURNISHERS.

FURNITURE REMOVED & STORED.
GOODS . TAKEN . IN . EXCHANGE.

Mr Cod.   6105.

Hawthorne Cottage Longsdon

Framing 4 Pictures in Gilt.		1	10	0
" 2 water Colors in Gilt		1	4	0

Office and Coal Depot:—Leek Station.

Exors
Mr John Brealey *Derby Street*

Bought of John Potts & Co.,

COAL MERCHANTS.

J. Goodwin, 7, Russell Street.

190*1*	COALS.	Tons cwt. qrs.	Price per Ton.	£	s.	d.
May 2	To Coke	1 2 0	15/-		9	.

Received 27/5/1902
With thanks
James Goodwin

for Joseph Abbott

Bought of JOHN POTTS,

SPOUT STREET.

	cwt.	qrs.		d.		£	s.	d.
Gross	17	0						
Tare	5	0						
Net weight delivered	12	0	Coals at 8 ₱ cwt				8	0

John ___ Carter.

Feby 15 1865

...e Bank
...REET.

		£	s.	d.
			7	1
"	Mrs Stubbs 10 0 "		7	1
"	Geo. Abbott 10 0 "		7	1
"	Mrs Stonehewer 10 0 "		7	1
"	H. Simpson 10 0 "		7	1
	J Abbott 12 9/	£ 1	15	5
			8	0

Settled
Feby 1866
J Potts

ONE PENNY

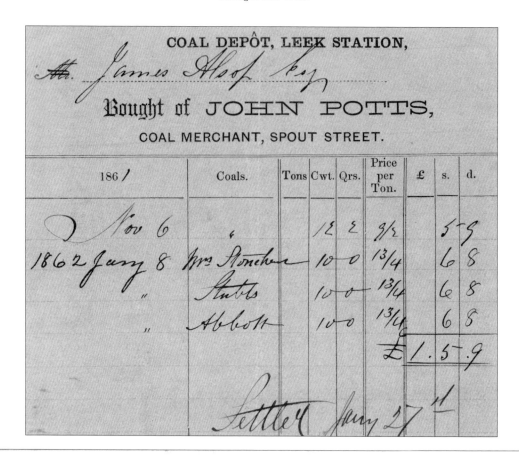

COAL DEPÔT, LEEK STATION,

Mr James Alsop Esq

Bought of JOHN POTTS,

COAL MERCHANT, SPOUT STREET.

186*1*	Coals.	Tons	Cwt.	Qrs.	Price per Ton.	£	s.	d.
Nov 6	"		12	2	9/2		5	9
1862 *Jany* 8	*Mrs Stonehear*	10	0		13/4		6	8
"	*Stubbs*	10	0		13/4		6	8
"	*Abbott*	10	0		13/4		6	8
						£1	5	9

Settled Jany 27

Telegrams:
PREMIER, LEEK.
Telephone:
139 LEEK.

Established 1838.

Telephone:
211 MACCLESFIELD.

THE PREMIER DYEING & FINISHING Co. Ltd.

FORMERLY
SAMUEL TATTON & SON

Proprietors of The Royle Dyeing Co. Macclesfield

Silk, Artificial Silk & Cotton Skein & Piece Goods

LEEK

REF. Nº

Received from Mr. William Brown, of Tittisworth
Farm, Near Leek, the sum of Twenty Pounds being the amount of
deposit on the purchase of dwelling house. No. 11 Arthur Street,
Leek, for the sum of Three Hundred and Twenty Pounds (£320),
and as now occupied by Miss Oliver.

GROCERIES & PROVISIONS.
One grade only – the HIGHEST.

Finest Hams & Bacon, Cooked Hams & Tongues.   Cheese & Butter.
Highest grade Tea & Coffee.   Tinned and Dried Fruits.
———— Shortbread and many Xmas Specialities. ————

ARTHUR PRIME, Grocer & Provision Dealer,
21, FOUNTAIN ST.   TELEPHONE : LEEK 443.

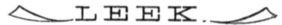

The Queen Laundry was in Cruso Street and the building can still be seen today.

WHITE'S DIRECTORY 1851

LEEK TOWN AND PARISH

LEEK, the largest market town in the hundred of Totmonslow, and one of the handsomest in the county, has long been extensively engaged in the silk manufacture, and covers the summit and declivities of a pleasant eminence, above the River Churnet, and nearly in the centre of a spacious valley, of a circular figure, the acclivities of which rise rapidly on every side to the distance of six or seven miles, and form one of nature's proudest and most stupendous amphitheatres, the foreground of which consists chiefly of fertile pastures, enlivened by several rivulets, the Caldon Canal, and many thriving plantations; whilst the more distant hills, rising tier above tier, partake of the general heathy character of the Moorlands, and are crowned on the north east side by a long range of lofty perpendicular rocks and crags, called the Leek Roches. Leek has a station on the Churnet Valley Branch of the North Staffordshire Railway; and is the head of a large parish and union, a polling and county court district, a rural deanery, and a petty sessional division. It is distant 10 miles N.E. by E. of Burslem, 10 miles S.W. of Longnor, 14 miles S.E. of Macclesfield, 10 miles N. of Cheadle, and 154 miles N.W. by W. of London.

LEEK PARISH comprises no less than 34,300 acres of land, extending six miles west and north of the town, and about four miles eastward; and rising from the picturesque valleys of the Churnet and other rivulets to some of the boldest heights of the Moorlands. It comprises many small villages and hamlets, and is divided into ten townships, as enumerated, with their territorial extent and their population in 1841. The whole parish had only 6810 souls in 1801 but its population amounted to 10,780 in 1831, to 11,738 in 1841 and to 13,294 in 1851.

The TOWN OF LEEK has several spacious and well built streets, and is nearly all comprised in the township of Leek-and-Lowe, which comprises about 6000 acres of land, including a number of scattered farm houses and cottages, at Birchalls, Leek Edge, &c, chiefly in the Lowe liberty. This township had only 3703 inhabitants in 1821, but in 1841 they had increased to 7233, and in 1851 to 8599 souls, nine-tenths of whom are in the town and its immediate suburbs.

The Earl of Macclesfield is lord of the manor of Leek, which includes the townships of Leek-and-Lowe and Leekfrith. The Earl also owns a great part of the soil, and the rest belongs to John Davenport, Jno. Cruso, Edw. Chorley, and Saml. and Wm. Phillips Esqrs, the Misses Gaunt, and a number of smaller proprietors. John Cruso, Esq. is the manor steward. The court leet is held in October, when two market lookers and other officers are appointed. The common was enclosed under an act passed in 1805, and a large portion of it has since been built upon, at Ballhaye green and Leek moor. Before the Norman Conquest, the manor was held by Algarus Ca; and in the reign of King Stephen by Ranulph, Earl of Chester, who gave the tithes of his mill here to the monks of St Werberge, at Chester. His grandson, the sixth Earl of Chester, gave this manor to the monks of the ABBEY of Dieu le Creyse, or Dieu Encres, which he founded in Leek Frith, in the vale of the Churnet, about half a mile north of the town. The following legend is recorded as immediately connected with the name and foundation of this abbey.

The Earl dreamt that the ghost of his grandfather appeared to him, and bade him go to Cholpesdale, near Leek, and found an abbey of white monks, near to a chapel there, dedicated to The Blessed Virgin, *"for by it"*, said the ghost, *"there shall be joy to thee, and many others who shall be saved thereby. Of this it shall be a sign, when the Pope doth interdict England. But do thou, in the meantime, go to the monks of Pulton, and be partaker of the sacrament of the Lord's Supper; and, in the seventh year of that interdict, thou shalt translate those monks to the place I have appointed."* Ranulph, having had this vision, related it to his wife, who, hearing it, said in French - *"Dieu encres! - God increase!"* whereupon the earl, pleased with the expression, said it should be the name of the abbey, which he speedily founded and furnished with monks of the Cistercian order, from Pulton, in Cheshire. He endowed it with divers lands and possessions, which his successors, Earls of Chester, confirmed and made considerable additions thereto. Robert de Menilwannin also gave to the monks, *"for the health of his soul, and of Ranulph, Earl of Chester and Lincoln, (his mother's brother,) in pure and perpetual alms, free common in the wood of Pevero, with housebote, and haybote, and pawnage for fifty hogs."*

At the dissolution, this abbey was valued at £243. 3s. 0d. per annum, and was granted, with most of its possessions, by Edward VI to Sir Ralph Baggenholt, who soon afterwards sold the abbey estate to the tenants; and it now belongs to John Davenport, Esq., of Westwood Hall. About 30 years ago, the ruins of the abbey, which had been so completely buried in the earth that cattle grazed over them, were dug up by the late owner, J.S. Daintry, Esq, of Macclesfield, and most of the materials used in erecting barns and stables for the use of the ancient farmhouse, which stands near the spot; but the shafts of the chapel columns are left standing to the height of several feet. The exterior walls of the farm buildings are decorated with many fragments of arches and capitals; and in one of them is a stone coffin, with a crozier and sword carved upon it.

Leek gave birth to Thomas Parker, the first Earl of Macclesfield, of his family, who was born here in 1666, in an ancient house still standing, near the churchyard. He was the son of Thomas Parker, an attorney, and, after receiving a grammatical education, applied himself to the study of the law, under the direction of his father. He became so eminent as a barrister, that he was appointed one of Queen Anne's counsel, and was exalted to the rank of Sergeant-at-Law, and had the honour of knighthood conferred on him in 1705. In 1710, he was appointed Lord Chief Justice of the King's Bench; and on the death of the Queen, he was one of the Lords Justices till the arrival of George I, from Hanover. In 1716, be was created Baron of Macclesfield, and in 1718 was raised to the dignity of Lord Chancellor of Great Britain. In 1721, he was created Viscount Parker, of Ewelme, in Oxfordshire, and Earl of Macclesfield, in the County of Chester. In consequence of some notorious mal-practices, he was impeached by the House of Peers on charges of gross corruption in the Court of Chancery, for which he was removed from office, and sentenced to pay a fine of £30,000, every shilling of which was exacted, and paid by his Lordship and his son, the latter of whom died in 1764, and was succeeded by his son, who died in 1795, and was succeeded by his son George, who died in 1842, and was succeeded by Thomas, the late Earl, who died in 1850. The Right Hon. Thomas Augustus Wolstenholme Parker, the present Earl of Macclesfield and Viscount Parker, was born in 1811, and his eldest son in 1843. His seats are Sherborne Castle, in Oxfordshire, and Buckfastleigh, in Devonshire. Before the Parkers, there were three Earls of Macclesfield, of the Gerard family, the title being created in 1679.

Near Leek are several pleasant seats. BALLHAYE, a stone mansion with a well-wooded demesne was held for many generations by the Davenports, and afterwards by the Hulmes and Unwins, but it is now in chancery, and unoccupied. WESTWOOD HALL, a neat mansion with beautiful grounds in the Lowe liberty, formerly belonged to Lady Vane, and afterwards to B. Grey, Esq., who sold it to the father of its present owner and occupant, John Davenport, Esq., who has greatly improved both the hall and the estate.

That the neighbourhood of Leek has been the scene of some signal action, fought between the Britons and the Romans, is evident from the circumstance of several pieces of Roman and British arms having been found at various periods, in the immediate vicinity of the town. In the churchyard is an upright stone, recording the death of Wm. Trafford, Esq., a distinguished royalist, who died at Swithamley Hall, in this parish, in 1697 and who saved himself from the fury of a party of Cromwell's soldiers, by disguising himself as a thrasher, and continuing his work in the barn. When the intruders found him, he answered their interrogations merely by uttering the words *"Now thus,"* between every stroke of the flail; upon which they considered him as a rustic idiot, and departed without further molestation. In this character, he is represented on his grave-stone, and his family introduced the words "Now thus," as the motto on their arms. Leek has not since been disturbed by any military events, except in the rebellion of 1745, when the Scottish insurgents, commanded by Charles Edward Stuart and the Dukes of Perth and Athol, marched through the town to Derby.

The SILK MANUFACTURE of Leek has long been in a flourishing state; and has been so considerably extended during the last 20 years, that several extensive mills and factories have been erected, and the population of the township has increased from 6372 to 8599. In the same period, several new streets have been formed, and many of the manufacturers have erected handsome residences in the suburbs. The articles in silk and mohair, for which the town is chiefly celebrated, are sewing silks, twist, buttons, ribbons, ferrets, galloons, handkerchiefs, shawls, sarcenet, and broad silk. Florentine buttons, consisting of wood, bone, or iron moulds, covered with worsted stuff, are also manufactured here, and give employment to many hundred women and children in the surrounding villages, who are employed in sewing the.cloth upon the moulds. In the silk trade many large fortunes have been made by the late and present manufacturers; and some of their weavers and other workmen have been enabled, by industry and economy, to build convenient houses for their own occupation. Opposite the entrance of the Hope Silk Mills is a fish pond, enclosed with palisades and stocked with upward of 600 gold fish, supplied with fresh water from the engine pump.

MARKETS AND FAIRS - As early as 1607, Leek is said to have had a good weekly market, which is now held every Wednesday and Saturday, and is well supplied with all kinds of provisions, exposed for sale in the spacious Market Place, which occupies the most central and highest part of the town, and has several good streets branching from it in different directions. A fat cattle market is held on every alternate Wednesday, between July 28th and Oct. 10th, in the spacious cattle market at the foot of Derby St. Here are also eight annual fairs for cattle, &c., held on the Wednesday before February 13th; Easter Wednesday; May 18th; Whit-Wednesday; July 3rd and 28th; the Wednesday after October 10th; and on Nov. 13th. The principal cattle fair is that on the 18th May. A statute fair, for hiring servants, &c., is held on the Wednesday after Christmas day. Cheese fairs were established here about 30 years ago, and are now held three times a year, on the second Monday in March, and the third Mondays in Sept. and Nov. The wake or feast is on the nearest Sunday to the 18th of October; and races are occasionally held on the succeeding Monday and Tuesday, in Birchall dale. In the town are many well-stocked shops, several good inns, and upwards of 40 public-houses. The Caldon Canal approaches within half a mile S. W. of the town, and opens a communication with the Trent and Mersey navigation, and with the coal and limestone districts. On the same side of the town is a commodious Railway Station, on the Churnet Valley branch of the North Staffordshire Railway, opened July 13th, 1849.

- The streets are generally well-paved and lighted, and the houses of some of the manufacturers and other principal inhabitants, are large, and handsomely built. In 1806, the old market cross, which stood at the foot of the Market place, was taken down, and removed to a field called Corn-hill. The TOWN HALL was erected on the site of the ancient cross, at the cost of about £600, and is now chiefly occupied as a news room and savings bank. The POLICE STATION, in Mill street, was built by the County Magistrates, in 1848, at the cost of about £800, and has a court room in which Petty Sessions are held every alternate Wednesday: a dwelling for the police inspector, and three large cells for the temporary confinement of prisoners. The magistrates, who usually sit here, are the Rev. T H Heathcote, the Rev. J. Sneyd, and J. W. Sneyd, T. Powys, M. Gaunt and John Cruso, Esqrs; to whom Mr. Fras. Cruso and Mr. W. Challinor are clerks. Capt. Lance is police superintendent and inspector of weights and measures, and here are also an inspector and 11 men belonging to the county police.

An Act of Parliament for Lighting, Watching, and Improving the Town, was obtained in 1825. The Commissioners of this act are empowered to levy rates upon the inhabitants, and some years ago they purchased the GAS WORKS, which were established in 1826 by 46 proprietors of 200 £26 shares. These works are near the wharfs, and have lately been enlarged. Consumers are charged at the rate of 5s. to 7s. 6d. per 1000 cubic feet; which is about half what they were formerly charged. Mr. George Nall is clerk to the Commissioners and manager of the Gas Works. Mr. Thos. Hulse, of Lane end, is lessee of the market tolls, under the Earl of Macclesfield; and Samuel Ball is the town crier. The Earl of Macclesfield is the proprietor of the WATER WORKS, which have been greatly improved and extended, under the authority of an Act of Parliament, obtained in 1827 so that the town is now well supplied with pure soft water from the springs on Leek moor, where there are two reservoirs, each about four yards deep, and one of them 120 yards long and 40 broad, and the other 60 yards by 40. They are now being enlarged. Cottage houses are charged for water only 4s. to 5s. per annum, or about 1s. per pound on the rentals. Mr. Edmund Clee has the management of the water-works and fire engine.

LEEK COUNTY COURT DISTRICT comprises all Leek Union and Superintendent Registrar's District, except Norton-in-the-Moors. The court is held monthly at the Red Lion Inn, and R. G. Temple, Esq., is the judge; Mr. James Bloore, clerk; and Mr. T. Price, high bailiff.

LEEK UNION comprises all the extensive parish of Leek and most of that of Alstonfield, as well as Horton, Norton, and Sheen. The following is a list of its nineteen townships, &c., with their POPULATION in 1851: Leek and Lowe, 8599; Leekfrith, 877; Bradnop, 447; Onecote, 438; Rudyard, 92; Heaton, 450; Rushton-Spencer, 355; Rushton James, 283; Endon, 658; Longsdon, 426; Stanley, 108; and Tittesworth, 606, in Leek parish; Warslow and Upper and Lower Elkstone, 715; Longnor, 561 Heathylee, 578; Hollinsclough, 400; Quarnford, 665; and Fawfield head, 923, in Alstonfield parish; and the three parishes of Horton, 967; Sheen, 395; and Norton-in-the-Moors, 3329. The total population of the Union in 1851 was only 21,827, though it comprises an area 82 square miles. The total expenditure of the 19 townships, &c., on their poor was £4551, in 1839; £5765, in 1849; and £5771, in 1850. The UNION WORKHOUSE is a large and handsome brick building, erected in 1838, at the cost of £6500, and having room for upwards of 250 paupers. It stands on a commanding eminence, about half a mile from the town, on three acres of land, which was given to Leek and Lowe by a late Earl of Macclesfield, towards the support of the workhouse of that township, built in 1768. Fras. Cruso, Esq., is the Union Clerk and Superintendent Registrar, and Mr John Perkin is the deputy-superintendent registrar. The Rev. E. F. T. Ribbans, BA., is the chaplain, and George Belfield and Harriet Bailey are master and matron of the Workhouse. Messrs. Thos. Rowley and Wm. Pickering are the relieving officers, the former for Leek and the latter for Longnor District. Mr. Geo. Rider is registrar of marriages; and the registrar of births and deaths are George Rider for Leek District; R. Hulme for Leekfrith District; John Millward for Longnor District; and J. Salt for Norton and Endon District. Besides the Union, Leek Superintendent Registrars District comprises Grindon, Wetton, and Butterton.

Leek Parish CHURCH is a large and venerable fabric, dedicated to St. Edward the Confessor, and standing on an elevated site near the head of the Market place, in a large burial ground, to which a considerable plot of ground was added many years ago, on the declivity which descends northward to the river Churnet. It is a Gothic structure, with a square tower, which contains a clock, six bells, and chimes. In 1816, eight pinnacles were added to the tower, and the whole edifice was thoroughly repaired at a great expense. In 1839, 269 additional sittings were provided, so that there are now 1400 sittings, of which 337 are free. In the interior are several neat mural monuments, belonging to the Daintry and other families; and in the churchyard stands the remains of an ancient pyramidal cross, ten feet high, with three steps at the foot, and adorned with rude imagery and fretwork, but bearing no inscription to designate its origin and purport, though it is generally supposed to be of Danish workmanship. In repairing one of the church buttresses adjacent to this monument in 1829, an inscription to the memory of Hugh, Earl of Chester, was found bearing the date 1180. In the lower churchyard stands a heavy stone building, erected in 1800 by the late Thomas Mills, Esq., of Barlaston Hall, as a burial place for his family. In the church is a copper plate, on which are engraved the date 1597, and figures representing John Ashenhurst, Esq., and his four wives and ten children. The higher part of the churchyard commands an extensive view of the 'Roches', and the other rocky hills to the north and west; and at the summer solstice, the sun appears to set twice on the same evening, behind the conical peak of one of these lofty mountains, called the Hen Cloud; for after sinking below the top of this hill, it breaks out again on the northern side of it, before it sinks below the horizon. The Vicarage, valued in KB. at £7. 19s. 2d., and now at £170, is in the patronage of the Earl of Macclesfield, and incumbency of the Rev. T. H. Heathcote, M.A., who has held the benefice since 1822, and has much improved the Vicarage House, which is supposed to have been partly built in the reign of Elizabeth, and partly in 1715. The Revs J. Barnes; MA., and E.F.T. Ribbans B.A. are the curates, and the former is also Rural dean of Leek. The tithes of the parish were all commuted for allotments of land many years ago.

ST. LUKE'S CHURCH on the eastern side of the town, is a handsome stone edifice in the decorated style, erected in 1848, at the cost of about £4100; for a district parish, formed in 1845, under Peel's Act, and comprising part of the township of Leek and Lowe, and the whole of Tittesworth, and embracing a population of about 4000 souls. The church was built by subscription and grants, and the site and churchyard were purchased with money left by the late Mrs. Brentnall; but the tower is not yet finished. The interior is neatly fitted up, and has 650 sittings, all free. The benefice is a perpetual curacy, valued at £170, in the alternate patronage of the Crown and the Bishop of Lichfield, and in the incumbency of the Rev. Benj. Pidcock, B A., who is not yet provided with a Parsonage House, but funds are being raised for the erection of one.

There are churches or chapels of ease at Endon, Meerbrook, Onecote, and Rushton in this extensive parish,as afterwards noticed, and in the town are seven DISSENTING CHAPELS, and one belonging to the Roman Catholics. The WESLEYANS have three chapels in Leek. Their first chapel, at Mount Pleasant, was built in 1787, but in 1811, it was converted into dwellings for two ministers, and adjoining it was erected the present chapel, which has 900 sittings, and cost £3400. Connected with it is a Sunday school, attended by about 450 children. Brunswick Chapel, in Ballhaye street, was erected in 1827, at the cost of £1700; and will seat 450 hearers. It has a Sunday and an Infant day school. The other Wesleyan Chapel is at Ball Haye Green, and was built in 1845. It has 200 sittings, and a Sunday school. The

Primitive Methodist Chapel, in Fountain street, was built in 1836, at the cost of £800, and has 300 sittings, and a small Sunday school.

The INDEPENDENTS, or Congregationalists, have two chapels, in Derby street and Union street, but both are now under the. ministry of the Rev R Goshawk. That in Derby street, was rebuilt about 70 years ago, after the seats had been pulled up and burnt in the Market place, during the religious commotion in Dr. Priestley's time. The lower part of the chapel has been converted into a library and reading room for the Mechanics Institution; and the upper part will seat 150 hearers. Union street chapel was built in 1833, at the cost of.£1300, and has 400 sittings, and Sunday and Infant Schools, built in 1845, at the cost of £450. At Overton's bank is an old Friends Meeting House, now but seldom used.

The ROMAN CATHOLIC CHAPEL, in Fountain street, was erected in 1829 at the cost of £700, and adorned with fine old paintings of St Helen, St Edward the Confessor, St. Lucius, and St. Editha, which were brought from a convent at Lisbon, by the nuns formerly at Aston Hall, near Stone, when they fled on the invasion of the French. The altar-piece is an excellent painting of the Virgin and Child, by Barney, an English artist. The chapel will seat about 250, and attached to it is a Day and Sunday School and house for the priest, the Rev. M.A. Power. Bible, Tract, Missionary and other Religious Institutions are liberally supported by the congregations of the churches and chapels; and besides the schools already noticed, here are large National Schools, and a Grammar School.

THE GRAMMAR SCHOOL stands near the church-yard, and was erected by the Earl of Macclesfield, lord chancellor, in 1723, and is kept in repair by the master, who has no endowment except £9. 13s. 10d. per annum, for teaching six free scholars to read, as the dividends of £323. 4s. 9d., purchased with a legacy of the Rev. George Roads, bequeathed in 1712. The Earl of Macclesfield appoints the master; but the six free scholars are admitted by the vicar. The present master is the Rev. E. F. T. Ribbans, B.A.

The National Schools, at Clerk's bank, attached to the parish church, were built in 1843, by subscription and grants, at the cost of about £700 and are attended by about 80 boys and 60 girls; on week days, and by a much larger number on Sundays. They have room for 400 children, and belonging to the trust are three adjoining houses, one of which is occupied by the master and mistress. St. Luke's National Schools were built in 1847, at the cost of £722, and are attended by about 100 boys and 50 girls.

Leek Mechanics' Institution, in Derby street, occupies the lower part of the old Independent Chapel. This useful and flourishing institution was established in 1837, and has now about 270 members, a library of 1500 volumes, a reading room, supplied with newspapers, magazines, &c.; classes for various branches of instruction; and occasional lectures. M. Gaunt, Esq., is the president; Mr. H. Brough, secretary; and Mr. C. Lees, librarian. There are News Rooms at the Town Hall and in Stockwell street. Leek Temperance Society has a lecture room in Stockwell street, open on Friday evenings, and has had a very beneficial effect on the habits and morals of a large portion of the operatives of the town and neighbourhood. There is an assembly room at the Red Lion Hotel, where the Leek and Moorland Troop of the Queen's Own Royal Yeomanry Cavalry have an annual ball.

The CHARITIES AND PROVIDENT INSTITUTIONS of the town are as follows:

The ALMSHOUSES, founded by Elizabeth Ash, in 1676, consist of eight houses, containing two apartments each, with a piece of garden ground apportioned among them. The foundress endowed them with a yearly rent charge of £40, to be paid out of a house and land, at Kewall green, in Leek, to the eight almswomen in weekly shares. She vested the nomination of two of the almswomen respectively in Thomas Joliffe and Wm. Ash, and their heirs; and the other six, in them and the vicar and overseers of Leek. All are to be of the age of 60 or upwards, and parishioners of Leek, viz., five from the town, one from Leekfrith, one from Endon, and the other from Bradnop and Onecote townships. This charity was afterwards augmented with £100 left by Lady Dethick in 1678, and laid out in 1723, (with £110 left to the poor of Leek generally), by Thomas Joliffe; and a Mr. Haywood, in the purchase of 18$\frac{1}{2}$ acres of land, in Rushton Spencer, called Great and Little Oulton, and now let for about £25 a year. Some timber, cut on this land, in 1803, produced £614. 18s., of which £562. 10s. was invested in the purchase of £900 three per cent. consolidated annuities. About every sixth year, upwards of £20 worth of underwood is cut on the land, and sold to the crate manufacturers in the Potteries. The almswomen are entitled to ten 21 parts of the rents and profits of the land and of the dividends of the stock. They have likewise the dividends of £436. 2s. three per cent reduced annuities, purchased with £400, given by Mrs. Rebecca Lowe, in 1765; so that they have each a weekly income of 2s; 6d., besides a surplus fund for the purchase of gowns once in two years; and coals to the amount of £15 yearly. The Vicar, and John Cruso, S. Phillips, and Hugh Sleigh, Esqrs., are the trustees. The almshouses were thoroughly repaired and covered with durable cement, in 1821.

The BENEFACTIONS to the poor of Leek, under the management of the Churchwardens, comprise the remaining eleven 21 parts of the property which has arisen from the gifts of Dethick, Joliffe, and Haywood, as noticed in the account of the almshouses, and the following donations, viz., the Leek field, left by Wm. Watson, in 1688, and now let, with an allotment made to it at the inclosure, for about £19 per annum;- £2. 10s. yearly from Thos. Joddrell's charity, (see Horton);- £33. 6s. yearly from three fields, near Cornhill Cross, left by Mrs. Ann Joliffe, in 1731, for poor widows; - 26s. as the interest of 40 marks, left by Wm. Hulme, in 1690; and 35s: 10d. yearly from an allotment, made in lieu of a rent-charge, left by John Hulme, in 1694. These benefactions produce collectively a yearly income of about £85., which is distributed in the church, at Christmas, in money blankets, and linen, and sometimes in coals. This distribution is called the Town Dole.

OTHER BENEFACTIONS To LEEK. In 1619, John Rothwell charged his lands, in Hellesend and Horsecroft, with ten guineas a year, to pay six poor persons of Leek 7d. per week each, and the residue to the Vicar, for four sermons yearly. At the inclosure, in 1805, that part of this rent-charge, belonging to the six widows, was exchanged for an allotment of 6A. 1R. 11P., and the remaining 18s. was compensated by part of an allotment of 7A 3R. 39P, set out to the vicar in lieu of this and other payments due to him. These, together with four other allotments set out in respect of other claims containing in the whole 18A. 3R. 22P, are let together for £31 per annum, which is apportioned as follows, - to the vicar, £16 2s. 3d.; to the six widows, £10. 7s. 6d.; to the poor, for weekly doles of bread, in respect of a rent charge left by James Rudyard, in 1709, £2. 15s.; and to the overseers, in respect of John Hulmes' charity, £1. 15s. 10d. Mrs. St. Andrew left 6s. 8d. to the vicar, and 13s. 4d. to the poor, out of Stringer's croft in Gayton. Mrs. Joan Armett, in 1665, bequeathed the following annuities, out of Nether Hay Farm, viz., 53s. 4d. to the poor of Leek and Mill street and 53s. 4d. to the minister, and 20s. to the poor of Meerbrook chapelry, Wm. Mills, in 1749, left £100, and directed the interest to be paid yearly as follows, viz., 20s. to the vicar, 5s. to the clerk, and the residue in bread to poor widows. Thomas Birtles, in 1755, left £100, now vested in £120. 13s. 3d. three and a half per cent reduced annuities, the dividends to be given to indigent housekeepers of Leek; on St. Thomas's day. In 1806, Wm. Badnall, silk dyer, bequeathed £1000, to be invested in the funds, in trust, to divide the yearly proceeds on November 5th, in blankets, quilts and other clothing, among 20 poor widows of the township of Leek and of the age of 60 or upwards. This legacy was invested in the purchase of £1646. 1s. 9d. three per cent, reduced annuities. The vicar is one of the five trustees. In 1738, John Naylor bequeathed to the town of Leek, two annuities, to be purchased out of his personal estate, viz. £50 to the poor, and £5 to the vicar for preaching a sermon on the day of distribution, Oct 23rd. This charity has undergone several changes, and now consists of £1620 new South Sea annuities, yielding only £48. 12s. per annum; so that the vicar has only £4. 8s.4d., and the poor £44. 3s. 8d. The latter is dispensed in various articles of food and clothing.

LEEK SAVINGS BANK is held at the Town Hall, but having a surplus fund of about £740, a neat building is intended to be shortly erected for its use. It is open on the 1st and 3rd Mondays of every month, from 12 to 1 o'clock. In Nov., 1850, its deposits amounted to £34,162, belonging to 1010 individuals, and 11 charitable, and 7 friendly societies. Mr. Sampson Gould is the actuary. At the Mechanics' Institution, a Penny or Preliminary Savings' Bank was established in 1850, and Mr. Joshua Brough is its secretary. Among the other institutions of the town are a number of Friendly Societies; a Lodge of Foresters, (with 350 members,) and several lodges of Odd Fellows. Eight of these societies hold their annual festival on the same day, early in August. The Leek and the Leek United Benefit Building Societies, were established in 1850, and are held at the Mechanics' Institution. Mr. Jas. Mycock is secretary of the former, and Mr. Robt. Belfield of the latter.

Leek Self-supporting and Charitable Dispensary was established in 1832. Adults paying 1d., and children $1/2$d. per week, are provided with medical and surgical aid, and have the choice of four surgeons. Honorary subscribers can recommend 5 or 6 patients for every annual subscription of 21s.; but a midwifery case is considered equal to two ordinary cases. Mr. Geo. Nall is secretary of this useful institution.

VILLAGES, &C., IN LEEK PARISH.

Bradnop, 2 miles S.E. of Leek, is a hamlet and township of 447 souls, and about 3000 acres of land, including CAWDRY, and belonging to a number of landowners; but John Sneyd, Esq., is lord of the manor, Ashenhurst is the pleasant seat of S. and W. Phillips, Esqrs. There is a Wesleyan Chapel at Bradnop. The poor of Onecote and Bradnop have 5 acres of land in the parish of Sheen, supposed to have been given by Thomas Stanley, Esq., for the benefit of the poor not receiving parochial relief. It is let for £10 a year, which is distributed at Christmas. In 1788, Joan Adsetts left to the poor of Onecote £30, which, in 1794, was laid out in land now let for 24s. per annum.

ENDON, a pleasant scattered village and liberty of 658 souls, 4 miles S.W. by W. of Leek, forms a township with Longsdon and Stanley, in the manor of Horton, of which G. C. Antrobus, Esq., is lord. The whole township comprises about 5000 acres, and 1192 inhabitants. The principal landowners are the Duke of Sutherland, the Earl of Macclesfield, T. Sneyd, Esq Saml. and Wm. Phillips, Esqrs., and the Rev. Jph. Dodd. The latter derived his estate from his father-in-law, the late Rev. Thomas Sutton, D.D. who died in 1851, and was vicar of Sheffield more than 45 years. Endon and Stanley form a chapelry, and the Church, or Parochial Chapel stands upon a commanding eminence at Endon, and has a tower and about 220 sittings. It is dedicated to St. Luke, and was erected by the inhabitants in 1730. It contains a neat marble tablet, in memory of the Heaton family, and another in memory of the late Francis Evans, Esq. In unconsecrated ground, near the church-yard, is the tomb of the late Mr. John and Miss Daniel. The perpetual curacy, valued at £125, is in the patronage of the Earl of Macclesfield, and incumbency of the Rev. Daniel Turner, who has upwards of 92A. of glebe, in Rushton Spencer, and Wolstanton parish. There is a Wesleyan Chapel at Endon, erected in 1836. Stone of excellent quality abounds in the vicinity, and an extensive quarry, at Moss Hall, is now being worked. Endon School, and the master's house were built by the freeholders of Endon, in 1750, upon land, given by John Wedgwood Esq. About a quarter of an acre, now used as a garden, was added to the school in 1797, by Ts. Harding. The master has £4. 10s. yearly out of an estate in Park lane, as the interest of £110 left by Thos. and Wm Sherratt for schooling six poor children. He has also £4. 10s. yearly from, the tollgate at Endon, for which he teaches two more free scholars, but the donor is unknown. Endon Chapel croft, worth £3 a year, was given by Gabriel Lees, for the use of the chapel. The poor of Endon have the following yearly doles, viz., 50s. from Thomas Joddrell's, and 60s. from John Wedgwood's charities, (see Horton;) 52s. in weekly doles of bread from sacrament money, and £40 left by John Ball; the interest of £10 left by John Boughey, in 1751; the interest of £30 left by Francis Evans, in 1826; and of £20 given in 1860, by Mr. Thomas Wood, in memory of his late wife, daughter of Charles Heaton, Esq. In Endon is an excellent public well, which was formed in 1845, at the expense of Mr. Thomas Heaton, and is honoured with an annual well-dressing, on the 29th of May.

HEATON is a hamlet and township of 2300 acres, and 405 souls, in Rushton chapelry, 4¼ miles N.W. by N of Leek. Wm. Brocklehurst, Esq., is lord of the manor, but a great part of the soil belongs to the Earl of Macclesfield, Thos. Yardley, Esq., Mrs. Gaunt, and a few smaller owners. On the river Dane, which separates this county from Cheshire, is a small cotton mill. Swithamley Hall, the ancient seat of the Traffords, is now the property and occasional residence of Wm. Brocklehurst, Esq., of Macclesfield. Heaton House, the neat modern residence of James Robins Esq., stands on a commanding eminence, where the high moorland heath has been much improved by him and Josiah Gaunt, Esq., and embellished with thriving plantations. Here is an old Wesleyan Chapel.

LEEKFRITH is an extensive township, between two branches of the river Churnet, and comprising 7500 acres, 877 souls, many scattered houses, and the hamlets of POOL END, 1¼ mile N.W.; WHITE'S BRIDGE, where there is a large dye-house, half a mile N.W.; ABBEY GREEN, half a mile N.; MEERBROOK, 3 miles N; BLACKSHAW MOOR, 3 miles N.N.W.; and UPPERHULME, 4 miles N.N.W. of Leek. At Abbey Green are the remains of an ancient abbey, noticed previously, and a Bowling-green. The abbey farm is the property of John Davenport, Esq. At the north end of the township are the moorland farms of Gunside, Rocheside, and Hazlewood. Leekfrith is in the Earl of Macclesfield's manor of Leek but most of the soil belongs to Wm. Brocklehurst, Esq., John Davenport, Esq, and many smaller freeholders. Upper or Over Hulme gave birth to Richd Caldwell, an eminent physician, who died in 1515. It has a silk mill in the dale, below the lofty mountain rocks, called Leek Roches, where, some years ago, an immense mass of rocks fell in such a manner as to leave under it a large cavern, which has since been occupied as a dwelling by a poor aged woman. Meerbrook Chapelry includes most of Leekfrith township. Its CHAPEL (St. Matthew,) was built and endowed by Sir Ralph Bagnall, who vested it with seven trustees, by deed, dated February, 2nd, 1564. It has about 250 sittings, mostly free. The living is a perpetual curacy, valued at £110, in the patronage of the Vicar of Leek, and incumbency of the Rev. James Turner, M.A., who rebuilt the Parsonage house, in 1828, and in 1845 settled upon the succeeding incumbents five acres of land and two buildings, at Roche Grange, for preaching additional sermons. Mr. William Condlyffe, of Leek, is heir-at-law of one of the original chapel trustees, and has an estate at Upper Hulme, which has been held by his family since 1647. John Stoddard, in 1673, bequeathed out of his lands at Thornyleigh and Leekfrith, three yearly rent charges, viz. £4 to the curate of Meerbrook, £10 to a schoolmaster for teaching 20 poor children of that chapelry, and £2 for the poor of Gunside. In 1679 Edm. Brough left out of his lands at Peakstones, 50s. yearly to the curate of Meerbrook, and 20s. to the poor of Rocheside and Hazlewood. Roger Morris gave £100, and directed one-half of the interest to be given to the schoolmaster, for the education of eight poor children of Leekfrith, and the other for a distribution, of bibles. The interest, £4. 10s., is paid out of the rent of Swines Moor Farm. Thomas Wood left £30, for which 30s. is now paid yearly out of Stock Meadow Farm, and distributed in bread among the poor of the liberty of Meerbrook.

LONGSDON is a hamlet of scattered houses and 426 souls, 2 miles W.S.W. of Leek, including the lofty ridge called Ladder Edge. J. Sneyd and J. Davenport, Esqrs., are owners of most of the soil. This high moorland hamlet forms a joint township with Endon and Stanley. At Wall Grange and Ladder Edge, are the copious springs and extensive reservoirs of the Potteries' Water Works.

ONECOTE is a scattered village, township, and chapelry, of 438 souls, and about 5000 acres, in the manor of Bradnop, 5 miles E. by S. of Leek, adjoining the Mixon copper mine, which has not been worked during the last 30 years. The Chapel is a small stone edifice, which was built in 1751. The living is a perpetual curacy, valued at £99, in the patronage of the Vicar of Leek, and incumbency of the Rev. Jeremiah Barnes, M.A., of Leek. Here is a Primitive Methodist Chapel, built in 1822.

RUDYARD is a small township of six farms, 2½ miles N.W. of Leek. The Earl of Macclesfield is owner of nearly all the land, and lord of the manor. RUDYARD LAKE, in this highly picturesque township, is an extensive Reservoir, which was formed many years ago for the purpose of feeding the Caldon Canal, which joins the Uttoxeter Canal, and extends from the neighbourhood of Leek to the Potteries, where it terminates in the Trent and Mersey Canal. Since the opening of the Churnet Valley Railway, which passes along the eastern side of it, this extensive sheet of water has been dignified by the name of Rudyard Lake, and is visited in summer by numerous pleasure parties from the Potteries, Manchester, Macclesfield, and other towns, especially at Easter or Whitsuntide, when there is usually a grand fete and regatta, attended by many thousand people brought by cheap trains. The lake covers about 400 acres, and is two miles long, and about a quarter of a mile broad. It is formed by the natural boundaries of a long and narrow valley, (a branch of the Churnet) and all that was necessary to form the reservoir was a short dam at the lower end of the valley. The principal supply of water is brought by a feeder more than three miles long, from near the source of the river Dane, amongst the neighbouring hills, on the borders of Cheshire and Staffordshire. The water thus conveyed and stored for the use of the canal is a portion of the torrent of that impetuous river after heavy rains. Herons and other aquatic birds resort to the lake, and it is well stocked with fish. The water is closely skirted on the eastern side by the railway, which has a station at Rushton, about three quarters of a mile north of the head of the lake, and another below the lake, in Horton parish, but called Rudyard Station. Here a new hotel has recently been established. On the lake are a number of neat boats, belonging to various gentlemen. The six FARMERS of Rudyard are: Samuel Bowyer, Wm. Brooks, John Fletcher, Robert Needham, Jph. Robinson, and Samuel Turnock. The Lake Hotel is kept by Mr. Peter Ullivero.

RUSHTON-JAMES is a hamlet and township of 283 souls and 1000 acres, N.W. of Leek, in G. C. Antrobus, Esquires, manor of Horton. RUSHTON-SPENCER is a village and township of 855 souls and 1000 acres, 5 miles N.W. by N. of Leek, in the chapelry of Rushton, which includes the three townships of Rushton-Spencer, Rushton-James, and Heaton. The small Chapel dedicated to St. Lawrence, is supposed to have been founded before Leek

Church; and a fruitless attempt was made about 20 years ago to establish it as a parish church. It was anciently called The Chapel in the Wilderness, and was thoroughly repaired in 1848. Near it is St. Helen's Well, which pours forth a very copious stream; but sometimes it happens that it will become suddenly dry, after a constant discharge of water for eight or ten years. The perpetual curacy is valued at only £91, though it is endowed with 60A. of land at Heaton. The Vicar of Leek is patron and the Rev. Geo. Mounsey, of Fairfield, Derbyshire, is the incumbent, for whom the Rev. James Turner, M.A., of Meerbrook, officiates. The manor is in five moities, belonging to the Johnson, Webb, Hardware, and Yardley families, except one moiety, which belongs to the freeholders. At RUSHTON MARSH, a village on the turnpike, half a mile S.W. of the Chapel, are three public-houses, a Methodist Chapel, and a School built by subscription in 1772, and endowed with land worth £3 a year. Here is a Railway station, on the Churnet Valley branch of the North Staffordshire Railway, and it is sometimes thronged with visitors to Rudyard Lake, as already noticed. The poor of Rushton-Spencer have a house and 1$\frac{1}{2}$ acre of land, let for £7 a year, and purchased in 1753 with £23 left by Alice Yardley and Mary Sidebotham. One-third of the rent is distributed in money at Christmas, and the remainder in monthly doles of bread. In 1725, Elizabeth Hulme bequeathed to the poor of Rushton James, a yearly rent charge of £4 out of her messuage, at Woodhouse Green, to be distributed in clothing on October 16th. Sarah Nicoll, in 1783, bequeathed £200, and directed the interest to be distributed in clothing on the 1st of January yearly, among poor men and women of Heaton and Leek-Frith. This sum was invested in the three per cent. annuities, in 1726, and products an annual income or £10.2s.0d.

STANLEY is a hamlet of 108 souls, on an eminence, 5 miles S.W. of Leek, forming a joint township with Endon and Longsdon. The soil belongs chiefly to the occupants. The hamlet possesses a charity estate of 69A. 2B. 39P. of land, with a house and outbuildings, let for about £70 par annum. This property was bequeathed by the Rev. Richard Shaw, and conveyed to the trustees by his heir-at-law, Wm. Furnival. The income is mostly applied in schooling poor children, and partly in weekly doles to poor families.

TITTESWORTH township, which contains 600 inhabitants, and about 1000 acres of land, adjoins the north-eastern suburbs of Leek, and includes part of the modern village of BALLHAYE-GREEN, the rest of which is in Leek township; and the hamlet of THORNCLIFF, 2 miles N.E. of Leek. The houses at Ballhaye Green have been erected during the last 30 years, since the enclosure of the common there, and many of them were built by members of building clubs. Edward Chorley, Esq., is the principal landowner, and has a seat here, called Haregate. Tittesworth township forms part of the new district parish of St. Luke. The resident FARMERs are Moses Ash, Isaac Bagshaw*, vict. Wellington; Isaac Bailey, Jph. Beardsley*, Wm. Bloore, Robt. Chadwick*, Jas. Critchley, Rd. Dean, and John Plant, Easing; Wm. Harrison, Jph Kirkham, Thos. Plant, John Plant, Blackshaw Moor; Wm. Robinson*, and Robt. Riley. Those marked * are in Thorncliff. Ballhaye Green is included with Leek Directory.

BRADNOP

Phillips Saml & Wm, Esqrs,
        Ashenhurst Hall
Bagnall Stephen, miller and
        maltster, Gorse Head
Bott Joseph, joiner, &c.
Chadwick George, schoolmaster
Cook John, vict., Red Lion
Farrall Samuel, vict., Hare & Hounds
Harrison Mary, shopkeeper
Lovatt Joseph, wheelwright
Mountfort Wm, miller, Ashenhurst
Plant Smith, wheelwright
Richardson Rev Harling, B.A.
        curate of Onecote
Turner Jas., vict., Blacksmiths' Arms

BLACKSMITHS
Cantrell Richard
Malkin Thomas
Morris Joseph
Turner James

SHOEMAKERS
Plant Eliza
Plant Joseph
Walwyn Francis

FARMERS (* are Owners.)
Bailey John
* Bassett Wm.
Beardmore John
Birch Joseph

*Birch James
Bloore John
Bloore Martha
* Booth George
Burnett John
Chappell Thomas
* Cook John
Cook Wm.
Cope Thomas
Corden George
Corden Geo.,jun.
Deaville Smith
Eardley Isaac
Fearns Thomas
Heath Abel

Hidderley Wm.
Hill Enoch
Hill John
Keeling Josh.
Kidd Wm.
Lovatt John
Meakin James
Moss George
*Needham James, Hare House

Oulsnam Chas.
Oulsnam John
Plant Samuel
Prince Uriah
Sant Joseph
* Simcock Mary
Stubbs John
Titterton Benjn.
Titterton George

Titterton G., jun
* Torr Adam
* Torr James
Walwyn Peter
Webster Ralph
Wheeldon Isaac
Whiston John

ENDON, LONGSDON, AND STANLEY

Marked 1 Longsdon, 2 Stanley, and others in Endon.

2 Docksey John, flint grinder
1 Goodwin Thos., earthenware mfr:
                    h Dunwood
2 Glover Wm., corn miller
Gosling James, vict., Black Horse
Heaton Charles, Esq.,Endon
Heaton Thos., land agent & surveyor
Hopkinson Thomas, vict., Plough
1 Lockett Thomas, quarryman
Minshull Mr John; and Misses,
        ladies' school, Sutton House
Salt John, schoolmaster & registrar
I Sigley Claas., vict., New Inn
Turner Rev Danl., incbt., Hallwater
Turner Misses
2 Weatherley Mr T.
Warrington Benj. and Jas., butchers
2 Willet Eliz., schoolmistress
Yates James, flint grinder

BEER HOUSES

Basnett James, and stonehewer
Frost Ellen
1 Morris James

BLACKSMITHS.

1 Turner Samuel
Walker Jno. & Ths.

BRICK MAKERS.

1 Alcock John
1 Alcock Sampson
1 Fernihough Sn.
1 Hargreaves Jph.
1 Hargreaves Rd.

BOOT & SHORMAKERS.

Baddeley James
Baddeley Noah
1 Bourne Herbt.

Durber Richard
I Stevenson Sol.

FARMERS. (* are Owners.)

Adams Jonathan
Bailey Joseph
1 Bentley Edw.
Bentley Thomas
2 * Billinge Isaac
Bolton George
Booth Henry
Bowyer Wm.
* Brindley Thos.
2 Browster Benj.
Critchlow George
Critchlow Thos.
Critchlow Wm.
1 Crompton Ths.
1 Corbitchly Jno.
2 Dean Hannah
I Edge Richard
Glover James
Glover John
2 Glover Wm.
Goodwin Jph.
2 * Grindey John
2 Hall James
Hall Wm.
Hammersley Rd.
Harrison Richd.
1* Harrison W. G.
Heath George
Heath John
1 Knight John
2 Leeke Ralph
Mountford Isaac
Mountford Wm.
1 Myatt Thomas
1 Nixon George

Oulsnam James
Pimlott Wm.
Plant Thomas
1 Read Wm.& Jane
Salt Jane
Shufflebotham Abel
Sims Thomas
1 Smith James
* Smith Thomas. -
Steel John
I Stubbs John
1 Stubbs Joseph
I Turner Samuel
Unwin Joseph
Warrington Jas
Weston Charles
1 West Henry, Wall Grange:
White Samuel.
Wooliscroft Ths Harracles
2 * Yates James
1 * Young Saml

SHOPKEEPERS.

Lowe Robert
Plant Mary
Stubbs Charles
2 Wrenshaw My.

TAILORS.

I Brooks Joseph
Gratton Thomas
2 Willet Wm

WHEELWRIGHTS

2 Kent James
Plant Thomas
Stubbs Joshua
1 Stubbs Samuel

HEATON.

Brocklehurst Wm., Esq.,
  Swithamley Hall (and Macclesfield)
Robins Jas., surgeon, Heaton House
Corbitchley Thomas, wheelwright
Dauber James, shoemaker
Earlam Thomas, blacksmith
Mycock Harden, butcher
Nadin John, shoemaker
Ratcliff John, vict. Black Horse
Salt James & Torr Daniel, shoemkrs

FARMERS

Allen Wm
Armett Joseph
Bateman Wm

Buxton Henry
Cooper Jas.,btchr
Dale John
Dale Joseph
Dawson James
Deakin Charles
Fletcher Wm
Gibson Henry
Goodfellow John
Goodwin Joseph
Hall Jacob
Heath Wm
Hine Thomas
Hulme Robert

Mayden Wm
Moss Sarah
Moss Wm
Shaw Widow
Slack James
Slack Wm
Smith Samuel
Steel George
Sudlow George
Swindles Michael
Torr Daniel
Tatton Ralph
Turnock George
Whiston Joseph

LEEKFRITH

Marked 1 are at Meerbrook, 2 Middle Hulme, 3 Thorny Lee, 4 Upper Hulme, 5 Wetwood, 6 White's bridge or Bridge end, 7 Abbey green, and 8 Pool end.

1 Brassington John, miller
Gaunt Matthew, Esq., Abbey green
6 Hammersley Wm., silk dyer
4 Hine Thomas, corn miller
8 Hulme James, wheelwright
1 Hulme Wm, day school
Nixon Robert, district clerk
4 Parker George, silk throwster
8 Plant Richard, tailor
1 Rider George, wheelwright
Tredwell Sol., Esq., Highfield Hall
1 Turner Rev James, M.A.,
      incumbent of Meerbrook

INNS AND TAVERNS.

7 Bowling Green, Ralph Dixon
1 Fountain, Charles Armett
1 Three Horse Shoes, Jas.Wheeldon
Three Horse Shoes, John Goodwin,
          Blackshaw Moor

BLACKSMITHS.

8 Finney Thomas
Rider Thomas

BOOT AND SHOEMAKERS.

1 Bratt Joseph
2 Brough John
4 Hand Abraham
Wood Wm

FARMERS. (* are Owners.)

Armett Mary
4 Ash Mary
Bailey Edward
Beswick Wm
Batt Ralph
* Brassington Ts. and 3 Samuel
Brocklehurst Jas
2 * Brough Wm
5 Brown Matthew
Brixton Thomas
* Carter Wm
Chappells Joseph
* Clowes John
Clowes Wm
3 Clowes Thomas
* Clulow James
* Clulow John
Critchlow James
* Findlow Samuel
Findlow John
Fisher James
* Fisher Thomas
Gould James
Gould Thomas
Hassall Edward
Hind George
5 Hind James
Hind Joseph

Hind Wm
7 Hulme James
2 Hulme John
Hulme Samuel
Hunt John
Lockett John
Lockett Wm
* Lomas Wm
Lownds Wm
Mellor John & Sml
Mills Joseph
* Mountford John
Mountford Saml
Needham George
Nixon John & My
4 Oulsman James
Pimlett Robert
* Plant John
3 Read Joseph
Riley John
4 Robinson Wm
* Rogers George
Taylor Thomas
* Taylor Wm
Turnock Martha
Wood Richard
7 Wooliscroft Ralph, Abbey
Yates Wm

ONECOTE

Allen James, blacksmith
Allen Wm., shoemaker
Beard Clement, butcher
Clews Elisha, shoemaker
Gibson George, wheelwright and
          vict. Dog and Partridge
Johnson John, blacksmith
Morris Thomas, vict. Bleak Meer
Smith Samuel, shopkeeper
Titterton John, vict., Jervis's Arms
Webster Ralph, Corn miller

FARMERS. (*are Owners.)

* Baker Wm
Baker Robert
* Ball Philip
* Bassett Thomas

Bentley Benjamin
* Booth James
Booth Wm
Burnett Thomas
Chadwick Thos
* Chapman Wm
* Cook Thomas
Critchlow Ann
Critchlow Richd
Critchlow Thos
Deaville Eli
* Deaville James
* Deaville John
Deaville Wm
Edge Joseph
Fernihough Wm
Frost John

Frost Joseph
Hambleton Thos Mixon Haye
Harrison Moses
* Harrison Sampsn
Harrison Thomas
Kidd Wm
* Kidd Sampson
Moss George
Naylor Jph & Ths
Pearson John
Sheldon Richard
Simcock John
Simpson Clement
* Smith Jno & Sml
Thompson Wm
Wood Thomas
* Woolley Edward and J.

RUSHTON-JAMES

Bostock Rev. James, incumbent of
          Wincle, Wolfdale
Bailey Moses, wheelwright
Dale Benjamin, blacksmith
Gibson Chas., wheelwgt. & vict. Fox
Hammond Chas., vict. Hanging Gate
Winkle Sml., vict. Crown, & blksmith

FARMERS. (*are Owners.)

Bailey Charles (and mason)
Bailey John
Bailey Thomas (and mason)
Bailey Samuel
Boon Thomas
Buxton Samuel

Clowes Thomas
Gibson Thomas (& rakemaker)
Hand Ann
Knight Thomas
Machin Widow
Mitchell John
Whittaker Thos

RUSHTON SPENCER
Marked 1 are at Rushton Marsh.

Batkin John, police officer
Bradburn Samuel, Shopkeeper
1 Chappells John, vict. Golden Lion
Cook James, silk dyer
Goldsmith George, station master
Hargreaves Mr Joseph
1 Kent George, vict. Robin Hood
Knight Thomas, shoemaker
Mayer Henry I., schoolmaster
Mitchell Thomas, nail maker
1 Rigby Jph., blacksmith & shopkpr
1 Spilsbury Fras., shoemkr. & beerhse

1 Tunnicliffe Mr Joseph
Vernon Joseph, corn miller
1 Vernon Charles, vict. Red Lion
1 Wilshaw George, shopkeeper

FARMERS. (*are Owners.)

* Bailey Josiah
Bailey Hannah
Chappells Nathan
Dawson Joseph
Dauber Hugh
Goodwin Widow
*Lockett George

*Lockett John
Machin John
Nixon Thomas
Sumner Thomas
1 Tomkinson Wm
Vernon John
Wright George
* Yardley Thomas Wallhill
Yates Henry

RAILWAY
Trains 4 times a day each way

LEEK

The POST OFFICE is in Custard street, and Mr. George Nall is the *post-master*. Letters are despatched by mail-cart to Newcastle-under-Lyme, at 7$^{1/4}$ evening, and received at 45 min. past 6 morning. Messengers daily to the surrounding villages.

MISCELLANY *of Gentry, Clergy, Partners in Firms, and others not arranged under the heads of Trades and Professions.*

Ainger Wm. D., clerk, King street
Allen Mrs. Phoebe S., Stockwell st
Alsop Jas., mfr.; h Stockwell street
Arkcoll Wm. Ja., veterinary surgeon, Russell street
Astles Mr. Jesse, Compton
Babbington Misses, King street
Bacon Thos., clerk, Compton
Badnall Wm. Beaumont, solr; and Mrs Sarah, Church lane
Bagnall Mr. Sampson, Compton
Bailey Harriet, matron,*Workhouse*
Ball Charles, accountant, West st
Ball John Cope, whsman., West st
Ball Samuel, town crier, Mill street
Barlow Edw., manager, London st
Barlow Jas., sexton, Stockwell St
Barnes Rev. Jermh., M.A., curate and rural dean of Leek, and incumbent of Onecote. Spout street
Belfield Robt., whsman., Fountain st
Belfield Geo., master of *Workhouse*
Bentley Jph., mfr.; h Fountain st
Bentley Mrs. Ann, King street
Birch Mr. Thomas, Overton's bank
Birch Joseph, whsman., Buxton road
Blackwell Jas., designer, Victoria gdns
Bloore Jas., sol. and clerk of County Court, Derby st; h *Compton*
Bloore John and George, warehousemen, Compton
Booth Thos., *tanner*, Ballhaye road
Booth Mrs., Stockwell street
Bowers Thos., traveller, King street
Brailey Rev Wm. (Wes.) Regent st
Brealey Thos., land agent, valuer, and surveyor, Stockwell street
Brookes Saml., rake maker, Mill st
Brough James, silk mfr.; h King st
Brough Joshua, mfr., Buxton Villa
Brough John, mfr., Regent street
Brough Henry, clerk, Buxton road
Brunt Mrs. Ann, King street
Butter Wm., goods clerk, Wall hill
Campion John Barry, *station master*, Wall hill
Carr Thos., silk mfr.; h Spout st
Challinor Wm., solr. and clerk to Comssrs. of Taxes; h *Pickwood*
Challinor Joseph, solr.; h Derby st
Challinor Miss Charlotte, Spout st
Chorley Edwood, Esq., *Haregate*

Clowes Saml., mfr.; h Prospect Hs.
Clowes Mrs. Ann, Mill street
Condlyffe Wm., gent., and Mrs. B., Derby street
Cooper Mrs Ellen, Ballhaye street
Crompton Misses, Spout street
Cruso Fras., clerk to magistrates and board of guardians, and superintendent registrar, Stockwell street
Cruso John, Esq., manor steward, Market place
Cutting Mr. Richard, King street
Davenport John, Esq., *Westwood Hall*
Davenport Mr. Nathan, Clerk's bank
Dawson Miss Mary, Ballhaye street
Deaville Jph, whsman., Market pl.
Dyson Rev. John B. (*Wes.*) King st
Ellis Lilley, silk mfr.; h Spout st
Fernyhough Mrs. Ann, Compton
Ferriar Miss, Spout street
Gaunt John, mfr.; h Queen's head sq
Gaunt Mrs Eliz., Ballhaye street
Gaunt Matthew, Esq., *Abbey Green*
Gaunt Misses, Derby street
Gee David, manager, Regent street
Gibson Jph., manager, Fountain st
Godkin Jno. Hy., police inspr., Mill st
Godwin Saml., whsman., Stockwell st
Goodwin Rd., overlooker, Buxton rd
Goostrey Wm., paper mfr., London rd
Goshawk Rev Rt. (Indpt.) Ballhaye street
Gould Joseph, mfr., Union street
Gould Sampson, secretary to Savings Bank, King street
Grosvenor Mrs Mary, Stockwell st
Hacker John Heathcote, solicitor; h Derby street
Hammersley Geo., mfr.; h Fountain st
Hammersley Wm., silk dyer; house Bridge end; and Robert, ditto; h *Browhill House*
Hammond Mr Isaac, Church street
Heathcote Rev Thos. Hy., M.A., *vicar*
Heaton Edwin, land agent and surveyor, Spout street
Hickson Rev Thos. (*Wes.*) Mt. plsnt.
Hine Mr. Thomas, King street
Ind Hy. W., overlooker, Buxton road
Jackson Wm. S., traveller, King st
Johnson Hr. Lionel, mfr.; h King st
Keates Wm., high constable of N. Div. of Totmonslow, Spout street
Lance Capt. Wm. Henry; supt. of police, and inspr. of weights and measures, Compton

Lea Wm., currier; h Spout street
Leech John, land agent & surveyor, Wall hill cottage
Lees Chas., whsman., Rosebank st
Littler C., architect & survr., Westwood
Lovatt John, mfr.; h Daisy bank
Mien John, Collector, Queen street
Mollatt Wm. S., clerk, Compton
Morley Mrs Mary, Ballhaye street
Moss Mr Joseph, King street
Newall John, manager, Buxton road
O'Donnell Jno., *pawnbroker* Spout st
Nicholson Jsha., travlr., Buxton road
Nixon James, builder; h Ballhaye st
Nixon Wm., builder; h Fountain Cottg
Perkin Joseph, assist. magistrates; clerk, Derby street
Phillips Mrs. Mary, King street
Phillips Saml. and Wm., Esqs., The Field,
                    and Ashenhurst Hall
Pickford Mrs Elizabeth, Church lane
Pickford Jabez, clerk, Britannia st
Pidcock Rev Benj., B.A., incumbt.
            of St. Luke's, Stockwell street
Pimlott John L., weigher, Derby st
Pointon Jas., paver, Prospect row
Power Rev Michl. A., (Cath.,) Fountain street
Price Thos., bailiff, Clerk's bank
Pyatt Mrs., King street
Ribbans Rev East Fdk. Thos., BA., curate, chap. to the
            Union, and mast. of the Gram. sch., Spout st
Rider Geo., parish clerk & registrar, Stockwell street
Rider Jas., dep. regr. Stockwell St
Robins Jas., mfr.; h Ballhaye street
Robson John, revenue offr., Albion st
Rowley Thos., relieving. offr., Church In
Russell John, silk mfr.; h Spout st
Scholefield Rd, overlooker, Queen st
Shaw Mrs., Ballhaye street
Shaw Miss Phoebe, Stockwell street
Sillitoe Mr Wm., London road
Simons Mrs Ellen, Derby street
Slack Thos., whsman., Derby street
Sleigh Hugh, silk mfr.; h Spout st
Sleigh Mrs Hannah, *Cawdry*
Smith John, colr., & assist. overseer, Derby street
Smith Wm. Fallows, gent., Prospect Cottage
Smith Geo. A., clerk, Rosebank st
Squire John, mfr., South Bank Hs.
Staley & Parr, fancy depot, Spout st
Stirling Robert, gent., Stockwell st
Stubbs Peter, manager, King street
Sugden Wm., architect, Ballhaye st
Swindles Saml., button mould mfr, Derby street
Thompson Geo. gent., Derby street
Van Tuyl Miss M. J., Spout street
Walker Chas., whsman., King st

Walker Peter, clk., Rose Bank st
Wamsley Mrs. Sarah, Church lane
Wamsley Pp. mfr., Mount pleasant
Ward John, silk mfr.; h Spout st
Ward Mrs. Frs. Ann, Derby street
Wardle James, Esq., Compton Ctge.
Webberley Mrs. Sar., Ballhaye st
Weston John, silk mfr., Buxton rd
Weston John, jun., mfr., do. Villa
Weston Mr. Wm., London road
Woolley Chas., silk mfr.; h King st
Worthington Andrew Jukes, mfr. house Spout street
Yates John, stay maker, Spout street
Young Geo. currier; h Clerk's bank

ACADEMIES AND SCHOOLS

Marked * take boarders.

*Bagnall Eliz., Compton street
*Chell Miss, Queen street
Mellor Misses, Stockwell street
Shufflebotham Joseph, Union street
Turner George, Ballhaye green
*Twemlow Ann, Stockwell street
*Wardle Elizabeth, Derby street
*Free Grammar School, Rev. E. F. T. Ribbans, B.A.,
      Spout street
Infant Schools, Miss Clarke, Union street, and Miss
      Moffatt, Brunswick Chapel
National Schools, Peter and Sarah Cannings, Clerk's bank;
& Mattw. Brindley, & Sarah Hargreaves, St. Luke's district
Roman Catholic School, Portland street, Sarah Cassin
Union Workhouse, Chas. Jno. Green, and Eliz. Smith

ALE & PORTER AGENTS

Fergyson Robt. (Burton,) Mkt place
Whistles John, (Burton,) Mkt place
Woolliscroft G. (Cheddleton Brewery,) Sheep market

APPRAISERS, &c.

Brealey Thos., Stockwell street
Fergyson Robert, Market place
Hilliard Wm. M. Sheep market
Keates William, Spout street
Leech John, Wall hill
Nixon William, Fountain street

ATTORNEYS

Challinor, Badnall, and Challinor, Stockwell St & Derby st
Hacker and Bloore, Derby street
Killmister Abin. Kershaw, Regent st
Redfern Thomas, Daisy bank

AUCTIONEERS, &c

Fergyson Robert, Market place
Hilliard William, Sheep market
Keates William, Spout street

BAKERS & FLOUR DEALERS

Abbott Jesse, Clerk's bank
Beard William, Compton
Brunt Micah, Ballhaye green
Bull Richard, Spout street
Burton Joseph, Stockwell street
Clowes William, Mill street
Davenport Thomas, Buxton road
Edge Rd., Market pl. & Church St
Heapy William, Stockwell street
Hodson Thos. Henry, Mill street
Hulme George, Derby street
Hunt Samuel, Mill street
Hunt Thomas, Mill street
Lowndes Wm. Wood, Market, place.
Magnier Peter, Derby st
Maskery Francis, spout street
Massey George, Sheep market
Nichols William, Canal street
Shallcross Thomas, Clerk's bank
Smith John, Derby street
Smith Samuel, Well street
Wardle William, London road
Warrington John Thos., Custard st

BANKS

Liverpool and Manchester District Bank, Church street,
(Branch of Hanley Bank) open Wednesday, 10 till 2.
Savings' Bank, Town hall, open the 1st and 3rd
Mondays in every month, from 12 to 1; S. Gould, actuary

BASKET MAKERS

Smith James, Custard street
Smith Noah, Derby street

BLACKSMITHS

Arkcoll Wm. J., Russell street
Beardmore Eliz. & Son, (& agricultural machine mkrs.)
      Spout st
Bold Peter, Mill street
Caiter John, Compton
Clowes Joseph, Compton.
Finney Samuel, Mill street
Hargreaves George, London road
Kidd Sampson, Buxton road
Lomas Jesse, Mill street
Rider George, London road
Weston Francis, London road

BOOKSELLERS, PRINTERS, STATIONERS, &c.

Hallowes Edward, Stockwell street
Hilliard Wm. Michael, Sheep mkt
Nall George, (library & stamp and post office) Custard st

BOOT & SHOE MAKERS

Beardmore Samuel, Ballhaye green
Birch James, Compton
Brown Joseph, Derby street
Done Joseph, Ballhaye green
Earls Henry, Mill street
Gratton John, Mill street
Hall Richard, Custard street
Harrison William, Mill street
Hiott Thomas, Fountain street
Hudson Joseph, Canal street
Jackson Thomas, Ballhaye green
Johnson Thomas, Spout street
Keates William, Derby street
Kirkham Thomas, Fountain street
Meakin Joseph, Compton
Olley Edward, Russell Street
Plant Henry, Custard street
Rigby Joseph, Derby street
Sales George, Canal street
Simister John, Custard street
Stevenson Charles, Mill street
Tatton Enoch, London road
Tipper Daniel, Spout street
Tipper George, Spout street
Tipper Thomas, Mill street
Walwyn John, Sheep market
Wood Ruth, Buxton road
Worrall William, London road

BRAZIERS & TINNERS

Howard Joseph, Market place
Ridgway Charles, Stockwell street
Travis Thomas, Spout street

BRICKLAYERS

Barlow Matthew, Regent street
Holroyd Joseph, Mill street
Mellor John, Fountain street
Tavernor Thomas, Spout street
Wilson James, Ballhaye green
Wilson Moses, Ballhaye green
Wright Thomas, Canal street

BRICK MAKERS

Carr & Brealey, London road
Hargreaves Thomas, London road

BUTCHERS

Bayley Benj., Mill street
Beard Henry, Spout street
Critchlow George, Church street
Godwin Joseph, London road
Goodwin Benjamin, Spout street
Henshaw John, Mill street

Hulme George, Spout street
Johnson George, Derby street
Knowles George, London road
Mitchell Thomas, Clerk's bank
Stevenson Joseph, Spout street
Tatton James, Mill street

CABINET MAKERS
(See Joiners & Furniture Brokers)

CHAIR MKRS. & TURNERS
Bassett Wm., Pickwood road
Booth Isaac, Spout street
Osborne Daniel, Queen street
Wain Richard, Derby street

COAL DEALERS
Birchenough Samuel, Cross street
Clarke John, Canal street
Doxey John, Mill street
Hall Joseph, Sheep Market
Lord Vernon, Russell street
Pimlott John Lomas, Derby street
Plant Robert, Mill street
Poultney Samuel, London road
Painter Thomas, Canal street
Reade Joseph, Workhouse street
Shenton Thomas, Ballhaye green
Smith Samuel, Well street
Smith Thomas, Stockwell st
Williams James, Mill street

CLOG & PATTEN MAKERS
Goodwin Ralph, Mill street
Millward Edward, Derby street
Wrigley Henry, Mill street

CONFECTIONERS, &c.
Edge Richd., Market pl & Church st
Heapy Wm., Stockwell street
Hodson Thos. Hy. (wholes.) Mill st
Magnier Peter, Derby street
Maskery Francis, Spout street
Massey George, Sheep market
Nichols Wm., Canal street
Smith John, Derby street

COOPERS
Deakin Samuel, Derby street
Slater Thomas, Custard street

CORN MILLER
Brindley James, Mill street

COW KEEPERS
Bloore Wm., Ballhaye green
Brunt Micah, Ballhaye green
Cumberlidge Wm., Buxton road

Gould Ann, Spout street
Mirfin Geo., Church street
Sanders Thomas, Ballhaye green

CURRIERS, &c.
Large Wm., Spout street
Young and Lea, Spout street

DRUGGISTS
Ball Thomas, Mill street
Blades Cphr., (tea dlr,) Custard st
Johnson Thomas, Derby street
Pickford Edwin, Market place

DYERS (See Silk Dyers)

EATING HOUSES
Alcock Ruth, Church street
Leese Henry, Derby street
Nadin James, Derby street
Perkin Joseph, Spout street
Taylor Joseph, Derby street
Trafford Chas. (tenpnce.) Derby st

FARMERS
Birch James, Lowe
Critchlow Richard, Lowe
Critchlow Wm., Market place
Dale James, Lowe
Dale Richard, Lowe.
Fernihough Thos. S., London road
Hocknell Saml. & Jno., Big Birchall
Hulme Wm., Mill street
Johnson Ralph, Leek Edge
Marsden Anthony, Cowhay
Oulsnam Benjamin, Bridge end
Rowley John, Sheep House
Smith Thomas, Knivedon
Steers Thomas, Debank House

FIRE & LIFE OFFICES
Atlas, Hacker & Bloore, Derby street
Birmingham, Edwin Pickford Mkt.pl
Crown & Legal, T. Redfern, Daisy bk
Equitable, Chas. Heaton, Custard st
Clerical and Medical, Thos. Brealey, Stockwell street
Imperial, J. Andrew, Custard street
Liverpool and London, John Leech, Wall hill
Manchester and Pelican, Thomas Johnson, Derby street
National Loan Fund, Chas. Heaton, Custard street
National Mercantile, Charles Ball, West st
Norwich Union, F. W. Jennings, Stockwell street
Notts. and Derbyshire, George Nall, Custard street
Royal Exchange, W. M. Hilliard, Sheep market
Star, J. S. Winfield, Market place
Salop, Wm. Challinor, Derby street
Sun Life, A. K. Killmister, Regent st
United Kingdom, Edwin Heaton, Spout street

GARDENERS & SEEDSMEN

Cartwright Daniel, Sheep market
Keeling Adam, Mill street
Nunns Wm., Ballhaye street
Painter Thomas, Spout street

FRUITERERS, &c.

Brassington Wm., Fountain street
Bullock Isaac, Market place
Lovatt, Francis, Russell street
Osborne Walter, Stockwell street
Swindles Jacob, Clerk's bank
Wardle Wm., Spout street
Yates John, Derby street

FURNITURE BROKERS

Beardmore Thomas, Derby street
Fergyson, H. E., Market place
Hall Richard, Custard street
Overfield Alfred, Queen street

GLASS, CHINA, &c., DEALERS

Ashton John, Sheep market
Barlow Francis, Spout street
Clee Edmund, Custard street

GROCERS AND TEA DEALERS

Bostock Henry, Church street
Braddock Samuel, Sheep market
Edge Richd., Church st. and Mkt. pl
Howes Jacob, Market place
Lowndes Wm. Wood, Market place
Middleton Isaac, Market place
Mountfort Ralph & Son, Custard St
Taylor John, Spout street
Thurstan Jas. & Co., Market place
Warrington John Thos., Custard st
Whittles John and Wm., (and guano and hop merchants) Market place
Williams Ann and Wm., (and coffee roasters) Spout st

HAIR DRESSERS

Bagshaw Noah, New street
Birch John, Custard street
Hassall Samuel, Derby street
Milner Elias, Mill street
Mycock James, Church street
Pilkington Wm., Spout street

HATTERS

Morley Thomas, Spout street
Tipper James, Sheep mkt

HORSE AND GIG LETTERS

Hyde John Kidman, Spout street
Lowndes Mary, Derby street
Painter Thomas, Canal street
Rowland Wm., Market place

INNS AND TAVERNS

Ballhaye Tavern, James Wilson, Ballhaye green
Bird-in-Hand, John Jackson, Mkt. pl
Black's Head, My. Chell, Custard St.
Black Swan, Wm. Fisher, Sheep mkt
Blue Ball, Richard Smith, Mill st
Bull's Head, Vernon Hulme, Spout st
Butchers' Arms, C. Wilson, Derby. St
Cheshire Cheese, Th. West, Sheep mkt
Churnet Valley Hotel, Henry Broadhurst, Station road
Cock, Saml. Lasseter, Derby street
Cock, (Old) John Cope, Market pl
Cross Keys, Wm.Capewell, Custard st
Crown, Francis Bromley, Church St
Dog and Partridge, Joseph Perkin, Derby street
Duke of York, Jph. Ward, Derby st
Dun Cow, J. Tomkinson, London rd
Dyers Arms, Rchd. Mellor, Mill street
Fountain, Wm. Jackson, Fountains st
Flying Horse, Wm. Wood, London rd
George Inn, Thomas Tatler, Spout St
Globe, Wm. Gorman, Spout street
Golden Lion, Geo. Murfin, Church st
Green Man, Wm. Barlow, Compton
King's Arms, Eli Plant, Mill street
King's Head., Enoch Cooper, Mkt pl
Nag's Head, James Johnson, Mill st
Plough, John K. Hyde, Spout st
Queen's Head, Jtn. Jackson, Custard. st
Quiet Woman, Joseph Hambleton, Spout street
Red Lion Hotel, (posting,) William Rowland, Market pl
Roebuck, Mary Lowndes, Derby st
Royal Oak, Eliz. Wilson, Buxton rd
Swan Inn, John Barlow, Spout st
Talbot, T. S. Fernihough, London rd
Unicorn, Thos. Johnson, Spout st
Union, Thos. Gascoigne, Stockwl. st
Wheat Sheaf, Chas. Stubbs,Custard st
White Lion, Wm. Fogg, London rd
White Lion, Wm. Hulme, Bridge end
Wilkes' Head, Whittles, Spout at
William IV., Abm. Howes, Church st

BEERHOUSES

Clowes Thomas, Mill street
Lowndes Joseph, Buxton road
Painter Thomas, Spout street
Simpson James, Russell street
Tatler John, London road
Williams Joseph, Mill street

IRONMONGERS

(And Nail Manufacturers)
Cartwright Daniel, Sheep market
Henshaw Wm., (nail only,) Mill st
Woolfe Benjamin, Market place

JOINERS AND BUILDERS

Cruse Jonathan, Compton
Eyre John, Cross street
Fernyhough Joseph, Rosebank at
Haynes Henry, King street
Howson Samuel, Cornhill street
Nixon Wm. & James., Stockwell st
Overfield Alfd., (cabt. mkr.) Queen st

LINEN & WOOLLEN DRAPERS

Andrew Joshua, Custard street
Fenton John, Market place
Gwynne Clement, Sheep market
Haynes George, Derby street
Phillips John, Custard street
Sutton John & George, custard st
Winfield John Sarson, Market place
Wood William, Derby street

MILLINERS, &c.

Ashton Mary, Spout street
Barlow Sarah, Stockwell street
Belfield Elizabeth, Fountain street
Benton —, Russell street
Birch Hannah, Stockwell street
Birtles Mary Ann, Custard street
Challinor Sarah, Buxton road
Critchlow Charlotte, Spout street
Crombie Ann, Fountain street
Davenport Ellzabeth, Stockwell st
Gosling Mary Ann, London road
Gould Mary, Mill street
Hall Harriet and M.A., Buxton rd
Hallowes M. A., Stockwell street
Hudson Elizabeth,Derby street
Jackson —, Ballhaye road
Johnson Frances, Union street
Meakin Martha, Derby street
Robinson Hannah, Spout street
Scotton Mary, Queen street
Simpson Mary, London road
Smith Susan, Portland street
Street Mary, Derby street
Twigg Mary, Spout street
Vickerstaff Ann, London road
Wardle Sarah, Spout street

MUSIC DEALERS, &c.

Barlow Benj., (organist,) Church lane
Clowes Jas., (news apt.) Workhouse st
Hilliard William Michael, Sheep mkt
Nall George, Custard street

NAIL MAKERS (See Ironmongers.)

PAINTERS, PLUMBERS, AND GLAZIERS

Ashton Edward, Ballhaye street
Ashton Henry, Spout street
Clee Edmund, (manager of the Water Works,) Custard st
Davenport William, Stockwell street
Johnson Thomas, Market place
Ratcliffe Thomas, King street
Stafford Edward, Stockwell street

PLASTERERS

Crompton William, Canal street
Staniforth Luke, Church lane
Staniforth William, London road
Stonehewer William, Mill street

RAG, &c. MERCHANTS

Howard Joseph, Market place
Wheeldon John, Clerk's bank

ROPE AND TWINE MAKERS

Mountfort Ralph & Son, Custard st; h. King street
Rogers, James, Spout street

SADDLERS

Allen George, Market place
Johnson Wm. Fynney, Derby street
Tatler James, Market place

SHOPKEEPERS (See also Bakers, &c.)

Abrahams John, Mill street
Alcock Ruth, Church street
Armishaw Hannah, Stockwell street
Beard William, Compton
Booth Charles, Russell street
Brunt Micah, Ballhaye green
Bull Richard, Spout street
Burton Joseph, Stockwell street
Carding Henry, Overton's bank
Carding Joseph, Workhouse street
Clowes William, Mill street
Crompton Peter, Mill street
Corbitt Benjamin, Mill street
Davenport Thomas, Buxton road
Critchlow James, Spout street
Forster Charles, Sheep market
Getliffe Simon, Market place
Goldstraw and Bold, Derby street
Gresty Sarah, Spout street
Harrison John, Ballhaye green
Hartley Ann, Stockwell street
Haynes Samuel Nixon, Derby street
Henshaw William, Mill street
Holroyd Olive, Mill street
Hulme George, Spout street
Hunt Samuel, Mill street

Keates John, Stockwell street
Keates Wm., London road
Kirkham Elizabeth, Derby st
Lovatt Susanna, Mill street
Magnier Peter, sen., Fountain st
Magson Martha, Compton
Naden John, Russell street
Pickford Wm., Buxton road
Rigby Jesse, Spout street
Salt Ts., Spout st.; and My., West st
Shallcross Samuel, Clerk's bank
Tatler John, London road
Trafford Louisa, Mill street
Wardle Wm., London road

SILK BROKERS
Jennings Fras. Wm., Stockwell st
Mitchell John S., Spout St

SILK DYERS
Ball Charles, Bridge end
Hammersley Wm. & Co., Bridge end and Mill street
Tatton Sml., Mill st; h Mount pleasant

SILK MANUFACTURERS
Alsop, Robins, and Co., New st
Beard Michl. John. & Son, Compton
Bermingham Jas. & Henry, Compton
Birchenough John, Compton; house Russell street
Brough J. and J. and Co., Union st
Brunt Josiah and Co., Derby street; house Daisy bank
Carr Thomas and Co., Hope Mills, Fountain street
Davenport George, (throwster) Mill st; house Clerk's bk
Davidson John & Co. Clerk's bank; house Stockwell st
Gaunt John, Globe Factory, Spout st; h Queen's Head sq
Goodwin James, Union street
Hammersley & Bentley, Fountain st
Johnson James, Portland st; house Queen street
Lovatt and Gould, Union street and Mill street
Mellor Wm., London street
Mien John, King street
Milner Wm., Union street
Reddish Fras. (throwster,) Pickwood rd; house Mill st
Ridout James, King street
Russell and Clowes, West st .
Simpson Miles, London st. Union st.and Victoria Mills
Sleigh and Wooley, Spout st
Smith Samuel, Kiln lane
Stubbs Pownal, King street
Tatton Wm., Pickwood rd
Trafford James, Pickwood rd
Wain John, London road; h Ballhaye street
Wamsley and Ellis, Albion st
Walmsley Mary & Son, (Jno.) Mill street; house King st
Ward Anthony & Co., Albion Mills
Weston John & Son, Buxton road

Worthington Andrew Jukes & Co., Fountain Mills, Portland st, (and London)
Wreford John and Co., London st

SILK TWISTERS (By Commission.)
Ball Wm., Mill street
Birch Wm., Ballh aye green
Broster Jesse, Mill street
Gibson Silas, Albion street
Hall John, Stockwell street
Hambleton Joel, King street
Malkin Benjamin, Spout street
Malkin Thomas, Mill street
Plant Wm., King street
Tuffley Wm. Edward, Stockwell st

SMALLWARE DEALERS
Booth John, Russell street
Brooks Fras., Derby st. (and sawyer)
Carter Mary Ann, Spout street
Clowes James, Workhouse st
Meakin Mary, Derby street
Milner Elias, Mill street
Pilgrim John, Derby street
Simister John, Custard street

STONE MASONS
Barlow Matthew, Regent street
Barlow Jas. (sexton,) Stockwell st
Coates Anthony, Ballhaye green
Holroyd Joseph, Mill street
Nadin John, Victoria place
Ratcliffe Richard, Stockwell st
Wilson James, Ballhaye green
Wilson Moses, Ballhaye green

STRAW HAT MAKERS
Beardmore Ann B., Derby St
Clowes Ann, Derby street
Gould Ann, Portland street
Hall and Hassall, Market place
Heapy Mary, Stockwell street
Walker Mrs., Buxton road

SURGEONS
Cooper Richard, Derby street.
Flint Charles, Compton House
Heaton Charles, Custard street
Turnock Richard, Spout street
Walters Edward Smith, (certifying surgeon to the factories,) Overton's bank

TAILORS Marked * are Drapers,
Armett Amos, Clerk's bank
Ball Samuel, London road
Bradley Frederick, Buxton road

Bradley Joseph, Spout street
Cade James, Mill street
Daniells Thomas, Mill street.
*Eaton Wm., Spout street
Hudson John, King street
Hudson James, Derby street
Keates Wm., London road
*Maddocks Thomas, Market place
*Needham James, Russell st
Orpe George, King street
Plant James, Mill street
Plant Wm, Overton's bank
Scott Thomas, Spout street
Sigley Elijah, Compton
Smith James, Church lane
Wood Wm., Fountain street
Woodings Wm., Compton

TALLOW CHANDLERS
Bull George, Derby street
Howes Jacob, Market place
Williams Ann and Wm., Spout St

TIMBER MERCHANTS
Brooks Samuel, Belle vue
Cruse Jonathan, Buxton road
Fernyhough Joseph, Ballhaye st
Howson Samuel, Compton
Nixon Wm. and Jas., Stockwell st
Shenton Thomas, Ballhaye st

WATCH & CLOCK MAKERS
Ashton John, Sheep market
Travis Wm., Market place
Walford John Austin, Derby st

WHEELWRIGHTS
Ball Thomas, London road
Bradley Henry, Overton's bank
Frost George, Mill street
Pimlott John Lomas, Derby st
Pointon Thomas, Spout street
Salt John, Canal street

WHITESMITHS
Cartwright Daniel, Sheep market
Heath James, Stockwell street
Murfin George, Cross street
Plant Jonathan, Spout street

WINE & SPIRIT MERCHTS
(And Ale and Porter Dealers.)
Evans Edward, Market place
Howes Abraham, Church street
Lightfoot Thos. Wm., Spout st
West Thomas, Sheep market

RAILWAY
Trains are despatched four times a day each way on the Churnet Valley Line, with passengers and goods for all parts. John B. Campion, station master.

OMNIBUSES
From the Red Lion Hotel and Roebuck Inn, to meet the trains.

CARRIERS
The North Staffordshire Railway Co. forward goods daily to all parts by rails and canal from the Station and Wharf. Wm. Butter, goods agt.

CARRIERS FROM THE INNS
(Every Wednesday.)

Places.	Carriers.	Inns.
Burslem,	J. Wood,	Black Swan
Butterton,	Ts. Stubbs, and P. Harrison,	Black's Head, Butchers' Arms
Buxton,	Wm. Cheshire,	Cock
Flash,	Wm. Wood, and Jph. Oliver,	Black Swan, Golden Lion
Hanley,	A. Forrister,	Crown
Hartington and Longnor,	Geo. Sutton,	Black's Head, Wed. & Sat.
Longnor, Bakewell, and Sheffield,	Joshua Knowles,	Butchers' Arms
Longnor,	Thos. Bradbury, and Wm. Bradbury,	Golden Lion, Black Swan
Longton, Stone, and Stafford,	Wm. Daniells,	Black Swan
Macclesfield &c	Anderton Co. daily,	Wilkes' Head
Newcastle and Salop,	J. Findlow,	Bird-in-Hand

Slater's Directory 1862

POST OFFICE, Custard Street, George Nall, Post Master. - Letters from all parts arrive (from Stoke-upon-Trent) at half past six morning, and are despatched at a quarter before eight evening. *Money Orders* are granted and paid from nine morning till six evening.

GENTRY AND CLERGY

Alsop James , Esq. (magistrate), Ballhaye st
Anderson Rev.Joseph, Buxton road
Badnall Mrs, Sarah, Church lane
Barnes Rev, Jeremiah, Spout st
Birch Mrs, Ann, Queen st
Boucher Rev, Alfred Fras, Cheddleton
Bradshaw Mrs, Eliza, Compton(
Bradshaw Rev.Samuel (magistrate) Basford Hall
Brough Miss Hannah, Fountain st
Brough Miss Sarah, Ballhaye st
Brown Mrs Sarah, King st
Carr Charles, Esq. Regent st
Carr Henry, Esq. Regent st
Carr Thomas, Esq. (magistrate) Regent st
Challinor Miss Charlotte, Spout st
Challinor Mrs. Mary, Derby st
Chell Mrs. Mary, Weston st
Clowes Mrs. Ann, Beech Villa, Park road
Condlyffe Mr. William, Derby st
Cooper Mrs. Ellen Gaunt, Ballhaye st
Critchlow Mr. William, Church st
Crompton the Misses Elizabeth and Dorothy, Spout st
Cruso John Esq. (magistrate) Market place
Dalgleish Hy, Richd, Esq. Ashcombe Park
Davenport Mr. Nathan, Clark's bank
Deacon Rev. George Edward, M.A., the Vicarage
Ellis Mrs Sarah, Spout st
Ferriar Miss Jane Cath, London rd
Flint Charles, Esq. Compton House
Galbraith Rev.James, Cheddleton
Gaunt Josiah, Esq. Horton Hall
Gaunt Matthew, Esq. (magistrate), Rudyard
Gaunt the Misses --, Derby st
Grosvenor Mrs. Mary, Stockwell st
Handley Mrs. Martha, Queen st
Hankinson Rev. Josiah, Queen st
Hooley Rev. Samuel, Mount pleasant
Hulme Mr. William, Villa Park, Cartledge
Jennings Francis William, Esq., Stockwell st
Lassetter Mr. Samuel, Crompton
Lawrence Rev. Philip Newman, Spout street
Lees Rev. William, King st
Lovatt John, Esq. Clark's Bank
Moore Rev. John, Regent st
Newby Mrs. Fanny, Derby st
Nixon Mrs. Eliza, Fountain st
Nixon Mr. James, Queen st
Nixon Mr. John, Fountain st
Phillips Wm. Esq. Overton's bank

Pickford Mrs, Elizabeth, Church la
Pidcock Rev. Benjamin, Park road
Pollock Rev.Thos.Benson, Rosebank
Rogers Mr. George, King st
Russell John, Esq. (magistrate), Spout st
Smith Miss Margaret, Stockwell st
Smith Mr. William, Spout st
Sneyd Rev. John, (magistrate), Woodlands
Squoire Mrs, Mary Ann, Buxton rd
Sutton Mrs, Mary, Fountain st
Turner Rev. Daniel, Endon
Vantuyle Miss Maria Jane, Spout st
Walmsley Mrs. Sarah, Church lane
Ward Mrs. Frances Ann, Southbank House
Wardle James, Esq. Compton Cottage, King street
West Mrs. Catherine, King st
West Mrs. Mary, Queen st
Weston Mr. John, sen, Buxton road
Wooliscroft Mrs. Eliza, Canal st

ACADEMIES AND SCHOOLS

Marked thus* are Boarding and Day; not otherwise described are Day Schools.
Bagnall Elizabeth, Compton
*Godbehere Hannah, Stockwell st
GRAMMAR SCHOOL, Clerk's bank - Rev. Philip Newman Lawrence, master
INFANTS' SCHOOLS:
Ballhaye st (Wesleyan) - Emily Shipp, mistress
Cheddleton (St. Edward's) - Sarah Barlow, mistress
Clerk's bank (St. Edward's) - Elizabeth Foden, mistress
Fountain st (St. Luke's) - Ann Morris, mistress
Union st (Independent's) - A. Bartlett, mistress

Mellor, Deansgate

NATIONAL SCHOOLS:-
Cheddleton (St Edward's) - Edwin Howarth, master; Sarah Barlow, mistress
Clerk's bank (St. Edward's) - Peter Cannings, master; Sarah Cannings, mistress
Fountain st (St. Luke's) - John Richmond, master
ROMAN CATHOLIC SCHOOL, Portland st - Sisters of the Institute of the Blessed Virgin, mistresses
*Smith Mary, Queen st
*Sykes Joseph C. M. BALLHAYE HALL
COMMERCIAL & BOARDING ACADEMY, Ballhaye green
WESLEYAN SCHOOL (boys) West st, Richard Groves, master

AGENTS
(See also Fire, &c. Office Agents and also Land Agents)
Dakin John (to Economic Loan Society), Stockwell st
Fergyson Robert (brewers'), Market place
Hilliard William Michael (new estate & house, and for
Milner's fire-proof safes & to the Liverpool, New York
    & Philadephia Steam Ship Co.), Sheep market
Mien John (house), Queen st
Moss William (to Uttoxeter Brewery Co.), Derby st
Whittles John & William (guano & linseed), Market pl
Whittles John Gibson (brewers'), Market place

APPRAISERS
(See also Auctioneers & Appraisers)
Brealey Thomas, Stockwell st
Hilliard William Michael, Sheep market
Leech John, Canal st
Nall George, Custard st
Nixon William B., Stockwell st

ATTORNEYS
Marked thus * are commissioners. + Chancery, and thus
for taking acknowledgements of deeds by married women
*+Challinor, Badnall & Challinor, Derby st & Stockwell st
*+Hacker and Bloore, Derby st
*+Redfern Thomas & Sons, Daisy bank
* Smith George, Church lane

AUCTIONEERS & APPRAISRS
(See also Appraisers.)
Fergyson Robert, Market place
Hilliard William Michael (& estate agent), Sheep market

BAKERS & CONFECTIONERS
Bateman Thomas, Church st
Beard William, Derby st
Bull Richard, Spout st
Burton George, Russell st
Clark William, Spout st
Eaton William Allen, Derby st
Heapy William, Stockwell st
Hulme George, Derby st
Keates James, Wilkes' Head yard, Spout st
Kidd William, Mill st
Leason Robert, Spout st
Magnier Peter, Derby st
Maskery Francis, Spout st
Massey George, Sheep market
Nicholls John, Mill st
Nichols William, Canal st

BANKS
LEEK BANK, Stockwell st - (draws on Bank of
London) - - Francis William Jennings, proprietor
MANCHESTER & LIVERPOOL DISTRICT
BANKING Co., Derby st - William Carse, manager

SAVINGS BANK, Russell st - (open every Monday
from 12 till 1) - William S. Mollatt, actuary

BLACKSMITHS
Arkcoll William James, Russell st
Beardmore Samuel (& agricultural implement maker),
                                  Spout st
Bold Peter, Mill st
Cantrill Richard, Bottom House
Carter John, Compton
Clowes James, Basford
Finney Samuel, Mill st
Finney Thomas, Poolend
Heath James, Stockwell st
Johnson John, Bottom House
Rider George, Bellevue road
Torr John, Derby st
Turner John, Bradnop
Turner John, Cheddleton
Turner Samuel, Ladderedge

BOOKSELLERS, STATIONERS, BOOKBINDERS & PRINTERS
Hallowes Edward, Stockwell st
Hilliard William Michael, Sheep market
Nall Robert, Custard st
Rider James, Spout st

BOOT AND SHOE MAKERS
Allen William, Ladder edge
Baimbridge Andrew, Stockwell st
Ball John, London road
Barber James, Cheddleton
Barber Joshua, Weston st
Barlow John, Cheddleton
Birch James, Duke st
Bourne Herbert, Ladder edge
Britton Wm. & Co. Market place
Brunt Thomas, Mill st
Byrne Walter, Canal st
Carter Elijah, Queen st
Clowes Isaac, Market st
Forster Samuel, Sheep market
Gratton John, Mill st
Hall James, Pickwood road
Harrison Henry, Mill st
Jackson Thomas, West st
Johnson Thomas, Canal st
Keates William, Russell st
Meakin George, London st
Newall John (dealer), London road
Rigby Joseph, Derby st
Sales George, Canal st
Salt John, West st
Simister John, Custard st
Sneyd John, Clark's bank

Stevenson Charles, Mill st
Stevenson Solomon, Latter edge
Tatton Enoch, London road
Tipper Daniel, Overton's bank
Tipper George, Spout st
Tipper Thomas, Mill st
Turnock Samuel, Fountain st
Walwyn John, Sheep market
Worrall William, Spout st

BRAZIERS AND TINMEN
Howard Joseph & William (& coppersmiths), Market pl
Wright William, Spout st
Yates Edwin, Golden Lion yard

BREWERS
Ford & Illsley, Cheddleton
Walker George, Canal st

BRICK MAKERS
Alcock John, London road
Alcock Solomon & Wm. Ladder edge
Carr & Brealey, London road
Hargreaves Richard, Ladder edge
Hargreaves Thomas, London road
Hodgkinson Samuel, London road
Porter Thomas, London road
West Henry, Ladder edge

BRICKLAYERS
Grace Thomas, Canal st
Plant Thomas, Clerk's bank
Taverner William, Aslop st

BUTCHERS
Beard Henry, South st
Blakeman William, Ladder edge
Chapman William, Bottom House
Critchlow George, Market place
Finney James, Ladder edge
Goodwin Benjamin, Spout st
Hulme George, Spout st square
Mitchell Thomas, Clerk's bank
Morris George Henry (pork), Market place
Plant Thomas, Ballhaye green
Smith Joseph, Russell st
Stevenson Joseph, Spout st
Taylor Joseph, (pork), Derby st
Wardle John, Derby st
Warrington Sampson, Cheddleton
Warrington William, Market st
Yeomans George, Fountain st

CABINET MAKERS
Billing Joseph (and picture framer), Stockwell st
Charles Henry, Derby st

Eyre John, Cross st
Nixon William & John, Stockwell st
Overfield Alfred & Co. (and picture frame), Russell st

CHEMISTS & DRUGGISTS
Blades Christopher (& tea dealer), Custard st
Bradbury Thos. Garmeson, Church st
Broadhurst Henry (and tea dealer), Market place
Johnson & Sons, Derby st
Pickford Edwin (and tea dealer), Spout st square

CHINA, GLASS & EARTHENWARE DEALERS
Alcock Elizabeth, Compton
Gee Edmund, Custard st
Spilsbury Timothy, Spout st
Wooliscroft Ralph, Market place

CLOG & PATTEN MAKERS
Bowcock George, Mill st
Millward Edward, Spout st
Wrigley Henry, Mill st
Wrigley J. Russell st

COAL DEALERS
Cheetham Thomas, Russell st
Critchlow James, Nelson st
Dean Thomas, Prospect place
Doxey Thomas, Mill st
Hall Joseph, Buxton road
Mycock John, Cross st
Pimlott John Lomas, Derby st
Potts John, Buxton road
Rider George, Bellevue road
Shenton Thomas, Ballhaye green
Smith Samuel, Cross st
Williams Joseph, Mill st

COAL MERCHANTS
Cheetham Thomas, Russell st
Potts John, Spout st; and Mortar Mill siding,
Macclesfield

COOPERS
Deakin Thomas, Derby st
Slater Thomas, Canal st

CORN MILLERS
Brindley James, Mill st
Broddok Smith, Mosslee
Mounford William, Bradnop

DYERS - SILK
Cook James, Rushton
Hammersley R. & Co. Mill st
Tatton Samuel, Mill st
Wardle & Son, Leek brook

EATING HOUSE KEEPERS

Hulme George, Custard st
Naden James, Derby st
Perkin Hezekiah, Spout st

ENGINEERS & MILLWRIGHTS

Gell Thomas (and machine maker), Park road
Sutcliffe Mark & Wilkinson, West st
Woodhead & Carter (and brass and iron founders),
Canal wharf

FARMERS

Alcock Ralph, Mosslee
Baley Edward, Leek Frith
Ball Benjamin, Abbey green
Barnett Thomas, Cheddleton Park
Beard Henry, Bottom House
Bennison James, Wall lane, Cheddleton
Beresford Joseph, Bottom House
Bermer John, Bradnop
Billinge William, Leek Frith
Birch James, Leek Lowe
Birch Joseph, Bradnop
Blakeman William, Ladder edge
Booth George, Bradnop
Brassington Charles, Hall House, Cheddleton
Brassington Charles, Cheddleton Grange
Broddok Smith, Mosslee
Brown Job, Bank end
Carter James, Leek Frith
Carter Thomas, Leek Frith
Chadwick Thomas, Bottom House
Chappell Joseph, Leek Frith
Chappell Thomas, Bradnop
Chell George, Basford Grange
Cook William, Bradnop
Cottrell John, Spicy Stone, Basford
Coxdon Grange, Bradnop
Critchlow George, Bradnop
Critchlow George, Leek Frith
Critchlow James, Ballhaye green
Crompton Thomas, Ladder edge
Cumberlidge Wm. Mount Pleasant
Deakin William, Finney Lane, Cheddleton
Deaville Eli, Bottom House
Docks Ephraim, Basford Bridge
Eardley Isaac, Bradnop
Finney James, Ladder edge
Finney Samuel, Leek Edge
Goodwin Joseph, Bank farm, Cheddleton
Hall Joseph, Buxton road
Hambleton John, Handfield
Heath John, Shafferlong
Hill Enoch, Cattledge
Hughes George, Dale House, Cheddleton
Hughes James, Felt House, Cheddleton

Hulme James, Abbey Green
Hulme Robert, Highfield
Johnson Benjamin, Leek Edge
Knight John, Ladder edge
Lesse Francis, Bottom House
Lockett Ann, Leek Frith
Lockett John, Leek Frith
Lockett Samuel, Barnfield
Massey Thomas, Basford Villa
Morris Hanson, Bottom House
Morris John, Basford Hall
Mountford - -, Leek Lowe
Myatt James, Ladder edge
Myatt Thomas, Wall Bridge
Mycock Wm. Oldfield, Cheddleton
Needham George, Leek Frith
Nixon George, Longedon Grange
Pimlott Robert, Leek Frith
Plant James, Ferny Hill
Prince Urin, Bradnop
Pulsman Jno, the Range, Cheddleton
Reid Sarah, Bank End
Robinson - -, Leek Lowe
Robinson Thomas, Cartlege
Robinson William, Bradnop
Rowe Joseph, Yew Trees, Cheddleton
Sant Joseph, Bradnop
Sharratt Hannah, Shafferlong
Sigley Charles, Ladder edge
Simcock John, Bradnop
Smith David, Leek Lowe
Stubbs Samuel, Ladder edge
Tatton George, Basford
Taylor George, Leek Frith
Timmis Richard, Flat Head, Cheddleton
Titterton John, Bradnop
Torr James, Bradnop
Turner Charles, Bank End
Warrington Thomas, Leek Brook
West Henry, Wall Grange
Wheeldon Thomas, Ferny Hill, Cheddleton
White James, Rowley gate
Williamson George, Felt House, Cheddleton
Williamson -, Hazelhurst, Cheddleton
Wooliscroft Thomas, Haracles

FIRE &C. OFFICE AGENTS

ALBERT, MEDICAL AND FAMILY ENDOWMENT
(life), James Rider, Spout st
ATLAS, William Challinor, Derby st
CLERICAL, MEDICAL & GENERAL (life), Thos.
Brealey, Stockwell st
FARMERS, Edwin Heaton, Basford Villa
IMPERIAL, Joshua Andrew, Custard st
LIFE, ASSOCIATION OF SCOTLAND, William Carse,
Derby st

LIVERPOOL AND LONDON, John Leech, Canal st
MANCHESTER (fire), and PELICAN (life), Thomas
    Johnson, Derby st
MIDLAND COUNTIES (fire), James Rider, Spout st
NORWICH UNION, Francis William Jennings,
     Stockwell st
NOTTINGHAM AND DERBY, George Nall, Custard st
ROYAL, William Michael Hilliard, Sheep market, and
    William Barlow Nixon, Stockwell st
SALOP (fire), Wm. Challinor, Derby st
SCOTTISH WIDOWS' FUND (life), Joshua Nicholson,
     Regent st
STAR, Thomas Johnson, Derby st
STATE, (fire and plate glass), Henry Broadhurst,
     Spout st square
WESLEYAN AND GENERAL, John Vigrass, Derbys st
WESTMINSTER, Geo. Smith, Church lane

FRUITERERS AND GREENGROCERS
Osborne Walter, Spout st
Prime Francis, Stockwell st
Swindells Jacob, Derby st

FURNITURE DEALERS
Beri & Dalera, Custard st
Clowes James, Spout st square
Fergyson Robert, Market place

GROCERS & TEA DEALERS
(See also Shopkeepers, &c.)
Ball Ralph (travelling) West st
Bostock Henry, Church st
Bull George, Derby st
Carding Samuel, Derby st
Goddard Joseph, Spout st
Gould Thomas, Compton
Howes Jacob, Market place
Hulme George, Spout st. square
Middleton Isaac, Market place
Mountfort & Son, Custard st
Pilkington John, Spout st
Pimlott John Lomas, Derby st
Poole Thomas, Mill st
Taylor Thomas, Sheep market
Thurston James & Co. Market place
Vigrass James (travelling), West st
Warrington John Thos. Custard st
Whittles John & William, Market place

HAIR DRESSERS
Birch John, Custard st
Mycock James, Market place
Parkinson Henry, Spout st
Speight George, Workhouse st
Trafford William, Derby st

INNS & POSTING HOUSES
(See also Taverns & Public Houses)
Red Lion, Wm. Mellor, Market place
Roebuck, John Flint, Derby st

IRONMONGERS
Cartwright Daniel (and nail manufacturer), Sheep market
Howard Joseph & William (and coppersmiths), Market pl
Woolliscroft Ralph (and seedsman), Market place
Wright William, Spout st

JOINERS & BUILDERS
Marked thus * are also Timber Dealers.
Brindley Robert, Buxton road
Clowes James, Basford
*Haynes Henry, Wilkes's Head yard, Spout st
Hudson Jas. & Joseph, Prospect place
Frost George, Mill st
Lees John, Roebuck lane
*Mathews John (and contractor), Buxton road
Nadin John, Derby st
*Nixon Wm. & John, Stockwell st
*Shenton Thomas, Ballhaye green
*Wardle John, London road

LAND AGENTS & SURVEYORS
Brealey Thomas, Stockwell st
Dean Richard Rapton, Derby st
Heaton Edwin, Basford villa
Leech John, Wall hill
Sugden William, Queen st

LINEN & WOOLLEN DRAPRS
Andrew Joshua, Custard st
Brooks Francis, Derby st
Carr & Bradley, Derby st
Carter Mary Ann, Spout st
Chell George, Derby st
Fenton John, Market place
Gwynne Clement, Sheep market
Heath George, Spout st
Keates Thomas, Stockwell st
Lovatt William, Russell st
Phillips John, Spout st
Sutton John, Custard st
Walker Samuel, Spout st
Walmsley Hezekiah, Mill st
Winfield John Sarson, Market place
Wood William, Derby st
Wright Edmund, Custard st

MARINE STORE DEALERS
Clowes James, Spout st. square
Eyre John, Cross st
Gossard Thomas, Derby st
Williams Joseph, Mill st

MILLINERS & DRESS MAKERS

Marked thus * are also Straw Bonnet Makers

Ashton Ann, Spout st
Ashton Mary Ann, Russell st
*Beardmore Ann Booth, Derby st
Beardmore Charlotte, Russell st
Birch Hannah, Custard
Booth Rebecca, Russell st
Carter Emily, Spout st
Challinor Sarah, Queen st
*Davenport Elizabeth, Stockwell st
Davenport Mary Ann, Stockwell st
Derbyshire Charlotte R. Mill st
Gossling Mary Ann & Anne, London road
*Gould Sarah, Buxton road
*Hassall Jane, Derby st
Meakin Harriet, Buxton road
Robinson Charlotte, Ballhaye st
Scotton Sarah, Stockwell st
*Street Jane, Derby st
*Twigge Mary, Spout st
Wardle Sarah, Spout st
Wright S. King st

NEWSPAPER & PERIODICAL DEALERS

Clowes James (& circulating library), Spout st. square
Hallowes Edward, Stockwell st
Hilliard William Michael, Sheen
Kirkham Charles, Market st
Nall Robert, Custard st
Raynor Peter Ascough, Spout st
Rider James, Spout st

PAWN BROKERS

O'Donnell John, Compton
Walker John, Clerk's bank

PHOTOGRAPHERS

Rayner Peter A. Spout st
Rendall Henry, Duke st
Wardle Henry, West st

PLUMBERS, PAINTERS AND GLAZIERS

Byrne John, Derby st
Clee Edmund, Custard st
Davenport William, Market st
Howard John Joseph, Wilkes's Head yard, Spout st
Johnson Thomas, Derby st
Stafford Edward, Stockwell st

ROPE MAKERS

Mountfort & Son, Custard st
Rogers James, Spout st

SADDLERS

Allen George, Market place
Brocklehurst Solomon, Church st
Hyde Charles Kidman, Spout st
Johnson William Fynney, Derby st

SHOPKEEPERS & DEALERS
GROCERIES & SUNDRIES

Abraham John, Mill st
Akers William, King st
Alcock Ruth, Church st
Armishaw Hannah, Stockwell st
Ball George, Buxton road
Beard William, Compton
Bishop Alexander, Leek brook
Bloore George, Spout st
Brunt Micah, Ballhaye green
Burton Joseph, Stockwell st
Carding Joseph, Spout st. Square
Clark William, Spout st
Co-operative Store, Clerk's bank
Corden Uriah, Cheddleton
Critchlow George, Wellington st
Crompton John, Duke st
Crompton Peter, Mill st
Cumberbatch Charles, London road
Daniels Vernon, Brunswick st
Davenport Thomas, Portland st
Dayson Ann, Fountain st
Earls Joseph, Cornhill st
Forster Charles, Russell st
Gettliffe Simon, Market place
Goldstraw & Bold, Derby st
Hall Robert, Spout st
Harrison John, Ballhaye green
Haynes Samuel Nixon, Russell st
Holroyd Olive, Mill st
Hughes John, Cheddleton
Hunt James, Mill st
Johnson Thomas, Canal st
Keates Mary, Canal st
Launder John, Wellington st
Leason Robert, Spout st
Lovatt Susannah, Mill st
Magnier Peter, Fountain st
Martin George, Cheddleton
Naden James, Derby st
Nichols William, Canal st
Nixon William, London road
Pickford William, Buxton road
Poultney Joseph, Park road
Prince Benjamin, Russell st
Ratcliffe John, Mill st
Read William, Allsop st
Redfern William, Stockwell st

Robinson James, Compton
Rogers Simeon, Queen st
Salt Mary, West st
Sharratt Isaac, Church lane
Shenton Thomas, Ballhaye green
Simpson John, Canal st
Smith Richard, Mill st
Smith Samuel, Cross st
Steel George, King st
Stubbs William, Mill st
Tomlinson Lewis, Mill st
Wall Mary, Canal st
Wardle Hannah, London road
Wardle William, Spout st
Warrington Ellen, Cheddleton
Weston Francis, Overton's Bank
Wheeldon Elizabeth, Regent st

SILK MANUFACTURERS
Allen Edward, Fountain st
Alsop, Downes & Co. New st
Bentley, Whittles & Walker, Fountain st
Bermingham James and Henry, Compton
Birch & Pickford, Ballhaye green
Broster Joseph, Mill st
Brough J. & J. & Co, Union st
Brunt, Fynney & Ridout, Market st
Carr Thomas & Co. Fountain st
Davenport George, Mill st
Davidson Myatt, Clerk's bank
Fogg Isaac (throwster), Pickwood rd
Gaunt John, Globe Factory, Spout st
Goodwin Stephen, London st
Gould Joseph, Union st
Hammersley Frederic, Mill st
Jackson Peter, Ballhaye green
Johnson Henry Lionel, Portland st
Lovatt William, Cornhill st
Mellor & Deane, Park road
Milner William, Union st
Reddish Francis, Cornhill st
Rushton Richard (baller), Joliffe st
Russell John, Britannia Mill, West st
Sleigh & Wooley, Spout st
Tatton William, Spout st
Thornton Edward, Union st
Trafford James, Pickwood road
Walmsley Mary & Co. Mill st
Ward Anthony & Co. Albion st
Weston John, jun. Buxton road
Widdall Thomas (throwster), Albion st
Worthington Andrew Jukes & Co. Portland st
Wreford John & Co. (and cotton), London st

SMALLWARE DEALERS
Bateman Hugh, Spout st
Counsell Edward, Church st
Gossard Thomas, Derby st
Lovatt William, Russell st
Pilgrim John, Derby st
Rayner Peter A. Spout st
Street Jane, Derby st

STONE MASONS
Barlow Matthew, Earl st
Nadin John, Buxton road
Robinson James, Canal st
Taylor Joseph, London road
Wilson James, London road

STRAW BONNET MAKERS
See under Milliners &c.

SURGEONS
Cooper Richard, Derby st
Heaton Charles (and physician), Stockwell st
Ritchie John James, Stockwell st
Turnock Richard, Spout st
Walters Edward Smith, Queen st

SURVEYORS
See Land Agents and Surveyors.

TAILORS
Marked * thus are also Drapers
Ball Samuel, Pickwood road
Bevins Edmund, Church st
Bowcock Thomas, Bellevue road
Bradley Charles, Pickwood road
Bradley Joseph, Spout st
Brocklehurst James, Spout st
Brocklehurst Solomon, Market place
Brough Thomas, Cheddleton
*Carr & Bradley, Derby st
*Eaton Elizabeth & Son, Spout st
Flanagan Bernard, Mill st
Furby Joseph, Spout st
Keates William, Rosebank st
*Needham James, Derby st
*Pattison & Ellerton, Market place
Peach Thomas, Russell st
*Phillips John, Spout st
Plant Charles, West st
*Scott Thomas, Spout st
Sigley Abraham, Buxton road
Vigrass John, Derby st

TALLOW CHANDLERS
Bull George, Derby st
Goddart Joseph, Spout st
Howes Jacob, Market place

TANNERS
Booth Thomas & Son, Ballhaye rd

TAVERNS & PUBLIC HOUSES
Angel, John Neesham Platt, Market place
Ballhaye, James Wilson, Ballhaye Green
Bird-in-Hand, Benjamin Wilks, Market place
Black Horse, Chas. Adams, Endon
Black Lion, Jas.Walker, Cheddleton
Back Swan, Enoch Mitchell, Sheep Market
Black's Head, Thos.West, Custard St
Blacksmith's Arms, John Turner, Bradnop
Blue Ball, Thomas Bullock, Mill St
Boat and Horse, James Mellor, Basford Bridge
Bowling Green, James Johnson, Abbey Green
Bull's Head, Saml.Boothby, Spout St
Cheshire Cheese, James Saunders, Sheep Market
Churnet Valley, Jas. Oakden, Canal Wharf
Cock, William Beardmore, Derby St
Cross Keys, Jos. Harrison, Custard St
Crown, James Smith, Church St
Crown & Anchor, Thomas Johnson, Canal St
Dog & Partridge, John Weston, Derby St
Dun Cow, Francis Brooks, London Road
Dyers' Arms, Hannah Bowcock, Mill St
Fountain, Thomas Nathan Jackson, Fountain St
George, Elizabeth Tatler, Spout St
Globe, William Gorman, Spout St
Golden Lion, Jas.Platt, Church St
Grapes, Thomas William Lightfoot, Spout St
Green Man, Mary Fernihough, Bottomhouse
Green Man, Chas.Cartledge, Compton
Hare & Hounds, Peter Walwyn, Bradnop
Kings Arms, Mary Plant, Mill St
Nag's Head, Samuel Birch, Mill St
Old Cock, Jos. Downs, Market Place
Old Plough, Wm. Capewell, Spout St
Plough, John Jackson, Endon
Pump, Richard Smith, Mill st
Queen's Head, Samuel Whittles, Custard St
Quiet Woman, John Kidman Hyde, Spout St
Red Lion, Thos. S Boswell, Cheddleton
Royal Oak, Henry Hubbart, Buxton Road
Scythe, George Tatton, Cheddleton
Sea Lion, James Walwyn, Russell St
Sneyd's Arms, Geo. Tatton, Basford
Swan-with-two-Necks, Jno. Barlow, Spout St
Talbot, Thos. Scarratt Fernihough, London Rd
Unicorn, George Griffin, Spout St
Union, Job Fatten, Stockwell St
Wheat Sheaf, Wm. Lovatt, Spout St
White Lion, Wm. Hulme, Bridge End
Wilkes's Head, James Brocklehurst, Spout St
William IV, Mary Ann Howes, Church St

RETAILERS OF BEER
Barlow Edward, Workhouse St
Broster Jesse, Park Road
Corden Uriah, Cheddleton
Kirkland James, Mill St
Knowles George, Buxton Rd
Knowles Joseph, London St
Martin George, Cheddleton
Mollatt Joseph, Leekbrook
O'Donnell Robert, Compton
Tomkinson Josiah, Osbourne St
Walker Peter, London Rd
Wardle Henry, West St
Wardle William, Spout St
Williams Joseph, Mill St
Wilson Moses, Ballhaye Green

TURNERS - WOOD
Bassett Ralph, Silk St
Booth Charles, Spout St
Sharratt Charles, (mould), Mill St
Wain Richard (& bobbin), Buxton Rd

WATCH & CLOCK MAKERS
Ashton Maria, Sheep Market
Baskerville George, Market Place
Faville John North, Market Place
Travis William, Market Place

WEIGHING MACHINE KEEPERS
Butter William Anwyl, Canal Wharf
Griffin George, Spout St
Pimlott John Lomas, Derby St

WHEELWRIGHTS
Clarkson Thomas, Cheddleton
Clowes James, Basford
Frost George, Mill St
Hulme Ann, Pool End
Pimlott John Lomas, Derby St
Poynton John, Buxton Rd
Salt John, Allsop St

WHITESMITHS
Beardmore Samuel (and gas fitter), Spout St
Cartwright Daniel, Sheep Market
Heath James, Stockwell St
Murfin George, Fountain St

MISCELLANEOUS

Arkcoll William Jas. veterinary surgeon, Russell St
Barlow Benj. teacher of music, Church Lane
Brooks Thomas, rake maker, Bellevue Rd
Findler Isaac, landscape painter, Cheddleton
Goostrey & Hulme, tissue paper makers, Cheddleton
Grosvenor William, nurseryman, Heath Ho, Cheddleton
Howard John, umbrella maker, Stockwell st
Keats, Shenton & Keats, sewing machine makers,
Cheddleton
Lightfoot Thomas William, wine and spirit dealer, Spout St
Lockett Chas. quarry master Ladderedge
Mitchell John Shepley, silk broker, Deansgate
Nunns William, nursery and seedsmen, Queen St
Osbourne Walter, town crier, Spout St
Pickford Jabez, fancy box manufacturer, Ballhaye Green
Pimlott John Lomas, manager of public baths, Derby St
Putman George, bird and animal preserver, Brunswick St
Slater William, livery stable keeper, Market Pl & Canal St
Smith James, basket maker, Custard St
Swindells Jacob, poulterer, &c, Derby St
Torr Ann, repository of the Society for Promoting
Christian Knowledge, Custard St
Tipper James, hatter, Sheep Market
Yates John, stay and umbrella maker, Spout St
Young & Lea, curriers & leather dealers

PUBLIC BULDINGS, OFFICES, &C.

Places of Worship and their ministers

St Edward's Church, Church St
Rev George Edward Deacon, MA, vicar;
Rev John Clarke, curate

St Edward's Church, Cheddleton
Rev. Alfred Francis Boucher incumbent
Rev. James Galbraith, curate

St Luke's Church, Fountain St
Rev. Benjamin Pidcock, incumbent
Rev Thomas B. Pollock, curate

Independent Chapel, Union St
Rev. Josiah Hankinson

Wesleyan Methodist Chapels, Ballhaye Gn,
Mount Pleasant, Market St, Ladderedge,
Endon, Cheddleton & Bradnop.

Primitive Methodist Chapel, Fountain St

Methodist New Connexion Chapel, Overton's Bank

Roman Catholic Chapel, Fountain St
Rev. Joseph Anderson, priest

POOR LAW UNION Workhouse, London Rd

Governor, George Belfield
Matron, Harriet Bailey
Chaplain, Rev. Philip Newman Lawrence
Schoolmistress, Hannah Turner
Surgeon, Charles Heaton
Relieving Officers, Thomas Rowley & William Pickering

COUNTY COURT

West St; Office Russell St
Judge, Sir Walter, Buchanan Riddell, Bart
Registrar, James Bloore
Assistant Registrar, William Allen
High Bailiff, John Minshull
Assistant Bailiff, William Warrington

REGISTRARS OF BIRTHS AND DEATHS

Superintendent Registrar - William Beaumont Badnall,
Stockwell St
Registrar for Leek District, Jas. Rider
(and of marriages), Spout St
Registrar for Leek Frith District, Robt Hulme, Heaton
Registrar for Longnor District, John Millward, Jun,
Longnor
Registrar for Norton District, John Salt, Endon
Registrar for Ipstones District, Thomas Martin, Ipstones

Almshouses, Compton

Cattle and Pig Market, London Road

Commissioners Offices, Derby St, Hacker & Bloore,
law clerks, Ralph Hammond Clerk to Commissioners

Fire Engine House, Cattle Market - Edmund Clee,
superintendent

Gas works, Canal wharf, Thos. Dickinson, manager

Inland Revenue Office, Red Lion Inn, Market place,
George Griffin, collector

Leek Association for the Prosecution of Felons,
Stockwell St, Challinor, Badnall and Challinor, solicitors

Leek Cemetery, Cornhill Cross, James Rider,
superintendent and registrar

Magistrates' Clerks Offices, Stockwell St, Joseph
Challinor, Clerk of sessions

Mechanics' Institution, Russell St, George Chell,
treasurer; Mr Henry Brough, secretary & librarian

News Room, Town Hall

North Staffordshire Rifle Volunteers Head Quarters, Town Hall

Police Office, Mill St, Thos Woollaston, superintendent; Henry Vernall, sergeant

Public Baths, Derby St, John Lomas Pimlott, manager

Saint Patrick's Convent, Fountain St, Elizabeth Haslam, superioress

Staffordshire Potteries Water Works, Wall Grange, Jas Trythall, manager

Stamp Office, Custard St, George Nall, sub-distributer

Town Hall, Market Place

Conveyance by Railway on

THE NORTH STAFFORDSHIRE LINE (CHURNET VALLEY BRANCH)

Station near the Canal wharf, Chas Hawkins, station master

Station near Cheddleton, Wm Weson, station master

Omnibuses from the Red Lion and Roebuck hotels attend the arrival and departure of trains

Carriers

To Alstonfield, W Bosley Allen from the Black Swan

To Bakewell, Joshua Knowles

To Burslem, W. Lightfoot, from the Black Swan, and Sandbrookes, from the Old Plough

To Butterton and Onecote, Harrison and Thomas Stubbs from the Red Lion

To Buxton, Thomas Brunt

To Cheadle, Thomas Spooner, William Daniel from the Bird in Hand

To Endon, Stubbs from Wilkes Head

To Flash, Ralph Oliver from the Golden Lion, and William Wood from the Black Swan

To Grindon, John Mycock from the Dog and Partridge, James Stoddard from the Cross Keys, and John Stubbs from the Old Plough

To Hollinsclough, Thomas Brunt from the Cock, and William Wood from the Black Swan

To Longnor, Belfield from the Golden Lion and Joshua Knowles

To Longton and Lane End, William Daniel from the Bird in Hand

To Macclesfield, The Anderton Carrying Co from the Wilkes Head daily

To Manchester, The Anderton Carrying Co from the Wilkes Head daily

To Reapsmoor, R. Lomas from Black Swan

To Sheffield Joshua Knowles

To Stafford and Stone, William Daniel from the Bird in Hand

To Tunstall, Beard and Smith from the Black Swan

To Warslow, F. Belfield, from Red Lion, Mon, Wed & Sat; Warrington and Watson Wednesday

To Waterhouses, Wheeldon from the Black Swan

To Wetton, Mart from the Cock

Conveyance by Water From the Canal Wharf

To London, Liverpool, Manchester &c, by the Cauldon Branch of the North Staffordshire Railway Co Trent and Mersey Navigation Canal, Wm Butter, wharfinger and agent.

Wharf Cheddleton, John Shaw, wharfinger.